ALEXANDER POPE

Modern Critical Views

Henry Adams
Edward Albee
A. R. Ammons
Matthew Arnold
John Ashbery
W. H. Auden
Jane Austen
James Baldwin
Charles Baudelaire
Samuel Beckett
Saul Bellow
The Bible
Elizabeth Bishop
William Blake
Jorge Luis Borges
Elizabeth Bowen
Bertolt Brecht
The Brontës
Robert Browning
Anthony Burgess
George Gordon, Lord
    Byron
Thomas Carlyle
Lewis Carroll
Willa Cather
Cervantes
Geoffrey Chaucer
Kate Chopin
Samuel Taylor Coleridge
Joseph Conrad
Contemporary Poets
Hart Crane
Stephen Crane
Dante
Charles Dickens
Emily Dickinson
John Donne & the Seven-
    teenth Century Meta-
    physical Poets
Elizabethan Dramatists
Theodore Dreiser
John Dryden
George Eliot
T. S. Eliot
Ralph Ellison
Ralph Waldo Emerson
William Faulkner
Henry Fielding
F. Scott Fitzgerald
Gustave Flaubert
E. M. Forster
Sigmund Freud
Robert Frost

Robert Graves
Graham Greene
Thomas Hardy
Nathaniel Hawthorne
William Hazlitt
Seamus Heaney
Ernest Hemingway
Geoffrey Hill
Friedrich Hölderlin
Homer
Gerard Manley Hopkins
William Dean Howells
Zora Neale Hurston
Henry James
Samuel Johnson and
    James Boswell
Ben Jonson
James Joyce
Franz Kafka
John Keats
Rudyard Kipling
D. H. Lawrence
John Le Carré
Ursula K. Le Guin
Doris Lessing
Sinclair Lewis
Robert Lowell
Norman Mailer
Bernard Malamud
Thomas Mann
Christopher Marlowe
Carson McCullers
Herman Melville
James Merrill
Arthur Miller
John Milton
Eugenio Montale
Marianne Moore
Iris Murdoch
Vladimir Nabokov
Joyce Carol Oates
Sean O'Casey
Flannery O'Connor
Eugene O'Neill
George Orwell
Cynthia Ozick
Walter Pater
Walker Percy
Harold Pinter
Plato
Edgar Allan Poe
Poets of Sensibility & the
    Sublime

Alexander Pope
Katherine Ann Porter
Ezra Pound
Pre-Raphaelite Poets
Marcel Proust
Thomas Pynchon
Arthur Rimbaud
Theodore Roethke
Philip Roth
John Ruskin
J. D. Salinger
Gershom Scholem
William Shakespeare
    (3 vols.)
    Histories & Poems
    Comedies
    Tragedies
George Bernard Shaw
Mary Wollstonecraft
    Shelley
Percy Bysshe Shelley
Edmund Spenser
Gertrude Stein
John Steinbeck
Laurence Sterne
Wallace Stevens
Tom Stoppard
Jonathan Swift
Alfred, Lord Tennyson
William Makepeace
    Thackeray
Henry David Thoreau
Leo Tolstoi
Anthony Trollope
Mark Twain
John Updike
Gore Vidal
Virgil
Robert Penn Warren
Evelyn Waugh
Eudora Welty
Nathanael West
Edith Wharton
Walt Whitman
Oscar Wilde
Tennessee Williams
William Carlos Williams
Thomas Wolfe
Virginia Woolf
William Wordsworth
Richard Wright
William Butler Yeats

These and other titles in preparation

Modern Critical Views

ALEXANDER POPE

Edited and with an introduction by
Harold Bloom
Sterling Professor of the Humanities
Yale University

CHELSEA HOUSE PUBLISHERS ◊ 1986
New York ◊ New Haven ◊ Philadelphia

821
PoP

7/86 Chelsea House

© 1986 by Chelsea House Publishers, a division of
Chelsea House Educational Communications, Inc.
133 Christopher Street, New York, NY 10014
345 Whitney Avenue, New Haven, CT 06511
5014 West Chester Pike, Edgemont, PA 19028

Introduction © 1986 by Harold Bloom

Printed and bound in the United States of America

∞   The paper used in this publication meets the
minimum requirements of the American National
Standard for Permanence of Paper for Printed Library
Materials, Z39.48–1984.

Library of Congress Cataloging-in-Publication Data
Main entry under title:

Alexander Pope.

   (Modern critical views)
   Bibliography: p.
   Includes index.
   Summary: Eleven previously published critical essays
on the works of the satirical eighteenth-century
English poet.
   1. Pope, Alexander, 1688–1744—Criticism and
interpretation—Addresses, essays, lectures. [1. Pope,
Alexander, 1688–1744—Criticism and interpretation—
Addresses, essays, lectures.   2. English poetry—
History and criticism—Addresses, essays, lectures]
I. Bloom, Harold.   II. Series.
Library of Congress Cataloging-in-Publication Data
   PR3634.A44   1986   821'.5   85–29062
   ISBN 0–87754–680–0

Contents

Editor's Note

This book gathers together a representative selection of the best criticism devoted to Alexander Pope, published over a thirty-five year span from 1949 through 1984, and arranged here in chronological order of its appearance. The editor is grateful to Ms. Jennifer Wagner for helping to select these essays. The introduction centers upon Dr. Samuel Johnson's powerful defense of Pope's greatness, while briefly examining the dialectical question of Pope's project of "refining" the poetic tradition.

The chronological sequence begins with the conclusion to Maynard Mack's influential essay upon Pope's imagery. It continues with William K. Wimsatt, Jr.'s equally celebrated essay upon the relationship between Pope's poetry and rhetorical theory. A triad of founding fathers of the modern criticism of Pope is completed by Earl R. Wasserman's study of *Windsor Forest*.

Another generation of critics—all indebted to Mack, Wimsatt, and Wasserman—is represented here by the work of Thomas R. Edwards, Jr., and Martin Price. Edwards, confronted by the speculative enigma of *An Essay on Man*, reaches the Johnsonian conclusion that "the poem's poetic failure is the curious measure of its human success." In Price's persuasive remarks upon the *Moral Essays*, we receive a clear sense of "an art that goes beyond mere beauty and weds its aesthetic power to moral vision." A sensitive reading of "Eloisa to Abelard" by David B. Morris follows, the first of two essays by this very Popean critic.

A larger social context is invoked in the next two essays, but in each instance with a very individual perspective. Writing on the verse epistles, particularly the magnificent one to Dr. Arbuthnot, Lawrence Lee Davidow concludes that Pope returns us not to an institutional norm, but to the personal virtues of an open heart. C. E. Nicholson, reading *The Rape of the Lock* as social history, usefully juxtaposes Pope and Karl Marx on reification, and commends Pope for his extraordinary insights into how the world of objects comes to live our lives for us. A contrasting and shrewd commentary upon Pope's Horatian imitations by Melinda Alliker Rabb moves our attention from social concerns to reflection on how Pope's persuasive mirror-images implicate his readers in a wilderness of multiple perspectives.

The social dimension and the ambiguities of perspectivism combine in Robert Griffin's brilliant recent account of Pope's strongest poem, *The Dunciad*. In a remarkable restoration of a neglected aspect of the poem, Griffin traces its relation to biblical prophecy, thus reinforcing our sense of the enormous complexity of Pope's poetic argument. This book ends by returning us to the youthful Pope, as David B. Morris analyzes *An Essay on Criticism*, finding in it a more valuable and original element of literary criticism than is generally conceded to it. Dr. Johnson loved *An Essay on Criticism*, and praised it for "extent of comprehension," "nicety of distinction," "acquaintance with mankind," and "knowledge both of ancient and modern learning." These are indeed virtues that work to refine the poetic tradition, even if they are hardly the prime virtues of poets like Milton and Blake, who stand on either side of Pope historically, and whose rather different strengths serve both to indicate Pope's limits and to acknowledge implicitly that he, and not they, labored to retain the middle ground, that bastion of civilization and its discontents that Freud named as our discomfort with culture.

Introduction

Dr. Samuel Johnson, the strongest critic in all the Western tradition (so far as I am able to judge), placed Pope ultimately in relation to Homer, greatest of precursors:

> if the writer of the *Iliad* were to class his successors, he would assign a very high place to his translator, without requiring any other evidence of genius.

Elsewhere in the *Life of Pope*, Johnson insists that Pope's *Iliad* "is certainly the noblest version of poetry which the world has ever seen." Pope, most modern critics would agree, is the poet of *The Rape of the Lock, An Epistle to Dr. Arbuthnot*, some of the *Moral Essays*, the astonishing *Epistle to Augustus*, and above all of *The Dunciad*. Translations, with rare exceptions, are for an age only. Yet what did Johnson hear when he read Pope's *Iliad*?

> Then thus to *Phoebus*, in the Realms above,
> Spoke from his Throne the Cloud-compelling *Jove*:
> Descend my *Phoebus*, on the *Phrygian* Plain,
> And from the Fight convey *Sarpedon* slain;
> Then bathe his Body in the crystal Flood,
> With Dust dishonour'd, and deform'd with Blood:
> O'er all his Limbs *Ambrosial* Odours shed,
> And with Celestial Robes adorn the mighty Dead.
> To the soft Arms of silent *Sleep* and *Death*;
> They to his Friends the mournful Charge shall bear;
> His Friends a Tomb and Pyramid shall rear;
> These unavailing Rites he may receive,
> These, after Death, are All a God can give!

This is from *The Episode of Sarpedon*, published with Pope's early *Pastorals* in 1709, and later incorporated into his complete version of the *Iliad*. It is not unrepresentative of Pope's Homer, and helps justify William Blake's savagery:

> Thus Hayley on his Toilette seeing the sope
> Cries Homer is very much improved by Pope

Still, it is unwise to dispute Johnson, and it is difficult to recall him ever praising a work so near to him in time as Pope's *Homer*, with anything like such unrestrained fervor:

> Pope searches the pages of Dryden for happy combinations of Dervick diction; but it will not be denied that he added much to what he found. He cultivated our language with so much diligence and art, that he has left in his *Homer* a treasure of poetical elegances to posterity. His version may be said to have turned the English tongue; for since its appearance no writer, however deficient in other powers, has wanted melody. Such a series of lines so elaborately corrected, and so sweetly modulated, took possession of the publick ear; the vulgar was enamoured of the poem, and the learned wondered at the translation.

That Pope's *Homer*, rather than Spenser, Shakespeare, and Milton, *may be said to have turned the English tongue*, was not Johnson's eccentric judgment, but the verdict of his age. The Augustan critical mythology that culminated in Johnson had its remote origins in the tripartite division of much seventeenth-century poetry into the schools of Spenser, Donne, and Ben Jonson. The line from Jonson to Johnson may be called the Neoclassic, a version of literary history that has its most influential manifesto in Pope's early *Essay on Criticism*, regarded by Johnson as sufficient in itself to "have placed him among the first criticks and the first poets," another uncharacteristic burst of Johnsonian hyperbole, doubtless traceable to ideological exuberance. "But most by *Numbers* judge a Poet's Song," the youthful Pope persuasively intones, while urging us to "praise the *Easie Vigor* of a Line, / Where *Denham*'s strength, and *Waller*'s sweetness join." If Eliot and Pound do not prove to have been the Cowley and Cleveland of our age, then perhaps time will show them instead to have been our Denham and our Waller, rather than our Dryden and our Pope. When the would-be Dr. Johnson, Hugh Kenner, tells us that Eliot and Pound may be said to have returned the Anglo-American tongue, then we listen to yet another revival of Augustan critical myth.

Pope's own elected precursor, Dryden, caused him no more anxiety than Homer did, a judgment in which I am happy to concur with David B. Morris. Morris remarks that "there is no more profound kinship between Pope and Dryden than the belief that poetry advances by refining the achievement of the past." Yes, but how do you refine John Milton? Pope and Dr. Johnson alike handle Milton *in their own poetry* in ways very different from Pope's refinement of Dryden or Johnson's reliance upon Pope. The exquisite parodies of Milton in *The Rape of the Lock*, and the wonderfully grotesque Miltonic mock-sublimities of *The Dunciad*, are remarkable instances of the Nietzschean, daemonic dance of influence-as-parody, much more than they are mimetic or mercantile refinements. Milton and nature are hardly everywhere the same, and *Paradise Lost* is a difficult native resource to convert into trade.

"Refinement," as a poetic trope in the context of literary history, is too large to be confined to tuning diction or metric. In Dryden and Pope, refining the tradition meant extending the realm of Enlightenment, by continuing to dispel the empire of Enthusiasm. Theodicy without enthusiasm might be described as the project of Pope's *Essay on Man*, an admirable project doubtless, but perhaps not suited to the Muse. Here is the poem's conclusion:

> Come then, my Friend, my Genius, come along,
> Oh master of the poet, and the song!
> And while the Muse now stoops, or now ascends,
> To Man's low passions, or their glorious ends,
> Teach me, like thee, in various nature wise,
> To fall with dignity, with temper rise;
> Form'd by thy converse, happily to steer
> From grave to gay, from lively to severe;
> Correct with spirit, eloquent with ease,
> Intent to reason, or polite to please.
> Oh! while along the stream of Time thy name
> Expanded flies, and gathers all its fame,
> Say, shall my little bark attendant sail,
> Pursue the triumph, and partake the gale?
> When statesmen, heroes, kings, in dust repose,
> Whose sons shall blush their fathers were thy foes,
> Shall then this verse to future age pretend
> Thou wert my guide, philosopher and friend?
> That urg'd by thee, I turn'd the tuneful art

From sounds to things, from fancy to the heart;
For Wit's false mirror held up Nature's light;
Shew'd erring Pride, WHATEVER IS, IS RIGHT;
That REASON, PASSION, answer one great aim;
That true SELF-LOVE and SOCIAL are the same;
That VIRTUE only makes our Bliss below;
And all our Knowledge is, OURSELVES TO KNOW.

The Muse here is the poet himself, trapped in the aesthetic impossibility of proclaiming that: "WHATEVER IS, IS RIGHT." This poetic disaster, if it refines tradition, does so at an outrageous price. The *Essay on Man* has its scholarly defenders, but they praise as paradox what the great Johnson properly dismissed as principles it was not his business "to clear from obscurity, dogmatism, or falsehood." We do not esteem *Paradise Lost* for its theodicy. Those who praise *An Essay on Man* for its moral and spiritual wisdom, its absurd abasement of theodicy, have done Pope ill service.

II

If *An Essay on Man* is Pope at his most dubious, then the "Epistle to Augustus," or "The First Epistle of the Second Book of Horace Imitated," displays him at very nearly his strongest. No poet before or since has written a satire either so subtle or so delicious. King George II, whose name was George Augustus, was renowned alike for his military vainglory and his contempt for poetry ("Leave such work to little Mr. Pope," he is reported to have said, "It is his trade"). Pope's revenge was at once decorous and perfect:

While You, great Patron of Mankind, sustain
The balanc'd World, and open all the Main;
Your Country, chief, in Arms abroad defend,
At home, with Morals, Arts, and Laws amend;
How shall the Muse, from such a Monarch, steal
An hour, and not defraud the Publick Weal?

George Augustus, or any monarch, could not ask for better. Unfortunately for him, he was inept at foreign policy ("sustain / The balanc'd World"), incapable of protecting British merchantmen from the marauding Spaniards ("open all the Main"), had just spent half a year abroad "in Arms," but those were the arms of his notorious German girlfriend, Amalie Sophie, and at home distinguished himself by the neglect of his duties, dislike of painting and literature, and the vigor of his performance with a harem of mistresses ("with Morals, Arts, and Laws amend").

Deftly, and with superb aplomb, Pope proceeds to destroy his victim and defend his own reputation:

> Oh! could I mount on the Maeonian wing,
> Your Arms, your Actions, your Repose to sing!
> What seas you travers'd! and what fields you fought!
> Your Country's Peace, how oft, how dearly bought!
> How barb'rous rage subsided at your word.
> And Nations wonder'd while they dropp'd the sword!
> How, when you nodded, o'er the land and deep,
> Peace stole her wing, and wrapt the world in sleep;
> Till Earth's extremes your mediation own,
> And Asia's Tyrants tremble at your Throne—
> But Verse alas! your Majesty disdains;
> And I'm not us'd to Panegyric strains:
> The Zeal of Fools offends at any time,
> But most of all, the Zeal of Fools in ryme.
> Besides, a fate attends on all I write,
> That when I aim at praise, they say I bite.
> A vile Encomium doubly ridicules,
> There's nothing blackens like the ink of fools;
> If true, a woful likeness, and if lyes,
> "Praise undeserv'd is scandal in disguise:"
> Well may he blush, who gives it, or receives;
> And when I flatter, let my dirty leaves
> (Like Journals, Odes, and such forgotten things
> As Eusden, Philips, Settle, writ of Kings)
> Cloath spice, line trunks, or flutt'ring in a row,
> Befringe the rails of Bedlam and Sohoe.

Maeonian or Homeric mountings are necessary to sing of Achilles or Odysseus. Every line in the passage above is a mortal insult, George Augustus being what he was, but to acknowledge the insult would be to accept the truth. The grand movement of "Your Arms, your Actions, your Repose to sing!" is as fresh now as it was in 1737, and as applicable to President Reagan's repose as it was to George II's. "When I aim at praise, they say I bite," Pope protests, and we recognize that no satirist since in the language, from Byron to Waugh, is Pope's peer. But if that were the limit of Pope's satirical art, we would not be obliged to admit him among the strongest poets in the language. What makes him so formidable, a Milton among satirists, is *The Dunciad*, certainly the poetic masterpiece of its century. *The Dunciad*, rather than Pope's *Homer*, ought to have received Johnson's highest praise. What inhibited a critic of Johnson's enormous discernment from receiving the poem as exuberantly as did William K. Wimsatt, Jr., the Johnson of our day?

Johnson, perhaps up too close to the person, judged it as the text where "Pope's irascibility prevailed" and where "Pope confessed his own pain by his anger; but he gave no pain to those who had provoked him." Clearly, Johnson strongly misread *The Dunciad*, since he refused to believe that the poem's design was moral. He found in it "petulance and malignity enough," granted it some beauties, and condemned "the grossness of its images," which he rightly found Swiftian. Certainly a comparison of the savagery of *The Dunciad* with the compassion of *The Vanity of Human Wishes* will convince us that Johnson had a profounder moral intellect than Pope, and was much the better man, but *The Dunciad* is immensely the finer poem, beautifully eloquent and humane as *The Vanity of Human Wishes* remains.

Yet one can sympathize with Johnson's uneasiness at Pope's freedom in expressing a personal rancor in his masterwork. It is difficult to read *The Dunciad* as a refinement upon the poetic tradition. At his rhetorical best, Pope is not quite the embattled defender of Enlightened England he declared himself to be. His fear of universal madness, of the return of a nihilistic abyss, is more than a personal pathology or ideology. The parallel fear is actually more personal in Johnson, which may be the clue to his reservations about the poem.

How rational a poem is *The Dunciad*? Compared to *Paradise Lost*, not very, must surely be the answer. The astonishing opening invokes Milton, thus enforcing a contrast at once dangerous and audaciously successful:

> Yet, yet a moment, one dim Ray of Light
> Indulge, dread Chaos, and eternal night!
> Of darkness visible so much be lent,
> As half to shew, half veil the deep Intent.
> Ye Pow'rs! whose Mysteries restor'd I sing,
> To whom Time bears me on his rapid wing,
> Suspend a while your Force inertly strong,
> Then take at once the Poet and the Song.

Satan, viewing the horrible dungeon of hell, discovers:

> yet from those flames
> No light, but rather darkness visible
> Served only to discover rights of woe,
> Regions of sorrow, doleful shades, where peace
> And rest can never duell, hope never comes
> That comes to all;

The cultural world is now hell, Pope avers, nor is he out of it. Dulness, a goddess as malevolent as Virgil's Juno, comes in all her majesty, to establish the Kingdom of the Dull upon earth, and her triumph is complete:

> Beneath her foot-stool, *Science* groans in Chains,
> And *Wit* dreads Exile, Penalties and Pains.
> There foam'd rebellious *Logic*, gagg'd and bound,
> There, stript, fair *Rhet'ric* languish'd on the ground;
> His blunted Arms by *Sophistry* are born,
> And shameless *Billingsgate* her Robes adorn.
> *Morality*, by her false Guardians drawn,
> *Chicane* in Furs, and *Casuistry* in Lawn,
> Gasps, as they straiten at each end the cord,
> And dies, when Dulness gives her Page the word.
> Mad *Mathesis* alone was unconfin'd,
> Too mad for mere material chains to bind,
> Now to pure Space lifts her extatic stare,
> Now running round the Circle, finds it square.
> But held in ten-fold bonds the *Muses* lie,
> Watch'd both by Envy's and by Flatt'ry's eye:
> There to her heart sad Tragedy addrest
> The dagger wont to pierce the Tyrant's breast;
> But sober History restrain'd her rage,
> And promis'd Vengeance on a barb'rous age.

This may have been justified in 1743; in 1985 it is simply the way things are. Every reader shudders (or should) as Pope ends the poem with a prophecy we continue to fulfill daily, even as we approach the domestication of a universal cultural disaster:

> In vain, in vain—the all-composing Hour
> Resistless falls: The Muse obeys the Pow'r.
> She comes! she comes! the sable Throne behold
> of *Night* Primaeval, and of *Chaos* old!
> Before her, *Fancy's* gilded clouds decay,

And all its varying Rain-bows die away.
Wit shoots in vain its momentary fires,
The meteor drops, and in a flash expires.
As one by one, at dread Medea's strain,
The sick'ning stars fade off th' ethereal plain;
As Argus' eyes by Hermes' wand opprest,
Clos'd one by one to everlasting rest;
Thus at her felt approach, and secret might,
Art after *Art* goes out, and all is Night.
See skulking *Truth* to her old Cavern fled,
Mountains of Casuistry heap'd o'er her head!
Philosophy, that lean'd on Heav'n before,
Shrinks to her second cause, and is no more.
Physic of *Metaphysic* begs defence,
And *Metaphysic* calls for aid on *Sense*!
See *Mystery* to *Mathematics* fly!
In vain! they gaze, turn giddy, rave, and die.
Religion blushing veils her sacred fires,
And unawares *Morality* expires.
Nor *public* Flame, nor *private*, dares to shine;
Nor *human* Spark is left, nor Glimpse *divine*!
Lo! thy dread Empire, CHAOS! is restor'd;
Light dies before thy uncreating word;
Thy hand, great Anarch! lets the curtain fall;
And Universal Darkness buries All.

The Gospel of John, and Milton's variations upon it, are reversed as:
"Light dies before thy uncreating word." Johnson, who dreaded something
like this return to chaos, may have been too strongly affected by Pope's
vision to have valued it properly. It cannot be an accident that Pope's most
Miltonic moments come in the apocalyptic opening and close of Book IV
of *The Dunciad*. The trouble at the core of Milton is also Pope's, whose
relation to Milton was very unlike his relation to Dryden. Whatever the
force of the poetic past was to Pope, that part of it he felt emanating from
Milton was beyond refinement. "Darkness visible," the Miltonic legacy after
all, returned as the inevitable trope for Pope's sense of what lay always
beyond the possibilities of the Enlightenment.

MAYNARD MACK

"Wit and Poetry and Pope"

The great pervasive metaphor of Augustan literature, including Pope's poetry, is the metaphor of tone: the mock-heroic. It is very closely allied, of course, to the classical or Roman myth [discussed earlier] and is, like that, a reservoir of strength. By its means, without the use of overt imagery at all, opposite and discordant qualities may be locked together in 'a balance or reconcilement of sameness with difference, of the general with the concrete, the idea with the image, the individual with the representative, the sense of novelty and freshness with old and familiar objects'—the mock-heroic seems made on purpose to fit this definition of Coleridge's of the power of imagination. For a literature of decorums like the Augustan, it was a metaphor with every sort of value. It could be used in the large, as in *Joseph Andrews, Tom Jones, The Beggar's Opera, The Rape of the Lock, The Dunciad,* or in the small—the passage, the line. It could be set in motion by a passing allusion, not necessarily to the classics:

> Calm Temperance, whose blessings those partake,
> Who hunger, and who thirst, for scribling sake;

by a word:

> Glad chains, warm furs, broad banners, and broad faces;

even by a cadence:

From *Pope and His Contemporaries: Essays Presented to George Sherburn*. Copyright © 1949 by The Clarendon Press, Oxford. Original title " 'Wit and Poetry and Pope': Some Observations on His Imagery."

> And the fresh vomit run for ever green.

Moreover, it was a way of getting the local, the ephemeral, the pressure of life as it was lived, into poetry, and yet distancing it in amber:

> That live-long wig, which Gorgon's self might own,
> Eternal buckle takes in Parian stone.

It was also a way of qualifying an attitude, of genuinely 'heroicizing' a Man of Ross, a parson Adams, a School-mistress, yet undercutting them with a more inclusive attitude:

> Rise, *honest* Muse! and sing the Man of Ross

Above all—and this, I think, was its supreme advantage for Pope—it was a metaphor that could be made to look two ways. If the heroic genre and the heroic episodes lurking behind *The Rape of the Lock* diminish many of the values of this society, they also partially throw their weight behind some others. Clarissa's speech is an excellent case in point. Her words represent a sad shrinkage from the epic views of Glaucus which reverberate behind them, views involving real heroism and (to adapt Mr. Eliot's phrase) the awful daring of a real surrender. Still, the effect of the contrast is not wholly minimizing. Clarissa's vision of life, worldly as it is when seen against the heroic standard, surpasses the others in the poem and points, even if obliquely, to the tragic conflict between the human lot and the human will that is common to life at every level.

This flexibility of the mock-heroic metaphor is seen in its greatest perfection in the *Dunciad*. There are, indeed, three thicknesses of metaphor in this poem: an overall metaphor, in which the poem as a whole serves as vehicle for a tenor which is the decline of literary and human values generally; a network of local metaphor, in which this poem is especially prolific; and in between, the specifically mock-heroic metaphor which springs from holding the tone and often the circumstances of heroic poetry against the triviality of the dunces and their activities. But what is striking about this metaphor in the *Dunciad*, and indicative of its flexibility, is that it is applied quite differently from the way it is applied in the *Rape of the Lock*. There, the epic mode as vehicle either depresses the values of the actors, as with Belinda, or somewhat supports them, as with Clarissa. Here, on the contrary, one of the two lines of development (the comic) grows from allowing the actors to depress and degrade the heroic mode, its dignity and beauty. Again and again Pope builds up in the poem effects of striking epic richness, only to let them be broken down, disfigured, stained—as the word 'vomit' stains

the lovely movement and suggestion of the epic line quoted above. Thus
the diving and other games in Book II disfigure the idea of noble emulation
and suggest the befoulment of heroic values through the befoulment of the
words and activities in which these values are recorded. Thus the fop's Grand
Tour in IV mutilates a classical and Renaissance ideal (cf. also Virgil's Aeneas,
to whose destined wanderings toward Rome the fop's are likened) of wisdom
ripened by commerce with men and cities. Indeed, the lines of the whole
passage are balanced between the ideal and the fop's perversions of it:

> A dauntless infant! never scar'd with God.
> Europe he saw, and Europe saw him too.
> Judicious drank, and greatly daring dined;

or between related ideals and what has happened to them:

> To happy Convents, bosomed deep in Vines,
> Where slumber Abbots, purple as their Wines.

or between epic resonances, the epic names, and the sorry facts:

> To where the Seine, obsequious as she runs,
> Pours at great Bourbon's feet her silken sons.

This is one line of development in the *Dunciad*. The other is its converse:
the epic vehicle is gradually made throughout the poem to enlarge and give
a status of serious menace to all this ludicrous activity. Here the epic circumstance of a presiding goddess proved invaluable. Partly ludicrous herself,
she could also become the locus of inexhaustible negation behind the movements of her trivial puppets; her force could be associated humorously, but
also seriously, with the powerful names of Chaos, Night, Anti-Christ, and
with perversions of favourite order symbols like the sun, monarchy, and
gravitation. Here, too, the epic backgrounds as supplied by Milton could
be drawn in. Mr. C. S. Lewis has remarked of *Paradise Lost* that 'only those
will fully understand it who see that it might have been a comic poem'.
The *Dunciad* is one realization of that might-have-been. Over and above the
flow of Miltonic echoes and allusions, or the structural resemblances like
Cibber's (or Theobald's) Pisgah-vision based on Adam's, or the clustered
names of dunces like those of Milton's devils, thick as the leaves that strew
bad books in Grubstreet—the *Dunciad* is a version of Milton's theme in
being the story of an uncreating Logos. As the poem progresses, our sense
of this increases through the calling in of more and more powerful associations
by the epic vehicle. The activities of the dunces and of Dulness are more
and more equated with religious anti-values, culminating in the passage on

the Eucharist. . . . The metaphor of the coronation of the king-dunce moves always closer to and then flows into the metaphor of the Day of the Lord, the descent of the anti-Messiah, the uncreating Word. Meantime, symbols which have formerly been ludicrous—insects, for instance, or sleep—are given by this expansion in the epic vehicle a more sombre cast. The dunces thicken and become less individual, more anonymous, expressive of blind inertia— bees in swarm, or locusts blackening the land. Sleep becomes tied up with its baser physical manifestations, with drunkenness, with deception, with ignorance, with neglect of obligation, and finally with death. This is the sleep which *is* death, we realize, a *Narrendämmerung*, the twilight of the moral will. And yet, because of the ambivalence of the mock-heroic metaphor, Pope can keep to the end the tension between all these creatures as comic and ridiculous, and their destructive potentiality in being so. Certainly two of the finest puns in any poetry are those with which he continues to exploit this tension at the very end of the poem, when Dulness finally *yawns* and Nature *nods*.

W . K . W I M S A T T , J R .

Rhetoric and Poems

When we seek to confront two such elusive entities as a theory of poems and poems themselves and to determine relations between these two, I think there is much to be said for placing them first, tentatively, in their most generic and noncommittal relation. There is much to be said for the conjunctional form of title commonly given to the academic paper: X *and* Y, Shakespeare *and* Hall's Chronicle, Theory *and* Poems. I for one find it convenient to distinguish five main types of relation between theory and poems, all five of which are frequently to be observed in critical and historical studies, though often more or less confused.

I.   There is for one thing the kind of relation between theory and poems with which we are concerned when our interest is chiefly in the theory itself, that is, when we try to describe and assess a given theory as objectively as we can with reference to whatever general norms for poems and hence for theory we possess. Is the classical theory of imitation in any sense a good or fruitful theory of poems? Or the classical theory of ornament and system of rhetoric? Or do these deserve to be completely demolished, as in the Crocean history of Aesthetic? Is Matthew Arnold's view of the high seriousness and critical function of poems the right view? Or, does it, as Tate and others have argued, deliver poems into the hands of science and morals? My purpose at the moment is not to maintain the importance of such questions, but merely to note their occurrence.

II.   It may at times be difficult to distinguish between such a general-evaluative interest in theory and what I consider a second kind of interest,

From *The Verbal Icon: Studies in the Meaning of Poetry.* Copyright © 1954 by The University Press of Kentucky. Original title "Rhetoric and Poems: Alexander Pope."

that with which we approach a theorist, especially a technical or rhetorical theorist and his cousins of the trivium, the grammarian and logician, for the purpose of borrowing tools which we shall put to the partly unpredictable uses of our own analysis: *fable*, or *character*, or *metaphor* from Aristotle, *antithesis* or *parallel* from the rhetoricians, *sentences*, for that matter, and *nouns* and *verbs* from the grammarians. To do this may imply that we think a theorist a good theorist of poems, and yet I believe it may come short of that, insofar as concepts themselves may come short of integrated or achieved theory, and also insofar as this borrowing extends readily, and perhaps most profitably, to the less literary philosophers, the grammarian and logician.

To look in the historical direction, I should say that when we take up the more generic concepts of rhetoric, grammar, and logic, we ought to be on our guard against imputing to them special connections with the poems of any specific period—as would happen if one were to note the Aristotelian "categories" in Renaissance logic and read in them an influence on the imagery of Drayton or Donne. Richards in his *Philosophy of Rhetoric* has found the concept of the morpheme as defined by Bloomfield a useful one for explaining certain powers of words. But it would be somewhat wide of the mark to learn that Auden had read either Richards or Bloomfield and from that go on to discover such elements as morphemes in Auden's poems. The idea of the circulation of the blood was expounded by Harvey in 1616, but we do not conceive that it was about that time that blood began to circulate in the human body.

III.   A third relation between theory and poems is that which obtains when a given theory does have a specific, historical relation to a poem, but has this in virtue of the special fact that it appears in the poem as part of the poem's meaning or content. One will recall numerous instances in the history of English poetry: Chaucer's burlesque of Geoffrey of Vinsauf in the mock heroic of the cock and the fox, Stephen Hawes' celebration of "golden" words in his *Pastime of Pleasure*, the Horatian arts of poetry (especially that of Pope), Mark Akenside's *Pleasures of the Imagination*, Wordsworth's *Prelude*, and Shelley's *Ode to the West Wind* (where the sparks from the unextinguished priestly hearth mingle with the sparks of "inextinguishable thought" which appear twice in his prose *Defense of Poetry*). This relation between theory and poems is that which for the most part obtains in historical studies of the neutrally observational type—but often with some implication that the relation established is of a more formal, or actually theoretical, sort.

IV.   A fourth relation between theory and poems which I believe it worthwhile to distinguish is again a specific historical relation, that which obtains when in a given era a theory helps to determine poems not as subject matter but as an influence or cause of why they are written in a certain way. Perhaps the most important thing to note about this relation is that (like number III) it does not require that the theory as theory be an adequate account of the poems. The classic theory concerning imitation of models, for instance, had a close bearing on the Augustan vogue of translations, paraphrases, and "imitations." Yet a theory of models is never really a literary theory, only a practical rule of inspiration. And the classic theory in particular seemed almost unconscious of the paramount factor of parody, or allusiveness, which worked in the most lively Augustan instances. Again, the massive theory of epic which prevailed in that day might be taken as a partial cause of Blackmore's *Prince Arthur* or, in jocular reversal, of *The Rape of the Lock*, or *The Dunciad*. But there are no successfully serious epics with which the theory can be compared. During the same period, the doctrine *Ut pictura poesis* may have joined with empirical views of imagination to determine the subject matter of some poems; it may have been responsible for certain instances of the pictorial fallacy or opaqueness in word painting; but, as Lessing was partly to show, the analogy between words and marble or paint is of limited service for analyzing the positive qualities of verbal art.

V. A fifth relation between theory and poems, that which will be the final focus of our argument, is that which obtains when in any historical era we can discern a specific affinity between theory as such and poems; that is, when what the theory says seems to be a specially appropriate description of what the poems are. Such a relation may of course coincide with the causal relation which we have just considered. There may be instances of a close causal connection between theory and poems and at the same time a high degree of validity for the theory as theory. A successful poet may be shown to have read a certain theory with profit, or he may even, though this I believe is rare, succeed in uttering a theory which explains his own poems. But these are matters for another sort of inquiry. It is only by keeping clear of such intentionalistic complications that we can focus upon the literary and critical issue: that is, the degree of resemblance between the theory and the poems or the adequacy of the theory to describe the poems.

To show a real correspondence between the theory of an era and the poems of the era would be, I take it, one of the most proper concerns of the student of criticism in its historical aspect, and to show that the theory gave an adequate account of the poems would be his masterpiece. Such an achievement, we ought at the same time to note, would be a special challenge to the student of either theory or poems who was interested in universal definitions or norms. Poems in different eras, it is assumed, will be to some extent different. But theory deals with universals. It is more disconcerting to find the theory of successive ages different than to find the poems different. No matter how well we, with our historical desires, succeed in localizing the theory or assimilating it to the poems of its own age, we can still see that the theory itself aims at the universal. If the poems and the theory vary in step with each other, then I suppose a great appearance of support is offered to historical relativism—unless indeed one's dialectic rises to reconciling certain valid special theories of poetry, say the metaphysical theory of wit and the romantic theory of imagination, in a more inclusive harmony. Or unless one is brave enough to decide in a given case that both poems and theory are bad—as Yvor Winters has not scrupled to say the poems of Poe are bad because they perfectly illustrate Poe's theory, a deliquescent version of romantic imagination.

Not every theory found in a given age is equally relevant to describing the poems of that age. There are not only bad theories which have no special bearing on any kind of poems, but another and more important kind, those of such general significance (if not complete truth) that they transcend a special application to the poems of their age. Such, for example, I should call the neoclassic doctrine that poetry reveals the generic or universal. Despite the game of omber and the all too specific and solid Dunces, the doctrine of the universal is if correctly interpreted a valid doctrine, and furthermore it is itself universal, that is, neither more nor less true of good neoclassic poems than of good poems in any other mode. Or the related doctrine that "Style is the dress of thought"—true poetry is "nature to advantage dressed." This would appear to be the Augustan version of a paradox which literary criticism has so far by no means solved. Today we speak of art signs as iconic or as calling attention to their own excellence, or we speak of poetry as intensely realized meaning, or as dramatized meaning, or perhaps as structure of meaning. Poetic meaning still seems to contain other meanings and to make use of them, but seems not to be tested in the end by the same norms. The doctrine that style is the dress of thought is as much our concern as it was Pope's, and, whatever its degree of truth, it applies no more specially to Augustan poems than to any other kind.

In somewhat the same way I believe we should have to discuss the whole classical theory of imitation and the antitheses deriving from the theory and flourishing in Pope's time, between art and nature, between invention and imitation of models, between wit and judgment, between genius and the rules. Or perhaps some of these theoretical formulas do show a special relation to the poems of the age, though one which will make acceptable sense to us only after a certain adjustment. One such example seems to me of importance here as a partial frame of reference for the more specific rhetorical ideas which I wish to discuss. I have in mind the Augustan concept of "correctness," which, distinguished from greatness or "genius," sometimes took the form of an ideal, as in the well known advice of Walsh to Pope: that there had been *great* English poets, but no great poet who was *correct*; but sometimes also was conceived as a fault or limitation, as in Addison's *Spectators*, Nos. 160 and 291, where the untrammeled productions of ancient Genius are preferred to the scrupulous nicety or correctness of the moderns. As Sir Joshua Reynolds was later to phrase it: "So far, indeed, is the presence of genius from implying an absence of faults, that they are considered by many as its inseparable companions." The paradox was still vital in the next century, when Ruskin preferred the *imperfections*, that is, the irregularities, of Gothic architecture to the *perfection*, that is, the regularity, of geometric ornaments in Greek architecture. This bizarre critical tradition seems to arise from the capacity of the term *correctness* to be taken not only (1) as a general term of value (certainly what is "correct" is right and good), but (2) as a more specially descriptive term, meaning something like symmetry and something like restraint and precision. It is in the latter sense, of course, that we shall have to take it if we apply it to Augustan poems—if we wish to say that Pope followed the advice of Walsh and became a *correct* poet. The other sense will hardly go with the liberal and usually accepted view that Shakespeare's verse and rhetoric fit what Shakespeare is saying, just as Pope's fit what Pope is saying. In the final sense of poetic value, each kind of good poetry is correct.

II

It is under the head of correctness in its limited sense that the most precise resemblances between neoclassic theory and neoclassic poems seem to be available—I mean in the rhetoric of the closed couplet. Perhaps it is not too much to say that the resemblance between theory and poems which obtains here is one of the most precise in the history of literature and criticism— that the hexameter couplets of Boileau and Racine and the pentameters of Dryden and Pope represent the maximum fulfillment of a classic technical theory. Yet the relation between theory and poems which obtains even here is not, as we shall see, strictly a synchronous one.

The year 1935 gave us two highly competent studies, one by Professor Williamson, concerning the history of English couplet theory from Puttenham in 1589 to Edward Bysshe in 1702; and one by Miss Wallerstein,

concerning the practice of English couplet writers, from the poems of Gri-
mald in Tottel's *Miscellany* to Denham's lines on the Thames in 1655.
Professors Williamson and Wallerstein, writing from these different directions, theory and poems, produced notably harmonious accounts of couplet
rhetoric; the sententious closure, the balanced lines and half-lines, the antithesis and inversion, the strict metric and accordingly slight but telling
variations, the constantly close and tensile union of what are called musical
with logical and rhetorical effects. The dates embraced in the works of these
two writers may, however, invite the reflection that so far as the couplets of
Alexander Pope (at the English neoclassic zenith) conform to a theory of
rhetoric, it is to a theory which had reached its full development a generation
or two earlier. For a good account in English of the figures of speech and
thought to be found in Pope's verse one will perhaps go even as far back as
Puttenham's *Arte of English Poesie*. In Puttenham one will find too the main
metrical rules and even the important emphasis on the caesura. Edward
Bysshe's *Art of English Poetry*, which may plausibly be taken as representative
of what had happened to English poetics by the time Pope was a youth,
says nothing at all of the figures, though it carries the metrics to a far greater
degree of rigidity than Puttenham and includes the now famous dictionary
of rhymes. The classical figures of speech and thought, joined with poetics
during the Middle Ages, had by Bysshe's time been reseparated from poetics
and confined again in the treatises on prose rhetoric—such as that of Thomas
Blount, *The Academie of Eloquence* (1654), or that of John Smith, *The Mysterie
of Rhetorique Unvail'd* (1657). Puttenham's *Arte* of 1589, though it is only
one of many English accounts of rhetorical figures up to Pope's day, remains
the most lively and informative and the most precisely focused upon poems.

     Pope himself in chapters 10 and 11 of *Peri Bathous* wrote a comic
treatment of "Tropes and Figures" (including "The Antithesis, or See-Saw"),
and he once observed to Spence that the "stiffness of style" in Wycherley's
plays was "occasioned by his always studying for antithesis." But neither in
his *Essay on Criticism*, nor in his remarks to Spence, nor in his letters, even
the elaborate letter on versification to Walsh, has Pope anything substantial
to say about the system of artful figures which later critics have considered
characteristic of his couplets. Pope talks of the metrical "niceties," of suiting
the sound to the sense, of caesura, of expletives, and of hiatus, or of avoiding
extravagance in diction. The rhetorical sinews of the kind of verse in which
he was the champion—the essential patterns where Waller's strength and
Denham's sweetness joined, where Dryden had achieved the long resounding
march and energy divine—these perhaps had been learned so well by Pope
as a boy that he could forget them. "It was our family priest," he told

Spence, "who taught me the figures, accidence, and first part of grammar."
In later life perhaps the figures were assumed by Pope under the general
head of "correctness." At any rate he seems to have been able to take them
for granted.

Among the hundred odd figures, "auricular," "sensable," and "sententious," presented by Puttenham, there are certain ones, a rather large number
if all subdivisions of the main types are counted, which would seem to be
fundamental to the logic of the formally ordered verbal style. Thus, *"Parison,
or the figure of even [clauses],"* *"Omoioteleton,* or the figure of like-loose [like
endings],"* and *"Anaphora,* or the figure of report"* (that is, repetition of a
word at the beginning of successive clauses) are the figures in Puttenham
which refer to formal parallels and which under one set of terms or another
are a constant part of the rhetorical tradition from Puttenham back to Aristotle. Contrast or antithesis is the natural accompaniment of parallel. This
appears in Puttenham as *"Antitheton,* or the quarreller, otherwise called the
overthwart or rencounter." Wherever there is a parallel, there is a distinction,
and wherever a distinction, the possibility of a paradox, an antithesis, or at
least a modulation. Thus, to illustrate now from the verse of Pope:

> Who sees with equal eye, as God of all,
> A hero perish, or a sparrow fall.

> Favours to none, to all she smiles extends;
> Oft she rejects, but never once offends.

> Survey the WHOLE, nor seek slight faults to find
> Where nature moves, and rapture warms the mind.

This brings us, still quite naturally, to a third group of figures, those
distinguished by Puttenham as *"Zeugma,* or the single supply" and *"Sillepsis,*
or the double supply." Zeugma is further distinguished by Puttenham into
Prozeugma (or the Ringleader), *Mezozeugma* (or the Middlemarcher), and *Hy-
pozeugma* (or the Rerewarder), accordingly as the zeugma, or yoking word,
occurs at the beginning, the middle, or the end of a total construction. He
treats zeugma among the figures "merely *auricular* in that they reach no
furder than the eare," and among figures "that work by defect," that is, by
the absence of "some little portion of speech." He does not say anything
about the relation of zeugma to parallel. But we might observe that zeugma
or ellipsis is almost the inevitable effect of a tightened and precise economy
of parallel. If A, B, C and X, B, Z are presented, then A, B, C and X, Z
is an easy result; or if A, B and X, B, then A, B and X—in the more usual
case, the parallel of two elements. Thus, in Pope's verse:

> *Who* could not win the mistress, wooed the maid. (Prozeugma)
>
> And now a bubble *burst*, and now a world. (Mezozeugma)
>
> Where nature moves, and rapture warms the *mind*. (Hypozeugma)

And, to note a special and significant kind of zeugma that occurs in Pope's verse, such examples as these:

> Or lose her heart, or necklace, at a ball.
>
> Or stain her honour or her new brocade.

This is metaphor. I mention it here not simply to list the figure of metaphor among Pope's accomplishments. Puttenham also duly lists *"Metaphora,* or the figure of transport." But here it seems to me curious, and worth noting, though it is not noted by Puttenham, that a series of several logical steps, distinction, parallel, then simplification or canceling a common element, has led us to metaphor, something that has often, and notably by some in Pope's day, been considered the very essence of the irrational or merely imaginative in poetry. Let us carry our series to its conclusion, returning to Puttenham for help. Consider the figure of *"Sillepsis,* or the double supply," which occurs according to Puttenham when a verb is used either with a double grammatical congruity, or in a double sense. The latter may be thus illustrated from Pope's verse.

> Here thou, great Anna! whom three realms obey,
> Dost sometimes counsel take—and sometimes tea.

> With earnest eyes, and round unthinking face,
> He first the snuff-box opened, then the case.

Worse and worse. We have now descended from logical parallel and ellipsis, through metaphor, into pun. In short, by starting with what might have been thought the most logical and prosaic aspects of Pope's verse (both *Antitheton* and *Parison* were mentioned by Puttenham as figures specially related to prose), and by moving through a few shades of meaning, we have arrived at the very things which the modern critic Empson noticed first in looking for the shiftiness or ambiguity of this kind of verse. We may note too, as we pass, that the distinction between the two figures last described, the metaphoric zeugma and the punning syllepsis, is not always easy. Take the couplet preceding that about counsel and tea:

> Here Britain's statesmen oft the fall foredoom
> Of foreign Tyrants and of Nymphs at home.

It depends on how technically and specifically we are accustomed to think of a "fall" from virtue, whether we take "the fall of tyrants and of nymphs" as metaphor or pun.

But now I should like to backtrack into an area of rhetoric different from antitheses and parallels, though joining them or branching off from them, in Puttenham's *Arte*, under the figure *Anaphora*, the word or phrase repeated at the beginning of successive clauses. Puttenham supplies a large battery of figures in this area: "counterturns," "redoubles," "eccho sounds," "swifte repeates," "rebounds," and "counterchanges," among which the pick is *"Traductio*, or the tranlacer."* This, says Puttenham, "is when ye turne and tranlace a word into many sundrie shapes as the Tailor doth his garment, and after that sort do play with him in your dittie." The principle of these figures is that a word or root is repeated in various syntactic positions, and sometimes in various forms, with a consequent shifting, version, turning, or translacing of the sense. These are the figures which Dryden in 1693 calls "turns, both on the words and on the thought," and which, despite a report by Dryden to the contrary, are nowhere better illustrated than in Milton's *Paradise Lost*. The turn is one of the main sinews of the sense variously drawn out from line to line. "So Man . . . Shall . . . die, And dying rise, and rising with him raise His Brethren, ransomed with his own dear life." Toward the end of the seventeenth century this kind of wordplay had fallen into comparative disfavor. We need not be surprised that in Pope's verse it is less heavily underscored.

> Yet graceful ease, and sweetness void of pride,
> Might hide her faults, if Belles had faults to hide.

> Jilts ruled the state, and statesmen farces writ,
> Nay wits had pensions, and young lords had wit.

These are lighter turns than Milton's—and at the same time wittier turns. By a different route we have arrived at somewhat the same terminus as when we pursued the forms of logical parallel, that is, at something like illogical pun—a difference being that whereas before we found the single word of two meanings, we find now two or more words of similar sound and one or another kind of play between their meanings.

In the couplet rhetoric which we have been examining, the abstract logic of parallel and antithesis is complicated and offset, then, by the turn and by the metaphoric zeugma and the punning syllepsis. It is complicated also by one other element of alogical counterpattern—the most important by far and, I believe, the apex of all the rhetorical phenomena which we have been considering—that is, rhyme. "Symphonie" or "cadence," says

Puttenham, meaning rhyme, is "all the sweetnesse and cunning in our vulgar poesie." And here we have too, as it happens, a theoretical statement by the master of practice. Pope told Spence:

> I have nothing to say for rhyme but that I doubt whether a poem can support itself without it in our language, unless it be stiffened with such strange words as are likely to destroy our language itself. The high style that is affected so much in blank verse would not have been borne even in Milton had not his subject turned so much on such strange, out-of-the-world things as it does.

Rhyme, in this offhand statement, seems to be something like a stiffening or support of verse, rather than the commonly conceived music. Puttenham remarks that the Greeks and Latins "used a maner of speach, by clauses of like termination, which they called *homoioteleuton*," a thing somewhat like vernacular rhyme, yet different. The difference between *rhyme* and *homoeoteleuton* is, in fact, one of the most profound of rhetorical differences. For *homoeoteleuton*, the repetition of inflected endings (morphemes) to support logical parallels of statement, is that which added to parallel and antithesis makes the rhetoric of pointed prose. But rhyme, the use of alogical or accidental sound resemblances between different morphemes, is that which added to parallel and antithesis makes the rhetoric of the pointed couplet. As the turn was the characteristic stiffener of classical Latin verse and of its English counterpart the blank verse of Milton, so rhyme was the characteristic stiffener of vernacular verse and especially of the couplet.

> Whatever Nature has in worth denied
> She gives in large recruits of needful Pride.

The music of the rhyme is mental; it consists in an odd, almost magic, relation of phonetic likeness which encourages us to perceive and believe in a meaning otherwise asserted by the words of the couplet. The nonparallel or chiastic chime (worth[1]-denied,[2] gives[2]-Pride[1']) is the phonetic expression of the unhappy receptivity of the mental void. The principle is well illustrated in a few of Pope's proper-name rhymes, where we may note an affinity for a certain old-fashioned and childish form of riddle to be found in the pages of *The Farmer's Almanac*. Why is A like B? Because the name of A or of something connected with A means B or something connected with B. Why is a dog dressed warmer in summer than in winter? Because in winter he wears a fur coat, and in summer he wears a fur coat and pants. Why is a

certain poet a dangerous influence upon married women? Because his name
sounds like something.

> Poor Cornus sees his frantic wife elope,
> And curses Wit, and Poetry, and Pope.

Why is a certain scholar a graceless figure? Because his name shows it.

> Yet ne'er one sprig of laurel graced these ribalds,
> From slashing *Bentley* down to pidling *Tibbalds.*

Here the words *sprig* and *pidling* play a part too in proving what it means
to have a name like that. *Paronomasia,* "*Prosonomasia,* or the Nicknamer,"
is Puttenham's name for this figure. "As, *Tiberius* the Emperor, because he
was a great drinker of wine, they called him by way of derision to his owne
name, *Caldius Biberius Nero,* in steade of *Claudius Tiberius Nero.*" But Puttenham, I admit, does not connect this figure with the "symphonie" or
"tunable consente" called rhyme.

Poetry, it would appear, is not an affair of pure ideas—where X or Y
could by agreement be substituted for any given word—nor strictly speaking
is it an affair of sound as such or verbal music. Poetry is both sense and
sound, and not by parallel or addition, but by a kind of union—which may
be heard in onomatopoeia and expressive rhythm and in various modes of
suggestion, extension, and secret verbal functioning. Of these the pun and
its cousin the rhyme are but the most extravagant instances. Poetry exploits
the *facts* of language, that words *do* mean so and so and acquire a kind of
prerogative to do this.

English critics of the Renaissance, among them Milton and latterly
even Dryden, were inclined to be hard on rhyme, calling it a jingling
bondage, rude, beggarly, and Gothic. (Even Puttenham remarks that rhyme
was brought into Greek and Latin by "barbarous souldiers out of the Campe.")
The Earl of Roscommon in polished couplets recited the bardic and monkish
history of rhyme and hailed the glorious day when the British Muse should
put on the rhymeless majesty of Rome and Athens. Critics of Pope's day—
Dennis, Felton, and Gildon—took the same cue and called rhyme "soft,"
"effeminate," "emasculating." At the same time, as we have seen, the basic
figures of parallel and antithesis originated as prose figures and by their
nature tended to abstraction, order, and regular lines. Other factors too in
the latter half of the seventeenth century—the scientific mistrust of inventive
imagination, the plain style of scientists and pulpit orators, a refined and
moderate way of talking adopted by society—are sometimes supposed to
have helped in making the Augustan couplet poems the nearest things to

prose poems in our language. Dryden and Pope, we remember Arnold said, are "classics of our prose." This, of course, we do not fully believe any more. Yet I suggest that we are confronted by an extremely curious and challenging situation in the heroic couplet of Pope: where a verse basically ordered by the rational rules of parallel and antithesis and showing at least a certain characteristic restraint of imagination, as contrasted say with metaphysical verse, at the same time is found to rely so heavily for "support" or "stiffening"—to use again the terms of Pope—on so barbarous and Gothic a device as rhyme.

In tracing the parallel between Puttenham and Pope we have observed perhaps the maximum degree of resemblance that obtains between the poems of Pope and any contemporary or nearly contemporary set of poetic rules. At the same time we have scarcely been able to refrain at each step from noting the incompleteness of Puttenham when compared to the fullness of the poetic actuality, even at the level specifically cited from Puttenham, the rhetorical. How far, we may now return and ask, does Puttenham or does any other rhetorician take us either in stating the main principles of couplet rhetoric or in exploring them? The answer, I believe, is: Not far. Puttenham can list and to some extent describe our figures of speech for us. He does little to show their interrelation or total significance. We can improve on Puttenham by going back to antiquity, where in the third book of Aristotle's *Rhetoric* we find a chapter (11) saying that the smartest expressions consist in a concurrence of antithesis, parallel, metaphor, and "metaphor of a special kind"—by the last of which it would appear that Aristotle means "homonym." All this may seem to relegate the rhetorical theory of Pope's age or that of earlier ages to the status described under the second heading at the start of this paper: rhetorical, grammatical, or logical theory upon which we draw merely for tools that we shall turn to the uses of our own analysis. Perhaps this is what happens. I do not know the remedy—unless in the interests of Puttenham and his fellows, we are to cut our criticism off from all that subsequent linguistics and rhetoric and our own insight may tell us.

"Rules," said Sir William Temple and was paraphrased by Sir Thomas Pope Blount in his *De Re Poetica* of 1694, "at best are capable only to prevent the making of *bad Verses*, but never able to make men *good Poets*." This might have been interpreted in Pope's day and by Pope himself according to the well known doctrine of the *je-ne-sais-quoi*, the "grace beyond the reach of art," the Longinian concession to genius and the element of the unpredictable in art. It ought to be interpreted by us in the further sense that the rules of a given age never contain even all that can be subsequently formulated

about the poems of the age and hence are never able to prescribe our interpretation or limit our understanding of the poems. Poems, if not always
prior to theory—in the case of the couplet they seem not to be—are certainly
always more concrete than theory.

III

What I have just said is the logical climax and completion of my argument.
What I shall say now, briefly, may be taken as a kind of tailpiece. In the
part of this essay where I made a brief survey of rhetorical theory in Pope's
age and the preceding, I suppressed one curious facet of that history, for the
purpose of introducing it at this point. It is a noteworthy fact that some of
the most penetrating technical remarks made by critics during the age of
Pope were made by those who disapproved of the devices they were describing. One will no doubt recall Addison's *Spectator* No. 62, where he mentions
doggerel rhymes and puns as instances of that "mixt Wit" which consists
"partly in the Resemblance of Ideas, and partly in the Resemblance of
Words." Addison also promises to tell us something, on another day, about
the "wit" of antithesis. Far more spectacular are some of the analyses made
by Pope's preromantic enemy John Dennis. "Rime," says Dennis in a Miltonic demonstration prefixed to one of his own blank-verse poems, "is the
same thing in Relation to Harmony that a Pun is in Relation to Wit. . . .
Rime may not so absurdly be said to be the Pun of Harmony." And so far
as puns proper and ambiguity are concerned, Empson was not the first to
detect their presence in the poetry of Pope.

> Nay wits had pensions, and young lords had wit.

"Here," says Dennis, "in the compass of one poor line are two devilish Bobs
for the Court. But 'tis no easy matter to tell which way the latter squinting
Reflection looks." Cleanth Brooks has noticed the indecent pun upon the
word "die" in the Fifth Canto of *The Rape of the Lock*. It is not to be supposed
that this had been overlooked by Dennis. "That is to say," observes Dennis,
"*He wish'd for nothing more than to fight with her, because he desired nothing more
than to lie with her.* Now what sensible Meaning can this have?" Puns, says
Dennis, are everywhere in *The Rape of the Lock*. "Puns bear the same Proportion to *Thought*, that *Bubbles* hold to *Bodies*, and may justly be compared
to those gaudy Bladders which Children make with Soap." Nor is it to be
supposed that Dennis had overlooked the kind of pun hinted by Puttenham
in the figures of syllepsis and zeugma. "A Receipt for dry Joking," says
Dennis. "For by placing something important in the Beginning of a Period,

and making something very trifling to follow it, he seems to take pains to bring *something* into a Conjunction Copulative with *nothing*, in order to beget *nothing*." Perhaps it is needless to add that Dennis chooses for illustration of this formula the same examples which I have quoted in my own admiring analysis—those about staining her honor or her new brocade, and taking counsel and tea. At a certain level, Dennis saw very well what Pope was up to. Not an innuendo got past him. This, however, was not the kind of poetry which Dennis prescribed. These were not the rules he would write. We are confronted in our final exhibit with a relation between theory and poems which we have up to now scarcely canvassed. In this version of the critic's role there is a marked correlation not between poems and contemporary poetics but actually between poems and contemporary antipoetics.

EARL R. WASSERMAN

Windsor Forest

Cooper's Hill is consistently and coherently political at its core. Its political thesis is supported, confirmed, and honored by the application of its governing principle to other areas of truth and thereby is fixed assuringly in an entire cosmic context. Consequently, neither are the descriptions of external nature merely suggestive of general truths and therefore disjunctive, nor are they the arbitrary metaphoric vehicles for political doctrines; they are symbolic in that they are the necessary embodiments of these doctrines: being the palpable law *of* Nature, *concordia discors* must be the law *for* men. On the other hand, if Pope did indeed read *Cooper's Hill* in this fashion—and the evidence is that he did—then his definition of the poem as alternately descriptive and reflective must have resulted from the lack of terms in his critical vocabulary to designate the presence of each of these factors in the other. But at the very least, if Pope's model is coherently political in purpose and highly integrated in artistry, we are justified in speculating on whether *Windsor Forest* may be an equally ordered and meaningful poem.

Even though, as he claimed, he may have adapted to the political circumstances of 1712 a poem he had written about nine years earlier, Pope obviously must have felt that in the earlier draft he had on hand a work bearing in some significant manner on the signing of the Peace of Utrecht, even if only by fortuity. Under any circumstance, he chose to publish a whole poem—not a poem and an appendix—and we have no choice but to attempt to read it as an artistic unity.

It is needless here to record the many verbal and structural parallels

From *The Subtler Language*. Copyright © 1959 by The Johns Hopkins University Press. Original title "Pope: Windsor Forest."

between Pope's and Denham's georgics. For our immediate purpose it will
be enough to recognize that just as the first half of Denham's poem consists
of descriptions of three hills and then an announcement of his all-embracing
theme of *concordia discors*, so *Windsor Forest* opens with a similar statement
of its cosmic principle and then describes three related events in the forest:
the hunting of William the Conqueror; the hunt as it is conducted now in
the age of Anne; and the transformation of the huntress Lodona. The clue
is broad enough to suggest that the opening statement of a cosmic design
governs Pope's entire poem, just as *concordia discors* governs Denham's, and
that the three hunts, like Denham's three hills, form a unit with a possibly
political center. Should we then add that, just as Denham contrasted Henry
VIII's destruction of the monasteries and Charles's preservation of St. Paul's,
Pope juxtaposes the levelling of churches by William the Conqueror and
Queen Anne's bill for fifty new churches, or should we add such a similarity
as that both poems fulfill themselves in symbolic descriptions of the Thames—
it becomes difficult to put aside the suspicion that Pope had considerable insight into Denham's poem and that the meaning of *Windsor Forest* is
in some way analogous to that of *Cooper's Hill*.

Only after his initial dialectical arrangement of the three hills could Denham
express in its largest and explicit terms his controlling doctrine that "the
harmony of things, / As well as that of sounds, from discords springs" and
that "All that we have, and that we are, subsists" in harmonious discord.
For Denham lacked a pervasive governing symbol. Cooper's Hill is his subject
only in the etymological sense of that word: it is not an operative symbolic
element of the poem, but merely provides him with a convenient platform
from which the topographical features of the countryside can be seen symbolically and in symbolic relationships; and his ultimate symbol of *concordia
discors*, the Thames, is only one of these features. Working with greater
artistic economy and coherence, Pope has made his titular subject, Windsor
Forest, his governing symbol rather than the ground for symbolism.

Then, since the Forest is to be the symbolic scene in which and against
which all the acts of the poem take place and from which they derive their
special values, it must be defined at the very beginning of the poem. It is
a paradise whose prototype is the "Groves of *Eden*" (7). It is, in microcosm,
the ideal order of Nature, since here the elements "seem to strive again,"

> Not *Chaos*-like together crush'd and bruis'd,
> But as the World, harmoniously confus'd:

> Where Order in Variety we see,
> And where, tho' all things differ, all agree.
>
> (13–16)

The Forest, like Denham's Thames, is the ideal physical expression in little of Nature's one law of *concordia discors*, the active harmonizing of differences.

This principle permeates almost all of Pope's writings and probably is even more central to his thought than the doctrine of the Great Chain of Being. His world, like Denham's, is a dynamic harmony, where "ALL subsists by elemental strife" (*Essay on Man*, i, 169) and where the great threats are the stagnation of mere harmony and the chaos of mere energy:

> So Waters putrifie with Rest, and lose
> At once their Motion, Sweetness, and their Use;
> Or haste in headlong Torrents to the Main,
> And lose themselves by what shou'd them maintain,
> And in th' impetuous Course themselves the sooner drain.

And on one occasion Pope commits himself, in effect, to this ancient view of world harmony. Commenting on a passage in the *Iliad*, he wrote:

> I was at a loss for the reason why Jupiter is said to smile at the discord of the Gods, till I found it in Eustathius; Jupiter, says he, who is the lord of nature, is well pleased with the war of the Gods, that is, of earth, sea, and air, &c. because the harmony of all beings arises from that discord: thus earth is opposite to water, air to earth, and water to them all; and yet from this opposition arises that discordant concord by which all nature subsists. Thus heat and cold, moist and dry, are in a continual war, yet upon this depends the fertility of the earth, and the beauty of the creation. So that Jupiter, who according to the Greeks is the soul of all, may well be said to smile at this contention.

Correspondingly, man occupies an isthmus of a middle state, being both "darkly wise, and rudely great" (*Essay on Man*, ii, 4), both "Virtuous and vicious" (ii, 231) because of his "mixed nature," and consequently is at the center of a network of oppositions that must be held in harmonious tension. His soul is governed by two powers, reason and passion, which, by mutual conflict, are capable of producing an energetic harmony: though they work by contrary means, "Self-love [i.e. Passion] and Reason to one end aspire" (ii, 87)—or, in Denham's phrase, "to the same center move." Even within the sphere of the passions, ordered vitality results from their elemental

strife, the harmonizing of pain and pleasure—a *concordia discors* whose ana-
logue for Pope is the chiaroscuro of painting:

> The lights and shades, whose well accorded strife
> Gives all the strength and colour to our life.
>   (*Essay on Man*, ii, 121–22)

And therefore virtue is not a heaven at the opposite pole from the hell of
vice, but a central point of tension:

> We s^d not speak agst one large Vice [he told Spence], without
> speaking agst its contrary.—As to ye General Design of Providence
> ye two Extremes of a Vice, serve like two opposite biasses to keep
> up ye Ballance of things. Avarice lays up (w^t w^d be hurtful;)
> Prodigality, scatters abroad (w^t may be useful in other hands;)
> The middle ye point for Virtue.

For Pope the harmony of art is due to the artist's reconciling the contrary
impulses of his wit and judgment; and the harmony of society springs from
the reconciliation of self-love and social love, just as the ordered motion of
the earth is its simultaneous revolutions about its own axis and about the
sun (*Essay on Man*, iii, 313–18). Because "Order is Heaven's first law" it is
basic to the structure of society that there be inequality among men, since
"All Nature's diff'rence keeps all Nature's peace" (iv, 49–56).

Clearly Pope has a presiding faith in a grand cosmic pattern of harmonious confusion and agreement through difference—a pattern governing
"Nature," the physical universe, human society, man, and the arts. "Extremes in Nature equal ends produce, / In Man they join to some mysterious
use" (ii, 205–206). And since this is Nature's great law, it is (or should be)
universal, fundamental even to the political state. In the development of
political systems, he wrote, wisdom at length

> Taught Power's due use to People and to Kings,
> Taught nor to slack, nor strain its tender strings,
> The less, or greater, set so justly true,
> That touching one must strike the other too;
> 'Til jarring int'rests, of themselves create
> Th'according music of a well-mixed State.
> Such is the World's great harmony, that springs
> From Order, Union, full Consent of things:
> Where small and great, where weak and mighty, made
> To serve, not suffer, strengthen, not invade;

More powerful each as needful to the rest,
And in proportion as it blesses, blest;
Draw to one point, and to one centre bring
Beast, Man, or Angel, Servant, Lord, or King.

(Essay on Man, iii, 289–302)

The passage echoes not only Denham's political doctrine and phraseology but also the whole cluster of ideas we have seen traditionally surrounding the doctrine, including its derivation from theories of musical harmony. Pope has inherited the entire tradition of *concordia discors*.

And yet the principle must have had an even greater significance to Pope than it could have had to Denham; for between the two stand not only the Civil Wars but also their final product, the Whig revolution of 1688. Although the Whigs continued to give lip-service to the political concept of harmony through opposition, it is essentially Tory in nature, since the Glorious Revolution had been grounded upon the popular right to determine the succession of the crown and therefore tended to make Parliament the major organ of government. An earlier symptom of this Whiggish tendency had been the argument of Harrington, who in defending the idea of a commonwealth claimed that equally balanced political powers must necessarily destroy each other, and so rejected governments "which are said to subsist by confusion." The Tories, on the other hand, were inclined to counter Whiggism by perpetuating the older doctrine of political *concordia discors* and arguing, as Pope did, that "Servant," "Lord," and "King" must equally be drawn "to one centre." Consequently, in opening *Windsor Forest*—a poem published to celebrate the Tory Peace of Utrecht—with the description of the royal forest as the ideal microcosm, where there is no mere warring of the elements but where the elements are "harmoniously confus'd" and where even "tho' all things differ, all agree," Pope was not only defining the cosmic plan but also expressing in its most inclusive terms a doctrine that, in the context of the Peace, could be read as an especially Tory thesis. For the faith in the harmonious tension of the conflicting political groups at home is also the ground for defending the Tory eagerness for a somewhat arbitrative peace with France—a *concordia discors* between nations—especially in view of the opposing desire of the Whigs to press on the "*Chaos*-like" crushing and bruising of war to undisputed victory. "And where, tho' all things differ, all agree" can be read as "All Nature's diff'rence keeps all Nature's peace" and then applied to the terms of peace that ended the Wars of the Spanish Succession.

Even apart from the direct commentary on the Peace of Utrecht at the end of the poem, a number of factors at the beginning impel the description of the Forest in terms of *concordia discors* to yield an especially political interpretation: (1) the opening address to Granville, Jacobite sympathizer, opponent of the Whigs' general, Marlborough, and one of the twelve recently elevated to the peerage to give the Tories control over the House of Lords and so to make the peace possible; (2) the fact that the place chosen to be described as the ideal microcosm is the royal Forest and the monarch's home, and so stands for England at large; and (3) the pointed statement that the peace and plenty of the Forest proclaim that a *Stuart*—not the Whigs' Nassau or the Whigs' Hanoverians—is on the throne. But much more subtly indicative that the political theme is at the heart of the poem is another, more complex reference to the Stuart line; for it is clear that Bolingbroke and many of his Tory associates had strong Jacobite sympathies, whereas the Whigs were necessarily committed to the terms of the Revolution settlement. In the process of describing the Forest, Pope praises its trees:

> Let *India* boast her Plants, nor envy we
> The weeping Amber or the balmy Tree,
> While by our Oaks the precious Loads are born.
>
> (29–31)

The passage is, of course, strongly nationalistic; has special reference to England's pride in her control over maritime commerce, which is carried in her ships of oak; and helps make the oak forests of Windsor a synecdoche for England. But in addition, by causing the last line of *Windsor Forest* to echo the first line of his *Pastorals*—just as the last line of Virgil's *Georgics* echoes the first of his *Eclogues*—Pope intended that they be recognized as companion pieces. Now, the first of the *Pastorals* had concluded with a Virgilian pair of riddles, both political in meaning. One of these asks Daphnis to tell "in what glad soil appears, / A wond'rous Tree that sacred Monarchs bears," and Pope, rather gratuitously, annotated the passage with the information that this alludes "to the Royal Oak, in which Charles II had been hid from the pursuit after the battle of Worcester." The precisely corresponding passage in Pope's georgic, then, is intentionally ambiguous, and the "precious Loads" borne by English oaks—Jupiter's sacred tree, the monarch of the woods, the sovereign over the seas, and the pride of the English forests—are both her commerce and her Stuart monarchs. Indeed, this is considerably more than a pun, since the ability of the figure simultaneously to make a surface statement about commerce and covertly to allude to the Stuarts indicates that a Stuart reign is so exclusively a condition for prosperity that a single linguistic expression conveys both the economic and the political senses. The oak, therefore, is at once the emblem of the Stuarts and of England's fleets, and consequently the lines prepare the way for the climax of the paragraph: "And Peace and Plenty tell, a STUART reigns." For Pope is not only praising Anne but, by identifying the commercially profitable Peace with the Stuarts, is pointing out that a hereditary monarch, Anne, has brought about a financially advantageous end to the wars of Nassavian William; and thereby he is following the party line of one group of Tories in exalting the Stuart succession at a moment when some Jacobites had visions of success.

But, coherently dominant though the political theme is throughout, it would be quite wrong to read the poem as a mere configuration of allegorical equivalents for the Peace of Utrecht and the political situations surrounding it. Pope's tightly integrated world-view taught that "the first Almighty Cause / Acts not by partial, but by gen'ral laws" (*Essay on Man*, i, 145–46) and that

> All are but parts of one stupendous whole,
> Whose body Nature is, and God the soul;
> . . . chang'd thro' all, and yet in all the same.
>   (i, 267–69)

In such a unitary conception of reality, human affairs are not significant in a merely temporal context, drawing their worth only from their causes and consequences, nor can they be autonomous fragments of reality with independent meanings. All events are but variant expressions of one fixed master plan, and meaning and value must derive from that plan, which the age loosely called the Law of Nature and which in *Windsor Forest* takes the form of *concordia discors*. A merely allegorical presentation of the Peace of Utrecht would therefore falsify it and deprive it of meaning by isolating it from the universal context in which all things exist. On the other hand, a poetic system of simultaneous references whereby the immediate occasion, the Peace, is seen in the context of, and in conformity with, the whole pattern of human life, and whereby the conduct of human life is evaluated in terms of Nature's all-embracing law, not only creates the proper philosophic view but also is the necessary means of validating the special event. Therefore, the poem is simultaneously general and particular—the Peace is but a special application of the universal and eternal Law of Nature; and it is simultaneously ethical and political—politics is but a special form of ethics. By presenting the various modes of human conduct and evaluating them in terms of the doctrine of *concordia discors* the poet can also subsume under these general forms of conduct the particular aspects of the Peace. And through the means of these simultaneously operative areas of reference the Peace gains its validity by being an expression of the universal law; the universal law stamps value upon the Peace.

What allows Pope to exploit this law as the ground for the Peace is the double role he assigns to Windsor Forest. For the Forest is both a principle and a place. We have already seen that the essence of this "Eden" is the cosmic principle of harmonious confusion, or ordered variety; and the opening paragraphs are devoted to giving the Forest this symbolic value. The complaints of critics like William Lisle Bowles that the description of the Forest forms no picture arise from irrelevant standards, which ask that the poem accomplish something it never intends. The description is not scenic, but thematic; we are not to see things, but to realize the principle of *concordia discors*. Having embraced the whole cosmic order as that in which "tho' all things differ, all agree," and having intellectually grasped this as perfection, Pope now offers it to us in substantial form. Consequently the entire description is organized around the natural harmonizing of contraries: here are both hills and vales, woods and plains, earth and water; here trees partly admit and partly exclude the light. "Here in full Light the russet Plains extend; / There wrapt in Clouds the blueish Hills ascend" (23–24); and in this couplet each factor in one line—place, condition, color, form, direction—is counterbalanced in the other, so that the blending of these parallel but contrary lines by the rhyme of the precisely antithetical "extend" and "ascend" is itself the artistic realization of *concordia discors*. Even the wild heath is rich with "Purple Dies," and fruitful fields arise in the midst of wastes (a passage reminiscent of Denham's expression of the same cosmic theme: the Thames "Cities in deserts, woods in Cities plants"). The tension of coexisting contrarieties that is the heart of the theme is most completely captured in the description of the trees that, shading, "shun each others Shades" (22) and in the comparison of the checkered grove to a coy nymph tensely suspended between indulging and repressing her lover's addresses (17–20). By manifesting in perfect form the harmonizing of contraries, Windsor Forest is the Law of Nature.

But the Forest is also, in two senses, a place. It is "as the World," and therefore it *is* the world. It is, in other words, the locale of all human actions. Any other forest or park or estate would have served equally well as a "paradise" to symbolize Nature's law, but few could have served as well as a world-place, a theater for the entire drama of human affairs. Here is the home of the monarch; here monarchs have been born and lie buried; here poets have lived and have written of the Forest-world; here men can hunt or retire from an active life to meditate; here is an Arcadia with mythic possibilities; and here flows the great artery of England's commerce. As the

Law of Nature, Windsor Forest is apart from man—it is notable that in the formulation of the Forest as the principle of harmonious confusion no human agent appears, but only the objects of external nature. But as a world-place, the Forest will be a scene for all the modes of human action: despoiling, hunting, poetizing, meditating, ruling, living, and dying. The meaning of the poem, then, will arise from the interaction of the Forest's function as place with its function as principle. The latter, having been established at the opening persists as the setting throughout the poem; the shifting and seemingly disparate place-aspects involve the varieties of human actions (or are symbolic of them) that are to be tested and evaluated against this setting.

However, at the same time that the Forest is the world it is also England in little, and therefore it *is* England. The Peace that Anne has brought about is but a special human action, and the double place-function of the Forest as both England and the world demands an evaluation of the Peace by the only possible valid standard, the standard of universal human conduct, which in turn is fixed by the law of *concordia discors* that the Forest symbolizes.

THOMAS R. EDWARDS

The Mighty Maze:
An Essay on Man

Pope is shown confronting a difficult poetic problem in *An Essay on Man* (1729–1734). As an "official" argument for philosophical optimism the poem cannot avoid simplification and direct statement; yet there are signs in the verse that Pope was uncomfortable with didactic strategies. He was not a very gifted thinker, if by that word we mean someone capable of clear and sound consecutive reasoning; by accepting the didactic role, he incurred an obligation to be rational that he could not fulfill. Yet the *Essay*, even though it is unsound at its avowed center, cannot be dismissed simply as a failure. The poem is partly redeemed by just those aspects of temperament and sensibility that made Pope's didacticism unsuccessful. By this I mean that the didactic impulse (whether it originated in Pope or in Bolingbroke makes no difference) is thwarted in the poem partly by the views of experience and expression that I have called Augustan. Though the *Essay* lacks thorough-going doctrinal coherence, still in some important ways it succeeds as a poem, even at the expense of its philosophy. What we have, I think, is a case of sensibility opposing and finally killing doctrine, as Pope's grasp of real experience stubbornly resists the use of such experience as a vehicle for rational abstraction. But sensibility kills doctrine only that it may assert positive values of its own, values firmly rooted in direct apprehension of the beautiful complexity of actual things.

From *This Dark Estate: A Reading of Pope.* Copyright © 1963 by The Regents of the University of California. University of California Press, 1963. Original title "The Mighty Maze."

THE VOICE OF GOD

In the opening address to Bolingbroke (I, 1–16) we seem, as has often been remarked, to overhear one of the participants in a conversation between well-bred Augustans. The contempt for the vulgarity of worldly aspirations in "leave all meaner things / To low ambition and the pride of Kings"; the discreet parenthetical admission that life is short and futile, followed by urbanely stoic determination to make the most of it; the action, an observant ramble through the woods and gardens of the world; the Chesterfieldian resolution to restrain mirth but to be "candid" about human folly whenever decorum permits—every detail works to define the speaker and his unheard companion as eighteenth-century gentlemen of leisure and cultivation. The extended metaphor of the world as a "Wild" or a "Garden" works nicely— in its rich variety the world exists to be explored by sophisticated men of sound judgment, who "expatiate" over it intellectually just as they range over their estates hunting beasts and birds. "Nature's walks" will mean more as the poem progresses; Pope has his eye on actual nature at the same time that his inner eye contemplates a larger, more abstract nature. But what is most significant here is simply the decorum of tone with which the subject is introduced.

This tone of urbane detachment is conversational, but without any of the colloquial raciness of rhythm and idiom so common in the satires. "Awake, my St. John" is a rather lofty kind of informality, and in fact the conversational element in the passage soon is counterpointed by another sort of speech: "Say first, of God above, or Man below / What can we reason, but from what we know?" These lines may be addressed to Bolingbroke, posing a rhetorical question as prelude to discussing a topic on which they generally agree, but it is hard not to feel that Bolingbroke has lost most of his dramatic individuality and become something like the epic muse. The dramatic situation changes and Bolingbroke disappears for a time as Pope pays his ironic respects to the astronautical fancies of John Wilkins and the Royal Society and to the Lucretian image of the speculative philosopher as supernatural voyager (23–34). It is obviously impossible for ordinary human reason to achieve such clear perception of the universe, and the consequent irony in "thy pervading soul" indicates a shift of situation. The "thee" being addressed is no longer Bolingbroke but "Presumptuous Man." Conversation becomes oratory, a change predicted by the elevation of tone in the opening line; and it is at the oratorical level that the poem will mainly conduct its argument.

This shift of tone is of course not complete. The conversational beginning persists in the inner ear throughout the poem, providing an implicit context for the oratory. We are both Pope's equals, sharing Bolingbroke's gratification at having our own ideas expressed so handsomely for us, and also his pupils, resisting in our ignorant pride the messages of reason that are being delivered. The didactic poet runs the danger of not being able to justify his knowledgeable tone. He must sound just a little like God, which is all right when the subject is crop rotation or beekeeping, something in which his *expertise* (or lack of it) can be assessed; but if he ventures upon high speculation, where authority is a more uncertain matter, his voice may grow uncomfortably pontifical. Pope often does talk like God in the *Essay*. His subject commits him to saying that human consciousness cannot comprehend orders of being higher than its own, and yet he must himself at times speak as if the whole hierarchy were visible to him: "All Nature is but Art, unknown to thee; / All Chance, Direction, which thou canst not see" (I, 289–290). The frame of conversation eases some of this pontificality. Our double identity in the poem—as the speaker's peers and as his congregation—allows us to feel the full weight of the sermon even as we participate in its delivery. Although we take the preacher seriously, we usually can remember that he is not a fanatic but a gentleman like us.

Still, our suspicions are not wholly allayed by the interplay of tones. When the voice becomes markedly aloof and judicative we tend to distrust it, and it does so too frequently to allow complete reconciliation. Pope's decision to cast the *Essay* in the form of direct and "sincere" moralizing involved a considerable problem of rhetoric. Disinterested sincerity in Swift, for example, is almost always a sign of irony, as Martin Price notes:

> The mask of impartiality, if it were not qualified by humor, was as much a questionable type as were those of partisan zeal. Constant claims of "modest proposals" to "universal benefit" were keys to pretentious and specious disinterestedness. "I burnt all my Lord——'s letters," Swift wrote to Betty Germain, "upon receiving one where he had used these words to me, 'all I pretend to is a great deal of sincerity,' which indeed, was the chief virtue he wanted."

Pope's later satires brilliantly demonstrate moral involvement; we are persuaded that he has chosen the right cause and that his vehemence marks a powerful and admirable indignation. The mask of cool disengagement, as worn by an Addison or a Chesterfield, seems unpleasantly lifeless when set next to Swift's or Pope's vigorous expressions of commitment. By choosing the disengaged man for his *persona* in the *Essay* Pope took on a difficult task, and the poem succeeds as much in the breaking of this dramatic fiction as in the observing of it.

HUMAN LIMITS AND NATURAL HARMONY

The theme of the *Essay on Man* is the familiar one of reconciling the apparent chaos of natural experience with man's intimations of ultimate order. The traditional concept of the "correspondences," the analogies that connect the human world with the natural below and the divine above, operates in the poem as a distinctly uncertain possibility. "Presumptuous Man" has questions to put to nature (I, 39–42, 61–66), but nature, while it seems in its variety to embody some principle of significant order, cannot tell him precisely what that order is. Both nature and man are ignorant, that is, but only man is cursed by the yearning to know. His "knowledge," as the passage (I, 99–112) on "the poor Indian" reveals, is essentially derived from mythmaking; the Indian simply projects, in all innocence, a "heaven" that is an idealized version of his known world. The results are not "true," but they serve the purposes of consolation, and the Indian, for all his pastoral naïveté, is happier than civilized man. It is the same predicament that so vexes Swift—one scarcely wants to be a fool, yet one suspects that ignorance and delusion are the only sources of serenity in a world which will not bear too much scrutiny.

Pope will not settle, however, for this view in its purest, most desperate form. Analogy *can* give a general sense of man's place in the scheme; man cannot look directly upward to the ultimate source of order, but he can look downward and make metaphors for his own lot from the relationships he perceives in the lower orders of the Scale of Being. But metaphor was not knowledge to the post-Hobbesian mind, and a steady skeptical undercurrent qualifies Pope's dogmatism. To assume, as Whitehead did, that Pope "was untroubled by the great perplexity which haunts the modern world," that he was "confident that the enlightened methods of modern science provided a plan adequate as a map of the 'mighty maze,' " is to ignore the complexity of Pope's view, as the lines on Newton (II, 31–38) show. Newton could answer all questions except the most important ones, those that concern the "movement of his Mind," "his own beginning, or his end." The irony places science in the right human perspective—Newton's unfolding of natural law must be contemplated in relation to his inability even to "describe," much less "explain," his own position in a universe of time and change.

This criticism of "reason" becomes explicit in the rest of Epistle II. It is a mistake to view the poem through the Victorian lens of "an age of prose and reason." As Professor Lovejoy observes, the most influential authors of the eighteenth century

> made a great point of reducing man's claims to "reason" to a minimum, and of belittling the importance of the faculty in human existence; and the vice of "pride" which they so delighted to castigate was exemplified for them in any high estimate of the capacity of the human species for intellectual achievement, or in any of the more ambitious enterprises of science and philosophy, or in any moral idea which would make pure reason (as distinguished from natural "passions") the supreme power in human life.

One of the strongest forces drawing Pope away from a simple confidence in reason is his understanding that like any human faculty, it operates within the confines of "the lurking principle of death" (II, 134). The phrase appears only as a simile within a passage whose main subject is the power of a "ruling passion" to undermine mental health; but the idea of life being a gradual dying reminds us of that area of the whole scheme which reason cannot investigate. Reason has its value, but Pope takes the Platonic view of it as "guard," not "guide" (II, 162), in a world whose springs of action are passionate.

In short, all that man can know about the processes of time and change are their fragmentary effects on nature and himself. His sense of his own identity, which he yearns to define in relation to these processes, must remain disconnected and dim. There is thus a tragic paradox in Pope's use of the Scale of Being, which has lost its former metaphoric potency as a true ladder by which man might transcend his earthly condition. The concept suggests that man is a part of a cosmic perfection, but he can never experience that perfection while he remains man. The problem for the moralist lay in man's discontent with his lot. If it is a condition of his middle status, how can he be censured for feeling discontent? And yet, the whole tenor of the poem insists, it is disastrous to him to feel it! Analogy is not a solution; to know something by analogy is painfully unlike knowing it by experience, and it is for experience of perfection that man yearns. But Pope's job in the *Essay* is to forbid despair; he evades this impasse, not very consistently, by occasionally giving ground before the theological pressure that bears on his position: "Hope humbly then; with trembling pinions soar; / Wait the great teacher Death, and God adore!" (I, 91–92). While one may "adore" perfection in this world, only in some world to come can one *know* it—if then.

Such difficulties in defining the ultimate reality lead Pope's sermon to its essentially negative center. Whatever man should be in this world, he should at least not be proud. He is neither the center nor the master of nature. The dangers of pride are clear in I, 131–140, where the ironies rebuke the arrogant anthropocentrism of supposing that the creation exists to serve man and mirror his feelings; it is equally clear in this fine "anti-pastoral" passage:

> Is it for thee the lark ascends and sings?
> Joy tunes his voice, joy elevates his wings:
> Is it for thee the linnet pours his throat?
> Loves of his own and raptures swell the note . . .
> The hog, that plows not nor obeys thy call,
> Lives on the labours of this lord of all.
>
> (III, 31–42)

The couplets play off the imagined nature invented by human pride against the real nature which exists as much for its own purposes as for man's. The natural world is full of life and feeling, but it is independent of "this lord of all." But there are consolations in man's position:

> he only knows,
> And helps, another creature's wants and woes.
> Say, will the falcon, stooping from above,
> Smit with her varying plumage, spare the dove?
> Admires the jay the insect's gilded wings?
> Or hears the hawk when Philomela sings?
>
> (III, 51–56)

Nature is not responsive to man, but man is responsive to nature in a way that no merely natural creature can be. Through his unique gifts of compassion and esthetic appreciation he can penetrate into nature and so in a sense participate in it. He achieves a moral dignity that no other creature can have, but by submitting to, not dominating over, the rest of creation. He is in fact a part of nature, though not in the way he would like to be. He is "Fix'd like a plant on his peculiar spot, / To draw nutrition, propagate, and rot" (II, 63–64). While his place in the Scale involves painful complexities of feeling from which the lower orders are free, he can nonetheless relate his own life and death to the rhythms of nature. The simile denies man's cherished illusions of freedom, even as it offers compensation in vegetable simplicity. Although reason distinguishes man from the other creatures, the "fruits" of virtue grow from "savage stocks" (II, 181–184)—the "wild Nature" working at man's roots is ultimately the same nature that gives productive life (and death) to the nonhuman creation.

The analogies of nature thus point down and not up. Man will find his place in the scheme not by yearning for higher status but by accepting his relationship with the lower creatures. Still, to know that man and nature are parts of a single order is not to resolve man's yearning for a direct, intimate bond with the things of this world. In Epistle III Pope postulates such a bond, in the pastoral innocence of Eden or the Golden Age from which man fell. Despite Hobbes, "the state of Nature was the reign of God" (148). Human history has represented a decline from this primal perfection, as man created the social arts, commerce, secular government, and ultimately tyranny and superstition through the exercise of reason. These inventions stemmed from natural promptings (171 ff.) to imitate the lower creatures, and thus were not originally wrong; the turning point, the beginning of man's alienation from nature, came when superstition replaced "charity" with "zeal" (261) and secular power no longer had to reflect a spiritual order that was fundamentally benevolent. Faced with such chaos, man was "Forc'd into virtue thus by Self-defence" (279); through the inspired examples of the poet and the lawgiver the "shadow," if not the "image," of true divinity was rediscovered (288), and secular organization again became a metaphor for the great hierarchy of nature. The pyramids of "Beast, Man, or Angel" and of "Servant, Lord, or King" (302) regained their congruence, with each order topped by the single point which is God.

Epistle III does not of course afford a very satisfying account of moral history. Nor is it poetically the strongest section of the *Essay*. Some of Pope's metaphors ring false; how true is it to say, for instance, that the "Ant's republic" provided a model for human society, or even (reading not historically but "mythically," as we probably should) that it affords a very enlightening analogy? Pope has his difficulties in leading the poem in a positive direction, for all the assurance of his tone. Yet in the great passage (283–302) on social harmony he comes as close as he can to solving the problem of the whole poem, through an Augustan appeal to the traditional concept of the *concordia discors*. Harmony is simply a special condition of discordance, and as Maynard Mack observes, the metaphor's power in the *Essay* stems from a doubleness associated with the figure from earliest classical times: "the image brought together in one perspective man's present suffering and his faith, the partial and the whole views; [and suggested] that in some higher dialectic than men could grasp the thesis and antithesis of experienced evil would be resolved." One may wish that the image were more solidly developed out of the argument of Epistle III, but its power is undeniable.

The stability of even the best human society resides in a rather precarious balance of stresses, but that even a limited harmony is conceivable in the secular world consoles us if we take that harmony as an echo, however faint, of the grand but unhearable cosmic composition. The original intimacy of man and nature vanished when man lost his innocence, but in a social order that is properly attuned to the order of nature, a measure of intimacy can be restored.

THE POWER OF TIME

This is as close as the *Essay* comes to expressing anything like "optimism" in our ordinary sense of the word. It is not very close, we see, when we ponder Pope's implicit comparison of the poem with *Paradise Lost*. The Fall of Man was marked by his subjugation to Sin and Death, which is to say to *time* and its fundamental enmity to human value. It is the fact of time, Professor Lovejoy argues, that ultimately invalidates the concept of the Scale of Being:

> A world of time and change . . . is a world which can neither be
> deduced from nor reconciled with the postulate that existence is
> the expression and consequence of a system of "eternal" and
> "necessary" truths inherent in the very logic of being. Since such
> a system could manifest itself only in a static and constant world,
> and since empirical reality is not static and constant, the "image"
> (as Plato called it) does not correspond with the supposed "model"
> and cannot be explained by it. *Any* change whereby nature at
> one time contains other things or more things than it contains
> at another time is fatal to the principle of sufficient reason.

Milton reconciles a temporal world to cosmic immutability by appealing to the orthodox concept of Redemption: because of the sacrifice of Christ, man can look forward to an eventual translation out of time into a realm of being which is perfectly changeless. The *Essay on Man* seems at times to yield to theological pressure, but Pope must generally exclude specific Christian doctrine. Whether or not he believed in the redemption of souls, in the *Essay* his subject is not eternity, which cannot be known, but this world and how to endure it. And the possibilities of earthly experience seem far from cheerful.

Epistle IV is especially rich in allusions to death, which (93–130) strikes capriciously, without regard for "justice." Even though by Pope's time the idea of an impersonal, mechanistic universe must have seemed considerably less terrible than it had to Shakespeare or Donne, the concept still could not have been a very comfortable one to entertain. Pope in fact does not entertain it fully; his rhetoric is addressed to the enormous task of making natural impersonality a source of comfort. Falkland, Turenne, and Sidney did not die *because* they were virtuous; nature cannot recognize either virtue or vice. But because the universe does not observe moral law, as men know it, does not mean that it obeys *no* law: "Think we, like some weak Prince, th' Eternal Cause / Prone for his fav'rites to reverse his laws?" The answer is "no"—the analogy of earthly order to supernal points out the weakness of the former only to assert the consoling perfection of the latter.

But this appeal to the "externalist pathos," the emotional power of the idea of immutability upon man's sense of his own involvement in time, cannot fully subdue the sobering fact of human mortality:

> What's Fame? a fancy'd life in others breath,
> A thing beyond us, ev'n before our death.
> Just what you hear, you have, and what's unknown
> The same (my Lord) if Tully's or your own.
> All that we feel of it begins and ends
> In the small circle of our foes or friends.
>
> (IV, 237–242)

In this paraphrase of *The Temple of Fame* (505–508) Pope again sees personal fame as sorry compensation for the necessity of dying. The lines, to be sure, state a positive view of personal relations, which Pope always cherished: "The only pleasure which any one either of high or low rank must depend upon receiving," he wrote to Ralph Allen, "is in the Candour or Partiality of Friends and that Smaller Circle we are conversant in." But this is tacit recognition that the pleasures of friendship are fleeting; they are valuable, they are in fact all that one has, but like everything else they will soon pass. Nor is wisdom any more reliable. When Pope returns to gentlemanly conversation (IV, 259–268) with Bolingbroke, it is only to place rueful emphasis on the futility of "Parts superior." Wisdom leads finally to frustration and loneliness:

> Truths would you teach, or save a sinking land?
> All fear, none aid you, and few understand.
> Painful preheminence! yourself to view
> Above life's weakness, and its comforts too.

As wise man, Bolingbroke stands as symbol of man's dissatisfaction with his mixed nature and his ambiguous role in creation. The cost of intelligence is fearfully high: " 'Tis but to know how little can be known."

HIERARCHY AND EXPERIENCE

The description of Bolingbroke has implications for the reader as well. Pope's rhetorical aim has been to put us in Bolingbroke's position, to improve our understanding so as to reveal how limited understanding must be. It is flattering to be admitted to such company, but the reader's new point of view is a difficult one—the "optimism" of the poem involves a serious recognition of its own limitations and of the oppositions that are all too likely to overcome it. But Pope's "official" theme will not permit so complex a view to prevail, and this inhibition leads to a crucial poetic difficulty. In Section vi of Epistle IV he undertakes to demolish "the false scale of Happiness" that prevents most men from understanding their roles in the true scale of Being. "External goods" cannot prevent "human Infelicity"—"the perfection of Virtue and Happiness consists in a conformity to the ORDER OF PROVIDENCE here, and a resignation to it here and hereafter." The trouble is that the false scale, since one knows it through immediate experience, lends itself more readily to poetic particularization than does the hypothetical, unexperienced "true" hierarchy.

The *Essay* both faces up to the difficult facts of human experience and attempts to make them bearable by assigning them functions in a hierarchical order. An appeal to hierarchy draws its rhetorical power from the useful changes of name that are made possible, and we note that Pope's arguments usually hinge on such redefinition:

> Respecting Man, whatever wrong we call,
> May, must be right, as relative to all.
>
> (I, 51–52)

> Cease then, nor ORDER Imperfection name.
>
> (I, 281)

> All Nature is but Art, unknown to thee.
>
> (I, 289)

> Modes of Self-love the Passions we may call.
>
> (II, 93)

> Know then this truth (enough for Man to know)
> "Virtue alone is Happiness below."
>
> (IV, 309–310)

Man, that is to say, tends to call things by their "wrong" names, and in so doing he confirms his own unhappiness, since he cannot make his vocabulary jibe with any consoling conceptual scheme of order. God, however, calls things by their "right" names. If man can translate his words for experiences into a vocabulary that fits an imaginative hierarchy extending beyond the limits of his knowledge, most of his anxiety about the human condition will turn out to have been the result of terminological muddles.

Like any example of sophisticated rhetoric, then, the *Essay* draws much of its persuasive force from a view of language that is fundamentally magical. The translation of our names for experiences into a new vocabulary is a therapeutic act, for to change the name is to change the "fact"—or at least to make it bearable—by providing a new context of ideas and feelings in which to contemplate it. Pope again is God, for he knows the right names. At the same time, however, this transformation of terms adds to our sense that the poem is "enclosed" by the speaking voice of an individual human being with whom we have a particular social relationship. The semantic shifts appeal to common sense: we share with Pope a firm identity within a community of intelligence and taste, and so he can confidently invite us to agree with him about names, since a defining characteristic of a community is the mutual acceptance of "proper" vocabularies. For example, we share his amusement at the Neo-Platonists who call "quitting sense" "imitating God" (II, 26). Like "Eastern priests,"they are somehow exotic, not a part of the community, and his manner of addressing us defines us as persons who share his belief that "sense" plays a vital part in any activity, religion not excepted. Once we have agreed about the right name for one kind of experience, we are inclined to accept the speaker's judgment about names in cases which are further from communal assumptions. Although the tone of such transformations is usually didactic, it is softened by our sense that we have come to occupy much the same ground from which Pope speaks.

But Pope's appeal to an explicit hierarchy of values involves him in poetic difficulties. In the *Essay* he expresses the complexity of human experience in a world that is at best indifferent to man; but he also attempts to resolve complexity into simplicity by relating experience to a predefined system of absolute values. In passages like Pride's speech in Epistle I (131–164) there is no poetic problem, since the "right" attitude is developed out of an initial "wrong" view which is nevertheless fairly (even beautifully) expressed. Both complexity and simplicity are there, in the verse, and the adjustment between them is dramatized as argument. But as the poem draws to its close, Pope must increasingly derogate the false scale in order to

emphasize the finality of the true one, as in the passage (IV, 361–372) on
the need for human love to "rise from Individual to the Whole":

> Self-love but serves the virtuous mind to wake,
> As the small pebble stirs the peaceful lake;
> The centre mov'd, a circle strait succeeds,
> Another still, and still another spreads,
> Friend, parent, neighbor, first it will embrace,
> His country next, and next all human race. . . .

Pope has no better luck than any other eighteenth-century moralist in bridg-
ing the gap between self-love and social. The metaphor seems arbitrary—
Addison would have called the play on "wake" and "stir" an example of
false wit, dependent upon "resemblance of words" rather than of ideas, and
there is nothing else to persuade us that self-love and pebbles are analogous—
and it seems positively muddled unless we exclude the entire metaphorical
vehicle from the "it" which embraces friends, parents, and the like. This
passage is the climax of Pope's final affirmation of the true scale, and it
simply does not work when we measure it against the Johnsonian description
of the fate of the worldly (IV, 289–308), the great "glory, jest, and riddle"
section that begins Epistle II, or any of the other passages in which Pope
treats human experience with full respect for its complexity. When he rises
from the individual to the whole something unfortunate happens to his verse.

The trouble seems due not only to Pope's weakness in rational argument
but also to the nature of his subject. Whitehead said that both the Greek
and medieval Christian views of nature were essentially "dramatic," which
is to say they supposed a nature that worked toward purposes which could
in some way be understood by human beings and that included human
experience in its operation. The nature Pope has to work with is a very
different one. He can deal dramatically with experiential reality in all its
complexity, but in the *Essay* he must also transcend experience to knowledge
of permanence and order; and since his "climate of opinion" presupposes a
cosmos which is not dramatic but mechanistic, and thus largely foreign to
human experience, his invocations of supernatural order are seldom fully
convincing. When he can find in the natural world some evidence of the
Scale—when he deals (as in I, 207–280) with the "esthetic" order his senses
perceive—the *Essay* achieves its great poetic triumphs by fusing rhetoric and
imaginative particularity. At such moments metaphor functions meaning-
fully, for the grand tenor is elucidated by solidly realized vehicles. But when
natural experience is left behind in the attempt to prove that one knows
what one insists is beyond knowledge, an attempt that must rely on rhetoric

alone, the *Essay* loses much of its power. Mechanism is not only unattractive as an idea, it is also nearly impossible to dramatize in experiential terms. It is immediate experience that sustains Pope's Augustan mediations, and when doctrinal considerations exert their thinning or confusing tendencies on the experiential vehicle, he shows his weakness in the kind of poetic reasoning that a Dryden or a Wordsworth might bring off. His tendency to resort to conventional pietism illustrates this weakness. He tries to soften the concept of mechanism by hinting that the Christian God is at the controls, but this scrambles his argument; for example, at the end of the poem, when he declares that virtue is not only the sole source of earthly happiness but also a way to ascend to God, we uneasily feel that he has come close to contradicting his earlier assertion that the quality of human life, *as man knows it*, has no relevance to the ultimate reality. But the main problem is a literary and not just a logical one. It is not that Pope tries to make us know what he himself has called unknowable, but that the quality of the knowledge we receive is flawed by his inability to manage an abstract poetic idiom. When he treats the "true Scale" his language is less rich, less interesting, and above all less intelligible than when he expresses the perplexing imperfections of actual experience. His sensibility was attuned to the concrete, the immediate, and the *Essay* is not fully alive at the moments when its oratory loses touch with natural particulars.

The poem finally seems most interesting when read not as philosophy but as an expression of a conflict between views of reality as excitingly terrible and as ultimately orderly and peaceful. In such a reading one sees Pope as a man whose strong sense of the value of order makes experienced disorder a dreadful thing to consider, and who yearns for an imaginative myth of cosmic immutability to sustain and console him. The myth does not work perfectly, to be sure; when the poetic speaker invokes a hierarchy that he has not fully grasped imaginatively, the poem falters, regaining its stride only when he returns to the world he can experience directly. But another kind of drama emerges from this conflict of experience and speculation, a drama in which a human being tries out ways of coming to terms with his situation and finds that though none are entirely adequate some work better than others. A man who was wholly convinced by his own vision of order would not need to test it so often against actuality; Pope's poetic concern for real things and real feelings (another way of saying his humanity) refuses to surrender to his speculations, and the result is poetry. The poetry is intermittent, to be sure. When Mr. Mack calls the *Essay on Man* the greatest speculative poem in English between *Paradise Lost* and *The Prelude*, we think as much of the decline such poetry suffered in the eighteenth century as of

Pope's achievement. No one could deny that the poem would be better if its argument were more consistently reasoned, if the didactic impulse were more cogently realized. But such "intentional" success would have taken the *Essay* even further from the Augustan mode's complex adjustment of ideal and actual, and the poem's poetic failure is the curious measure of its human success.

MARTIN PRICE

Character and False Art

In the poems of Pope we have considered there are three kinds of art: the art of Nature or of God; man's humble and reverent imitation of that in his own; and, finally, man's arrogant constructions in defiance of Nature. The last of these can be seen in the *Essay on Man*, with suggestions of the Tower of Babel; the Titans' piling Pelion upon Ossa in their effort to dethrone Zeus; the fallen angels' building of that travesty of heavenly splendor, Pandemonium, in *Paradise Lost*; and the "kings of the earth" of the Second Psalm:

> Oh sons of earth! attempt ye still to rise,
> By mountains pil'd on mountains, to the skies?
> Heav'n still with laughter the vain toil surveys.
> And buries madmen in the heaps they raise.
>
> (IV, 73–76)

The point lies in the materialism and the *hubris*, the insensibility and the blasphemy. The attempt to traverse the incommensurable distance that separates the order of flesh from the order of charity with heaps of earth is a telling instance of the constructions of false art.

Throughout his major satires Pope uses the mock order of false art as a symbol of moral failure. We can see this in his discussion of the splintered brilliance of false wit in the *Essay on Criticism*:

From *To the Palace of Wisdom: Studies in Order and Energy from Dryden to Blake*. Copyright ©
1964 by Martin Price. Southern Illinois University Press, 1964. Original title "Pope: Art
and Morality."

> Poets like Painters, thus, unskill'd to trace
> The naked Nature and the living Grace,
> With gold and jewels cover ev'ry part,
> And hide with ornaments their want of Art.
> (293–96)

> False Eloquence, like the prismatic glass,
> Its gaudy colors spreads on ev'ry place;
> The face of Nature we no more survey,
> All glares alike, without distinction gay.
> (311–14)

Here false art becomes all the more dazzling by sacrificing form to glitter: "one glaring chaos and wild heap of wit" (292), seeking to tyrannize over us by making an immediate appeal to the senses and closing off the more deliberate and demanding aesthetic response that is concerned with formal structure.

Pope's finest instance of the mock order of false art occurs in his second Moral Essay, the epistle *To Burlington* (1731). Originally called *Of False Taste*, the poem is an important document in the history of eighteenth-century sensibility, especially in the matters of architecture and landscape gardening. It celebrates the Earl of Burlington's classicism as a return to Roman manliness and severity, to public spirit and sober piety—a return from extravagance and ostentation, from the triviality of an art that has lost the sense of function in the pursuit of ornament. Burlington was, in effect if not design, the inheritor of Shaftesbury's artistic legacy. Like Shaftesbury, he renounced the baroque strain in Wren. Shaftesbury rejected "false and counterfeit . . . magnificence," and coldly dismissed two of Wren's great public works: the public can no longer bear "to see a Whitehall treated like a Hampton Court, or even a new cathedral like St. Paul's." Burlington turned back to the work of Inigo Jones and Palladio, collecting and publishing their designs; and his own architectural inventions are closely based upon their example, although he moves even further back toward Roman models than they.

Burlington inherited Shaftesbury's concerns in another, more striking way. His villa at Chiswick is an adaptation of Palladio's Villa Rotonda (given a saucer dome like that of the Pantheon), but the gardens, which were begun in 1715 and were not completed until 1736, became one of the earliest instances of the new interest in the "natural" garden. Shaftesbury, we may recall, admired the wildness of the natural scene for its authenticity. His devotion was to "the chief degree or order of beauty . . . that of the rational life, distinct from the merely vegetable and sensible," but he found natural wildness free at least of the mock order of false art. Burlington, in turn, sponsored the irregular garden. It had at least some classical precedent. In 1728 Robert Castell published his *Villas of the Ancients*, a work sponsored by Burlington and probably available to him earlier. In it the garden of Pliny's villa is described, and, although it was largely regular, it contained areas of irregularity: the *pratulum*, where "nature appears in her plainest and most simple dress" and, particularly, the *imitatio ruris*, where "hills, rocks, cascades, rivulets, woods and buildings, etc., were possibly thrown into such an agreeable disorder as to have pleased the eye from several views, like so many landskips." Here again we have the dialectical interplay that we see in the literary criticism of the period. The return to a severe classicism is one statement, the irregular garden a counterstatement; they have in common a rejection of mock order and an imitation, in different ways, of a true order. Within the mathematical precisions of Chiswick House occur the varieties of form we find in the three rooms along the garden front (round, apsidal, and octagonal, in turn). Within the irregularities of the garden itself are those formal controls that are meant to be only glimpsed or sensed, without being sharply visible.

In *To Burlington*, Pope questions the nature of taste: is it a discrimination of genuine pleasures or a conformity to fashion, a means of self-cultivation or of self-display? The fool does not buy for himself but at others' bidding and for others' eventual enjoyment; for he cannot possess these things with his own mind—

> Think we all these are for himself? no more
> Than his fine wife, alas! or finer whore.
>
> (11–12)

The last line has incredible richness of suggestion. We are invited to contemplate a marriage that is little more than an act of acquisition by a man of wealth. His "fine wife" is another adornment or stage property, and it is not surprising if she is unfaithful. But in this world of display, one can achieve most conspicuous consumption with objects of luxury—the mistress must be even "finer" than the wife.

For the man who has no substantial self, who lives only for the creation of a public image, every act of self-display becomes an unknowing act of self-exposure. The proud worship of taste requires that man violate nature in order to satisfy his transient whim; in turning to his private will for a standard, he has lost touch with nature and has lost the stability of an excellence founded on something outside himself. Villario's formal gardens are pleasing enough, although suspiciously artful and pseudo-pastoral. But they are an imposition upon nature for the sake of a taste that is easily cloyed ("He finds at last he better likes a field"). Again Sabinus' son, fond of an "opener Vista," destroys the trees his father planted, and we find again the inversion of nature for the sake of an artificial taste:

> The thriving plants ignoble broomsticks made,
> Now sweep these alleys they were born to shade.
>   (97–98)

These lines contain what Donald Davie has called "a little tragic plot." There is at least a suggestion of the heroic queen transported into drudging slavery, and this only reinforces the contrasts of living plants and stiff, dead broomsticks, or of "stretching branches" and rectilinear alleys. All of these themes are summed up in Timon's villa itself, where all is artful, dull, and unnatural. The interior crowns the effect: learning gives way to display, religion to comfortable self-flattery. In the chapel, the "pride of prayer" is overarched by ceilings "where sprawl the saints of Verrio or Laguerre." The grossness and overblown ripeness of the fleshy saints and of the "soft Dean" ("Who never mentions Hell to ears polite") point finally to an art that, in its essentially decorative or ostentatious end, is self-defeating, just as the scale of the dinner ("In plenty starving, tantaliz'd in state") is the frustration of true hospitality or service.

But Timon's pretensions accomplish what they least intend: service to many who are indifferent to his state, the laborers his "charitable Vanity" supports. The comic view is completed by the reclamation of the land from the usurper, as Nature regains her throne and produces a truer splendor:

> Another age shall see the golden ear
> Embrown the slope, and nod on the parterre,
> Deep harvests bury all his pride has planned.
> And laughing Ceres reassume the land.
>   (173–76)

The regal notes of *golden, nod,* and *reassume* effect a reconciliation of art and nature, of just rule and living energy. And again there is a suggestion of vast extent—the reaches of the estate are large vistas of grain—and of framed and ideal landscape. The *Essay* closes with a return to Roman building ("whate'er Vitruvius was before," "Imperial works") and to the constructive power of human art in its true sense—no less in control of nature ("And roll obedient rivers through the land") but serving "happy Britain" and creating a new harmonious order.

The divine force in nature is embodied in the "Genius of the Place," with its reminiscence of the classical deities who inhabit and inform both men and places. To consult the Genius of the Place is to serve nature rather than to coerce her; the true artist "helps" the hill to rise, "calls in the country," "joins willing woods." And that miraculous harmony one recognizes as a work of art seems to leap into being:

> Parts answering parts shall slide into a whole,
> Spontaneous beauties all around advance,
> Start even from difficulty, strike from chance;
> Nature shall join you; Time shall make it grow.
>
> (66–69)

In contrast we have the sterile mock order of Timon's villa:

> No pleasing intricacies intervene,
> No artful wildness to perplex the scene;
> Grove nods at grove, each alley has a brother,
> And half the platform just reflects the other.
>
> (115–18)

The topiary artist produces an "inverted Nature" by forcing artful forms upon the natural—"Trees cut to statues." And this is balanced by the profusion that loses all sense of design, "Statues thick as trees." The displacement of life is nicely caught in the final image of the impotent river god: "And swallows roost in Nilus' dusty urn" (126).

Milton's Eve must turn from her Narcissus-like love of her own "smooth wat'ry image" to love for Adam and learn "How beauty is excell'd by manly grace / And wisdom, which alone is truly fair" (IV, 490–91). So, too, Bernard Berenson remarks of Raphael that he was "not artist enough to do without beauty." Here Burlington represents the standard of dignified severity:

> You show us, Rome was glorious, not profuse,
> And pompous buildings once were things of use.
>
> (23–24)

We move back from the ornamental to the functional, and in a deeper sense from the aesthetic to the ethical.

> 'Tis Use alone that sanctifies Expense,
> And splendor borrows all her rays from sense.
>
> (179–80)

The word *sanctifies* should not be underestimated; the light of Heaven now descends, through sense, to inform genuine art. Burlington, as artist, becomes himself a transmitter of the light of Heaven; it is but for kings to "call forth th' ideas of your mind" (195) and create works of authentic magnificence, "which alone is truly fair."

The theme of true magnificence draws together the use of riches and the problem of taste. Aristotle writes, in the *Nicomachean Ethics* (IV, 2):

> The magnificent man is like an artist; for he can see what is fitting and spend large sums tastefully. . . . Magnificence is an attitude of expenditures of the kind which we call honorable, e.g., those connected with the gods—votive offerings, buildings, and sacrifices . . . and all those that are proper objects of public-spirited ambition. . . . [The] magnificent man spends not on himself but on public objects . . . (trans. W. D. Ross).

In contrast for Aristotle is the man of "tasteless showiness." As Pope puts it, "never coxcomb reach'd Magnificence" (22). We are back to the "sons of earth" and "the heaps they raise."

The art that defies nature lies behind the central metaphor of the second Moral Essay, *To a Lady* (1735). The metaphor is drawn from painting, and it works in two principal ways: a discussion of the difficulty of painting the character of women, who are mercurial and unstable, and a criticism of the kind of painting they require. Running through the poem is an implicit analogy between the variability and ostentation of vain women and the broken light and color of dazzling but superficial painting:

> Pictures like these, dear Madam, to design,
> Asks no firm hand, and no unerring line;
> Some wand'ring touches, some reflected light,
> Some flying stroke alone can hit 'em right:
> For how should equal colors do the knack?
> Chameleons who can paint in white and black?
> (151–56)

With these lines we may contrast those written twenty-three years earlier, to the painter Jervas:

> O, lasting as those colours may they shine,
> Free as thy stroke, yet faultless as thy line;
> New graces yearly like thy works display,
> Soft without weakness, without glaring gay.
> (*Epistle to Mr. Jervas*, 63–66)

The kind of painting, then, that these ladies require, is precisely the kind that was regarded with distrust and alarm by such a critic as Shaftesbury: the Venetian school and its issue in Rubens.

Pope is alluding to the conflict between the claims of *disegno* and *colore* that culminated in the French academic debate between Poussinists and Rubenists. The doctrine that draughtsmanship and line have priority over color goes back at least as far as Aristotle's *Poetics*, where the primacy of plot over character invokes the analogy:

> Compare the parallel in painting, where the most beautiful colors laid on without order will not give one the same pleasure as a simple black-and-white sketch of a portrait.

So Pope on "versifiers": "Their coloring entertains the sight, but the *lines* and *life* of the picture are not to be inspected too narrowly" (to Cromwell, 17 December 1710, *Correspondence*, I). Colorist painting, with its broken areas, its touches and strokes, becomes the counterpart of the false architecture Pope treats in the epistle to Burlington:

> Load some vain church with old theatric state,
> Turn arcs of triumph to a garden gate.
>
> (29–30)

A mere "dog-hole eked with ends of wall" becomes an entrance or "frontispiece" with the addition of a few touches of ornament and rustication:

> Then clap four slices of pilaster on't,
> That, lac'd with bits of rustic, makes a front.
>
> (33–34)

Just as the dog-hole is dressed with pretentious sham, so the ladies in Pope's epistle try on various roles of historical or mythological painting:

> Let then the fair one beautifully cry,
> In Magdalen's loose hair and lifted eye,
> Or dressed in smiles of sweet Cecilia shine,
> With simpering angels, palms, and harps divine.
>
> (11–14)

Here the lines are worked out with a cruel incisiveness. What adverb can overwhelm its verb more than the self-conscious "beautifully" does the supposedly spontaneous "cry?" Or how better than with "in" suggest the assumption of a costume? And how more neatly catch the ambiguity of mock piety and self-display than in the sensual detail of the "loose hair," with

Magdalen's humility in washing Christ's feet played off against the artful negligence of the lady? We can recall the iconography of the Magdalen's tear-filled eye and see it converted to histrionic imitation, which as readily turns to the rapt smiles of Cecilia. The lady is surrounded at last with all the furniture of divinity: cosmic harmony provides a musical setting, and angels can only simper their adoration.

The very grotesqueness of bad art has a fascination, for in the failure or misdirection of intention the ambitions of art are made all the more conspicuous; bad art cannot conceal art, and it becomes as a result monumental in its futility, its aspirations nakedly unrealized and imposingly asserted. So in the portraits of *To a Lady*: Atossa's vehemence and strain, her unconscious but unerring commitment to failure, her "brave disorder," which cannot come to terms with the world but still has neither integrity of aim or stable object of its own—these have a grandeur that approaches tragic stature. The forces at work within Atossa acquire more than human dimensions, and their magnification is insistently stressed. Such phrases as "by turns all womankind" or "all her life one warfare upon earth" create a vastness of scale that intensifies the shifting motives and unstable will. The vastness that cannot be composed becomes monstrous.

Yet, even as Pope creates this effect, he composes the picture; the thrusts of will and eddies of feeling are given a regularity of effect that Atossa cannot see. The implicit logic, to which Atossa is blind, is made inescapably neat:

> Strange! by the means defeated of the ends,
> By spirit robbed of power, by warmth of friends,
> By wealth of followers! without one distress
> Sick of herself through very selfishness!
>
> (143–46)

The clarity of pattern makes Atossa's blindness seem all the more mechanical; every effort she makes accomplishes her defeat the more precisely. She becomes a near-tragic figure locked in a pattern of satiric transparency, and, like Timon's, her dreadful self-assertion is blandly assumed into a comic pattern as her wealth "wanders, Heaven-directed, to the poor" (150).

These lives are themselves failures of art; if Pope shows us "character as a creative achievement" in the *Essay*, he shows us here the inability to create the stable self-knowledge which makes for a true self.

> Fair to no purpose, artful to no end,
> Young without lovers, old without a friend,

A fop their passion, but their prize a sot;
Alive, ridiculous, and dead, forgot!
(245–48)

Flavia's desperate thrusts are an instance. She is a woman who disdains every common thought and convention, who seeks for an intensity of experience that life can never give her. Her search, by its very nature, must be disappointed with every attainment, and she veers between impossible hope and utter despair. What casts her spirits down? "A spark too fickle, or a spouse too kind" (94). What does it mean? Does she fear her husband's pity? Or is he also unfaithful? Or does his loyalty stir her guilt? Or is he drearily trying to win her back? Or is he foolishly in the way? All kinds of guesses are possible, for "true no-meaning puzzles more than wit" (114). The formless work of bad art teases us with the forms it might have assumed. We cannot help taking for granted that nonsense is aspiring to meaning. But it turns out that we are looking at the wrong level. We cannot

Infer the motive from the deed, and shew,
That what we chanc'd was what we meant to do.
(*To Cobham*, Moral Essay I, 53–54)

Only in light of the ruling passion do the wild seem constant and the foolish consistent. The work which seems formless composes if one stands at the right distance. So with Flavia:

You purchase pain with all that joy can give,
And die of nothing but a rage to live.
(99–100)

The last lines fix compassionately on the helpless self-destruction that underlies the worldly wit and overrefinement.

But it is toward the order of a true work of art, a true character, that Pope moves. Character, Aristotle tells us, "is that which reveals the moral purpose of the agents" (*Poetics*, vi), and it demands the power of choice. The ladies we have seen so far act through involuntary passion, but at the close as we come to the Lady addressed (presumably Martha Blount), we move from intense femininity to a woman who is a "softer man." The Lady is capable of self-knowledge and self-control; even more, of generosity and tact. Pope looks back here, as in much of the epistle, to *The Rape of the Lock*, where a lovely order composed without true consciousness is easily lost. This Lady is "Mistress of herself, though China fall" (268). She becomes a fusion of the charm, variety, and energy of feminine passion, and the stability, directness, and strength of masculine reason. Pope has come close to defining the art toward which he has moved in his later satires, an art that goes beyond mere beauty and weds its aesthetic power to moral vision.

DAVID B. MORRIS

"The Visionary Maid":
Tragic Passion and Redemptive
Sympathy in "Eloisa to Abelard"

Samuel Johnson dismissed with curt and undisguised contempt one of the
most intensely erotic poems Pope ever wrote. "Poetry," he judged, "has not
often been worse employed than in dignifying the amorous fury of a raving
girl." The remark, significantly, was not inspired by "Eloisa to Abelard"
but by the equally impassioned "Elegy to the Memory of an Unfortunate
Lady." Unlike many modern readers, who lump the poems together as
evidence that the heights of emotion were not entirely beyond Pope's reach,
Johnson apparently found reason to discriminate carefully between them.
He balanced his scorn for Pope's unfortunate lady, whose suicide in his view
no passion could justify or excuse, with praise excessive even by Johnsonian
standards: "The *Epistle of Eloisa to Abelard* is one of the most happy productions of human wit: the subject is so judiciously chosen that it would be
difficult, in turning over the annals of the world, to find another which so
many circumstances concur to recommend." Certainly Johnson's grounds for
approval, which include what he took to be Pope's reverent treatment of
"religious hope and resignation," do not always coincide with those of subsequent readers. Yet, with recent accounts generally agreeing that the poem
betrays drastic flaws, Johnson's authority offers some comfort to admirers of
"Eloisa to Abelard" and suggests the need for a detailed defense and explication—tasks Johnson does not undertake—stressing the principles or attitudes which seem to govern Pope's treatment of his subject. Such an inquiry

From *Modern Language Quarterly*. Copyright © 1973 by University of Washington. Original
title "'The Visionary Maid': Tragic Passion and Redemptive Sympathy in Pope's 'Eloisa to
Abelard.' "

has the special virtue of heeding the advice Pope himself thought fruitful in *An Essay on Criticism*:

> A perfect Judge will *read* each Work of Wit
> With the same Spirit that its Author *writ*,
> Survey the *Whole*, nor seek slight Faults to find,
> Where *Nature moves*, and *Rapture warms* the mind;
> Nor lose, for that malignant dull Delight,
> The *gen'rous Pleasure* to be charm'd with Wit.
>
> (233–38)

In addressing critics, Pope elevates passion far above mere propriety as a source of literary delight, and the redeeming power which he attributes to sympathetic insight and to emotional generosity should raise at least the possibility that his attitude toward Eloisa, like his idea of criticism, is based ultimately in a deep commitment to the saving value of human affection.

An effective defense requires some knowledge of predictable avenues of attack. Although individual writers may blur the lines of demarcation, the most common objections to "Eloisa to Abelard" fall into several distinct categories, and these categories have remained stable since the eighteenth century, despite the shifting theoretical and personal biases which underlie some two hundred years of critical activity. In appraising the attacks on "Eloisa to Abelard," then, it will be useful to avoid commentary on specific arguments of contemporary critics—which might be unfairly represented when detached from context for the purposes of rebuttal—and to study the general categories of objection. These can be identified loosely as the aesthetic, the ethical, and the moral.

The aesthetic objection takes many shapes. In practice, the diverse complaints against Pope's artistry often reduce to the single claim that rhymed couplets and an artfully patterned rhetoric are inappropriate to Eloisa's impassioned meditations. If this claim is valid, "Eloisa to Abelard" would fail by Pope's own standards: his idea of poetry, as Edward Niles Hooker has shown, demands a harmony among subject, style, and form. At first glance, however, the objection can seem justified, for the poem hardly resembles a spontaneous effusion of passionate speech. Despite its extravagance and the fiction of spontaneity, the marks of Pope's craftsmanship are conspicuously evident, revealing a deliberation and latent control which far exceed the trace of artifice implicit in even the most conversational Popean couplets. Aesthetic objections concerning Eloisa's unrealistic diction and contrived style recognize a distinctive feature of the poem, and in order to appreciate the formal aspects of "Eloisa to Abelard" we must read with at least some awareness of Pope's intentions.

Pope understood, of course, that correspondents who write in the grip of immediate passion do not normally compose in rhymed iambic pentameter. Nor do they trifle with the rhetorical intricacies of wit. On the death of his father, for example, Pope wrote to Lord Burlington with a spare directness which, especially in contrast with the intellectual and stylistic gamesmanship of his earlier letters, conveys an authenticity of feeling almost (as was said of the sublime) too powerful for language. The sheer exuberance of Eloisa's diction and style, then, implies that Pope did not intend the poem as a faithful imitation of her actual words and thoughts. The insistent artifice suggests instead that the poem should be accepted as a literary creation in which Eloisa's experience is not reproduced exactly but rather is infused with the interpretative vision of the poet. Pope does not seek fidelity to a real language of feeling, as Wordsworth did on occasion. He means the diction to be accepted as a poetic hybrid created in order to interpret the meaning of Eloisa's struggle. Her artificial language, as it evokes and controls genuine feeling in the reader, serves the natural end of ordering and of clarifying the poet's raw materials of life-uninterpreted.

If one acknowledges that the nature which Pope imitates in "Eloisa to Abelard" is the truth of experience rather than of language, his contrivances of diction, of style, and of form assume an appropriateness consistent with his own declaration in the Argument prefixed to the poem. "Eloisa to Abelard," he explains, is intended to offer a *"lively . . . picture of the struggles of grace and nature, virtue and passion"*—and perhaps the most revealing aspect of the statement is its stylized balance and opposition. Whereas a modern poet might show Eloisa fragmented by a multitude of conflicting pressures, Pope views her struggle as essentially dualistic: grace and virtue compete with nature and passion for control of a psyche divided between the opposing claims of soul and of body. In emphasizing the particularly dualistic nature of her struggle, the rhetorical features analyzed by Jacob H. Adler find added significance. "Zeugma, chiasmus, and anaphora," he tells us, "are typical; but simple balance is more frequent, more typical. Eloisa's mind simply works—or is made to work—in pairs and in series. Almost everything is in conjunction with something else." Rhyme itself, like the balance of opposites, helps to dramatize the conflict within Eloisa's mind. The poem, Adler reports, exhibits a greater proportion of off-rhymes than all but one of Pope's major works. In a poet who consistently labored to make the sound of his verse echo its sense, the slight dissonance of imperfect rhyme suggests the clash of uneasily juxtaposed forces within the speaker, just as other rhymed pairs express many of the poem's overt oppositions: restrain/in vain (27–28), bloom/gloom (37–38), night/light (143–44), pray'r/despair (179–80), repose/glows (251–52), sleep/weep (313–14), destroy/joy (337–38). Even the contrast between passages of somewhat exaggerated romantic diction ("Ye grots and caverns shagg'd with horrid thorn!" [20]) and moments of direct plain speech ("I have not yet forgot my self to stone" [24]) probably reflects Pope's attempt to picture Eloisa within the extremes of divided possibility. These devices, and others of similar function, imply that Pope worked consciously to create a correspondence between subject and style. Although the manipulated contrasts may not suit every taste, they are certainly appropriate to Pope's main design.

Even readers who grant the propriety of Eloisa's language, however, are liable to raise ethical objections which can equally distort the poem's meaning. Such ethical objections center on the character of Eloisa. She is, her critics claim, an irrational creature, unhinged by love and sinfully obstinate in rejecting her duty to God. Among the multitude who have been (in the tolerant eighteenth-century phrase) no better than they should be, Eloisa achieves a modest notoriety for her open defense of the indefensible, and Pope's early biographer Owen Ruffhead is not the last to discover peril and iniquity in the depiction of her unsanctified love:

> The glowing lines which express the extravagance of Eloisa's fondness, her contempt of connubial ties, and the unbounded freedom of her attachment, have been often repeated with too much success by artful libertines to forward the purposes of seduction, and have as often, perhaps, been remembered by the deluded fair, and deemed a sanction for illicit deviations from the paths of virtue.

The progress of sexual revolution in the post-Augustan world gives Ruffhead's warning a nostalgic charm, but even that cannot redeem it as criticism. Eloisa's sensuality is linked with an equally strong love of God, and the Old Testament might be condemned by the same logic which Ruffhead employs to censure Eloisa. Yet it is still possible to claim, as has been maintained recently of the speaker in the "Elegy to the Memory of an Unfortunate Lady," that Pope portrays Eloisa's passion ultimately to discredit her. Like Atticus, Atossa, Sir Balaam, and Cibber, one can argue, Eloisa stands as a model of improper conduct: her extravagance is self-incriminating. This possible resemblance to Pope's method elsewhere should not be too hastily accepted, for "Eloisa to Abelard" is in many ways a unique venture, an experiment unparalleled in Pope's earlier and later works. Its spirit does not seem even

obliquely satirical. Pope continually invites our compassion for his belea-
guered heroine and concludes with a passage implying his direct personal
sympathy. We must take Eloisa as we find her, with her mixture of flaws
and virtues, not measure her conduct against the standards of everyday
propriety. Understanding, not censure, is Pope's goal.

Unfortunately, ethical and aesthetic objections can seem strengthened
and confirmed by the ease with which they support more general moral
objections to the poem. While the ethical judgments center on the character
(ethos) of Eloisa herself, moral objections consider the broadest implications
of structure and of development, what eighteenth-century critics of epic and
of drama usually included under the heading of *fable*. The fable or moral of
a work referred to its unifying vision (in practice often simplified to an
acceptable moralistic tag) which embraces the diversity of separate episodes.
Homer's moral in the *Iliad*, according to Pope, concerned the relationship
between personal anger and social discord. As he wrote of Achilles, "*Homer*
proposes him not as a Pattern for Imitation; but the Moral of the Poem
which he design'd the Reader should draw from it, is, that we should avoid
Anger, since it is ever pernicious in the Event." Pope did not restrict himself
to such a reductive interpretation of Homer, and "Eloisa to Abelard," falling
outside the generic demands of epic and of drama, would not necessarily
require the embodiment of a ponderously Homeric moral. But Pope did
require moral significance of all serious literature. "No writing is good," he
told Joseph Spence, "that does not tend to better mankind some way or
other." He would ask himself, and expect readers to ask of the poem, what
general ameliorating purpose underlies the portrayal of Eloisa's intense and
disjointed struggle, from her first startled, hesitant questioning to her final
repose.

The moral purpose, as claimed earlier, is not to expose Eloisa as a
woman justly afflicted for her uncontrolled passion and willful disobedience
to God. Like Achilles, she is hardly a pattern for imitation; but she is equally
inappropriate merely as an *exemplum* of culpable misconduct. If neither praise
nor blame adequately defines Pope's intention, however, can the poem be
said to embody a moral purpose at all? Here opinion divides. And the division
grows when readers consider, through an analysis of the poem's broad pattern
of development, the implications of Eloisa's final state of mind. Some find
her peacefully composed to die in full acceptance of God's will, penitent for
her sins and trusting in the forgiveness of a merciful Redeemer. This reading
has the benefit of conforming with historical accounts of Eloisa's life and
probably reflects Pope's own view, as it certainly does Johnson's. Its defect,
aside from carrying little conviction for many readers because the progress

toward penitence seems haphazard or unclear, is that the poem appears to reward fornication and impiety with the solace of a blessed end. Still other readers find Eloisa at the conclusion merely lapsed into quiescence: although her passion is spent, her conflicts remain unresolved. This view exposes Pope to attack for daring to sympathize with a creature hardened in sin. Either reading can lead to charges of moral confusion. At this point, waiving a lengthy theological explication of a poem which seems more deeply concerned with Eloisa's mind than with her soul, it is not enough to reply that Pope's idea of moral purpose in "Eloisa to Abelard" has little to do with precepts of morality. That reply itself requires taking a positive step toward under-standing the poem's attempt "to better mankind." In particular, many of the common objections vanish completely when one considers "Eloisa to Abelard" as an exploration of two closely related concepts: tragic passion and redemptive sympathy.

It is one of the inert facts of literary history that Pope modeled "Eloisa to Abelard" on the Ovidian heroic epistle. Yet Pope's most valuable legacy from Ovid was a spirit which has no necessary connection with direct bor-rowings, and a too detailed source-study can obscure what to Pope, and also to Dryden, was clear, important, and stimulating in Ovid's work: its relation to drama. Dryden called attention to the dramatic properties of Ovid in a passage quite relevant to "Eloisa to Abelard":

> Though I see many excellent thoughts in Seneca, yet he of them [the Ancients] who had a genius most proper for the stage, was Ovid; he had a way of writing so fit to stir up a pleasing admiration and concernment, which are the objects of a tragedy, and to show the various movements of a soul combating betwixt two different passions, that, had he lived in our age, or in his own could have writ with our advantages, no man but must have yielded to him.

Pope's subject in his Ovidian epistle is precisely what Dryden called the various movements of a soul "combating betwixt two different passions." Eloisa's love for Abelard and her duty to God—like the poles of inclination and of honor in Restoration heroic plays—are the ingredients of dramatic tragedy. By understanding the poem's dramatic qualities and its kinship with tragedy, we gain an illuminating perspective from which to understand Pope's attitude toward Eloisa.

The decision to cast Eloisa's story in the highly dramatic mode of the Ovidian epistle, rather than in the form of drama itself, was doubtless instinctive. No amount of genuine interest in the theater could induce Pope to turn dramatist. Early experience taught him "how much everybody that did write for the stage was obliged to subject themselves to the players and the town." Critics too stood poised to hamper the playwright with their annoying and often barren controversies, among which a current dispute over the propriety of love as a tragic passion would have assured Eloisa a stormy debut, especially since Pope's dedicated enemy John Dennis had strong views on the subject. It is even likely that Pope knew his own limitations at the sustained give-and-take of drama: there is substantial truth in Macaulay's jaundiced observation that "Pope writing dialogue resembled—to borrow Horace's imagery and his own—a wolf, which, instead of biting, should take to kicking, or a monkey which should try to sting." His ear for phrases failed him when riposte prolonged itself into conversation. Yet, if he avoided formal drama except for minor collaborations at farce, he also deliberately infused his own nondramatic works with many of the qualities of drama. *The Rape of the Lock* may owe its final shape to the influence of traditional five-act theatrical plotting, and Donald J. Greene is correct in stressing the "dramatic texture" which characterizes many of the later satirical poems. As poet, translator, editor, and critic, Pope reveals a lasting appreciation for the blend of narrative and dramatic elements in a single composition—Shakespeare's set speeches, for example, placed within a context of dialogue and action—and this taste appears to have governed his treatment of Eloisa's story. In the rambling, sententious discourse of the original letters, he recognized the possibility of creating a highly concentrated dramatic episode. In effect, he isolates a moment of intense passion in a drama of connected events and discards the shell of plot. Despite her role as correspondent, Eloisa is essentially a tragic heroine.

Eloisa's posture as tragic heroine frees Pope from certain limited ethical and moralistic responsibilities which critics like Ruffhead wish to impose on the poem. Particularly when she is viewed in the traditional, complementary tragic roles of actor and of victim—at once the willful agent of her own suffering and the prisoner of circumstances—she joins the class of fictive protagonists whose histories are too tangled for simple moralistic judgment. *King Lear* can be forced to yield the allegorical lesson that discord follows the division of rule, although the play provides no assurance that not dividing the kingdom will preserve harmony. Few responsive readers, however, would wish to apply a simple moral judgment to Lear himself or to Cordelia. It is not true that they get exactly what they deserve. That is one reason why Johnson found the conclusion of *King Lear* too painful for rereading and why eighteenth-century audiences, obsessed with the mechanics of poetic justice, enjoyed the play in the sweetened version of Nahum Tate, who married Cordelia to the deserving Edgar. Although Shakespeare permits Lear and

Cordelia to earn a measure of wisdom and of self-knowledge, at terrible cost, he does not permit the audience to indulge in a reassuring balance of loss and gain. Pope restored Shakespeare's original ending in his otherwise flawed edition of 1725, and he seems to have understood the force of Shakespeare's tragic vision. Like Lear, Eloisa both acts and suffers in ways too complex to point her tale with an edifying maxim.

Eloisa as victim evokes the pathos which eighteenth-century readers admired in tragedy. Yet the pity for someone trapped in the coils of passion and of chance never degenerates into sentimentality, as it can in Nicholas Rowe's bombastic she-tragedies. The difference may involve Pope's care in establishing a complexity of motive which locates the source of Eloisa's anguish in something beyond her own intensity of feeling and powers of speech. Certainly, like most tragic protagonists, she is in part the victim of her own impulsive and passionate nature—a point which recent criticism has rightly stressed, although it is rarely mentioned that she is also the victim of her own best qualities: generous instincts and a vast capacity for love. In addition, however, she is beset by a complicated series of forces essentially outside her control, including chance, historical circumstance, and the passions of those around her. Especially because readers continue to see Eloisa as a woman too weak and foolish to control her own emotions, it is worth looking briefly at the various outside forces which have contributed to her misfortune.

"Eloisa to Abelard," like a history painting, presupposes a series of actions which generate the single moment delineated by the artist. It also presupposes an established idea of character to which the poet, no matter how he shades his interpretation, must pay homage. The legend of Eloisa—supplemented in Pope's day by John Hughes's *Letters of Abelard and Heloise* (1713), a translation of a romanticized French version of the original Latin correspondence—by no means pictured her as the witless agent of her own perplexity. Whatever exaggerations have attended her legend, Hughes explained, she "may deservedly be placed in the Rank of Women of the greatest Learning." Erudition certainly is no shield against folly; Pope delights in exposing the absurdities of mad learning. But Eloisa's accomplishments assure us that, however strong her passions, she possessed extremely well-developed powers of reason. Further, she did not dizzily fling herself at Abelard, but succumbed only after a carefully plotted and relentlessly pursued seduction by the greatest philosopher of his day, who was abetted in his design by the stupidity and greed of her worthless guardian uncle. Even once deeply in love with Abelard—which surely is no crime—she resisted his pressing demands for marriage, countering his passion with a rational

and selflessly inspired argument emphasizing the irrevocable damage which
marriage would inflict upon Abelard's reputation and ability as a philosopher.
It is not that on principle she preferred being a mistress to a wife; rather,
faced with the prospect of ruining Abelard's philosophic stature if she con-
sented to his demands for marriage, she resolutely refused to put her own
interest above his. Dido maintained no such regal dignity in love.

Virtually forced into compliance by Abelard, she obediently yielded at
last to his ill-conceived sequestrations, although only Abelard could have
been blind enough to anticipate no unpleasantness from the avuncular Ful-
bert. When revenge came, in the violent and humiliating castration, Abelard
once more commanded her obedience, instructing her to take the veil at the
convent of Argenteuil. Her friends dissented—sensibly thinking "the yoke
of monastic rule intolerable for one of her youth"—but she replied by quoting
the words of Cornelia, wife of Pompey, that she gladly atoned for causing
the misery of her husband, an exceedingly generous idea of causation. Although it later pained her to learn that Abelard had cautiously delayed his
own vows until certain she was securely immured, she maintained her fidelity
to him while earning almost universal admiration in her subsequent role as
the efficient and devoted Abbess of the Paraclete. If Pope had wished to
write about the dangerous propensity of amorous fury to overwhelm the
reason, Abelard would have suited his purpose much better than Eloisa.

These external pressures might have bowed even a saint, and Eloisa,
although genuinely devout, was unluckily no Saint Theresa. But it is possible
that Pope wished us to recognize an additional weight which increased her
difficulties, for hers were not propitious times in which to reconcile the
demands of reason and passion. When meditating on the dissociation of
those two fundamental and complementary human powers—which ought to
be linked in a cooperative friendship—Pope in *An Essay on Man* traced its
source directly to the nominal distinctions established by the scholastic
philosophers of Eloisa's day:

> Let subtle schoolmen teach these friends to fight,
> More studious to divide than to unite,
> And Grace and Virtue, Sense and Reason split,
> With all the rash dexterity of Wit:
> Wits, just like fools, at war about a Name,
> Have full as oft no meaning, or the same.
>
> (2.81–86)

Eloisa's struggle between the apparently counter claims of "grace and nature,
virtue and passion" owes something to the historical split between man's

rational and passionate faculties which it was one main purpose of *An Essay on Man* to heal. And, ironically, Abelard's rash dexterity as a philosopher is at least indirectly related to the torment he causes Eloisa as a lover. Hughes tells us of Abelard:

> Of all the Sciences to which he applied himself, that which pleased him most, and in which he made the greatest Progress, was Logick. He had a very subtle Wit, and was incessantly whetting it by Disputes, out of a restless Ambition to be a Master of his Weapons. So that in a short time he gain'd the Reputation of the greatest Philosopher of his Age; and has always been esteem'd the Founder of what we call the *Learning of the Schoolmen*.
>
> *(Letters of Abelard and Heloise)*

Although the poem does not exploit the irony of Abelard's philosophic responsibility for Eloisa's plight, Hughes's description certainly suggests added reason for Pope's sympathetic attitude toward his heroine. Eloisa, while admittedly not blameless, is nevertheless a victim of forces far beyond her control, just as even the weather seems to conspire against Lear. Born in a bad time, nurtured by a pernicious guardian, seduced by an unscrupulous lover, virtually forced into marriage, wedded to a passionless castrate, shut away in a convent, and deceived by a philosophy which taught the eternal opposition of reason and desire, Eloisa inspires something like tragic admiration simply by her power to endure. Her suffering is sharp and continuous, but she refuses to give in.

While Eloisa as victim arouses the pity and fear appropriate to tragedy, it is not as victim that she achieves the full tragic stature with which Pope invested her. A virtuous individual struggling with misfortune, which Addison (quoting Seneca) thought the fittest subject for tragedy, did not satisfy Pope's more Shakespearean imagination. Although he had warm praise for the sentiments and moral earnestness of *Cato*, Addison's bookish tragedy which traps a near saint in the fatal net of history and military power, it seems unlikely that he entirely admired Cato's passivity and suicide. Misfortune may buffet him continuously, but the storms of passion never budge the well-anchored reason of Addison's flawless hero. Eloisa, as we have seen, is far less irrational than some have pictured her. Reason repeatedly asserts the claim of her duty to God, intensifying the emotional force of her divine love. By implication, she steadfastly rejects the easiest and in some ways most logical responses to her dilemma: she never contemplates suicide, and she refuses to go mad. Especially when throughout Pope's work madness and death-in-life constitute major threats and even temptations, Eloisa's rational will to endure signifies her possession of admirable and vigorous qualities of mind. The Paraclete is for her no refuge but a setting for struggle— often in fact the projection or symbol of one portion of her mind— and she never retreats, despite her pain, into the state of potentially delusive solipsism which (as Freud wrote of neurosis) replaces the cloister in modern life. Although partly the victim of forces beyond her control, she also displays active powers of character which must not be ignored. To some extent these powers simply increase her anguish by increasing her range of awareness. Yet, through the exercise of her active powers of mind, she emerges as the agent of a heroic struggle, affirming the dignity and worth of human qualities which even the combination of chance, error, and the pressures of history cannot overwhelm or render wholly self-destructive.

Among the various aspects of Eloisa's character which Pope might have discovered in Hughes's translation or invented from his own analysis, two recur in the poem so frequently that they become almost defining traits. They are summarized in the phrase she once uses to describe herself—"the visionary maid" (162)—for it is preeminently her distinguishing powers of memory and of imagination which create for her a striking, singular, and even heroic identity. Many women have found themselves, as an appropriately nameless voice tells her from a nearby tomb, "Love's victim" (312). What raises Eloisa above this sorority is her clearly defined character based upon extraordinary powers of remembering and imagining. These traits—which center the poem in the psychology of Pope's heroine and justify, as Brendan P. O Hehir has argued, the instances of "pathetic fallacy" when altars blaze and statues tremble—were not an inevitable choice for emphasis however natural they now appear. The letters translated by Hughes reveal at least as much concern with doctrine as with Eloisa's mental processes, and the diffusion of focus weakens even what psychological interest Hughes manages to convey. In creating a unified, emphatic, and consistent idea of character from his hodgepodge source, Pope achieves a remarkable feat. By adding some details, by omitting others, by compressing, arranging, and substituting various parts of the original letters, he transforms a wandering and heterogeneous correspondence into the concentrated drama of Eloisa's mind. Indeed, the immediacy of her quasi-dramatic situation enhances Pope's attention to psychological and interior processes. It is a drama not of action but of thought and feeling which can find no outlet in events. We should notice also that Eloisa emerges from this transformation as a convincing tragic heroine not simply because she experiences misfortune but because she remains amid misfortunes acutely sensitive to the workings of her own mind. She exhibits what Shakespearean drama offers at its best: a self defined not through the accidents of history or through the exaggerations of type-character but through the process of inwardly perceived tragic experience. Eloisa transcends the faceless horde of Love's victims because she is not merely victimized. Through her extraordinary powers of memory and imagination she virtually creates an identity, and this process of individual self-creation both augments her suffering and gives significance to her pain.

This general claim can be illustrated by the practice of Augustan satire, where perhaps the cruellest and most effective technique involves the deprivation of full human identity. The technique is not limited to the outward and pictorial dehumanizing of caricature. It deliberately robs the individual of any cohesive quality of inwardness. The human object of satire becomes a mere shell enclosing either emptiness or formless confusion. Eliot's phrase "the hollow men" aptly characterizes numerous figures of Augustan satire, from Buckingham's Bayes to Pope's Bufo, Cibber, and Atossa, whose interior vacancy or swirling chaos in effect negates identity. The effect of this technique can be comic as well as savage, but it is nearly always disquieting: a slight vertigo accompanies even the most lighthearted suggestion that human identity is nothing more than names and clothing stretched upon a void. Yet, for Pope, the moral force of this suggestion derives from its recognizable perversity. Appearance of "the hollow men" in Augustan satire is necessarily based upon the conviction that genuine identity, whatever peculiar expression it may receive through the influence of humour, of ruling passion, or of benign obsession, is fundamentally a creation of two forces: memory and complexity of awareness.

If in the Middle Ages and Renaissance memory could become a means of ordering the universe, as Frances A. Yates has shown, or a means of reconstituting through meditation the meaning of history, as Louis L. Martz has shown, memory in the Augustan age holds the humbler but no less crucial function of ordering the individual. Memory enables eighteenth-century man to assert a continuity with his own past, without which he might grow as fragmented and incoherent as Swift's impersonated modern author in *A Tale of a Tub*, who pointedly both laments and celebrates the unhappy shortness of his memory. Pope himself tells us in *The Dunciad* that "Wits have short Memories, and Dunces none" (4.620)—which helps to explain why, despite the profusion of real names, Scriblerus can insist that the dunces are mere inhuman "phantoms." Memory provides the basis of coherent reasoning and of substantial identity: not to remember is ultimately not to exist. There are, of course, evident dangers in an undiscriminating attention to the past, whether personal or historical; as Pope observes in *An Essay on Criticism*, the predominance of memory inevitably restricts the force of understanding, just as the immediacy of imaginative experience invariably overpowers the less compelling figures of memory (56–59). Pope's ideal, as always, is a harmonious balance, without which the personality faces potential uncreation, a lapse into stupor or meaningless contradiction. Both fates afflict Buckingham's Bayes, whose hasty adherence to opposite points of view effectively cancels awareness, leaving a blank of nonconsciousness in place of the poet's reconciling intelligence. "Pope thinks of human character," writes Maynard Mack, "as a creative achievement, an artistic result, something built out of chaos as God built the world." And, while many of the satiric victims reveal the possibility that human identity may dissolve into a primal incoherence, Eloisa demonstrates the contrary process by which identity can be created and sustained upon the flux of human nature. Man may be, as Pope calls him in *An Essay on Man*, a "Chaos of Thought and Passion, all confus'd" (2.13), but he still retains the creative power of self-discovery through an intelligent perception of his dilemma, through connecting himself by means of memory with the past, and through sharing a charitable concern for the life around him. These activities—for they require powerful and continual exertion—create the fully human, complex, and sympathetic identity which the satiric victims so obviously lack. They are among the activities which raise Eloisa to the stature of a tragic heroine.

No illustration is needed to prove Pope's emphasis upon Eloisa's powers of memory and of imagination. The entire poem varies between her excursions into fantasy and her vivid recollections of the past, both played upon a consciousness wholly alive to the controlling presence of reason. Although her understanding may seem to veer with each new image, in fact the shifts occur because, while allowing free play to the imagery of past and of possibility, she never allows memory and imagination to overwhelm her perception of the actual state of things. The result is a complexity, not a distortion, of awareness. Further, while the scenes unfolded in memory and in imagination certainly help to fire Eloisa's already kindled passions, her emotional fervor may be unphilosophical without being irrational or inappropriate to the occasion. Just as Fielding's Parson Adams, in contradiction of all his sermons, experienced a period of frenzied grief on receiving news that his youngest son had drowned, Eloisa reacts to a sudden shock in discovering Abelard's letter, and the violence of her reaction is, as with Parson Adams, high tribute to the powers of human affection. In one context Pope could exalt the temperance of Martha Blount, "Mistress of herself, tho' China fall." But Eloisa's loss is not the breaking of a teacup. Undiscriminating equanimity, after all, is no better than Belinda's undiscriminating grief in *The Rape of the Lock*. Unlike some of the later sentimentalists, neither

Pope nor Fielding believed that emotional outbursts were necessarily good, but they also rejected the duty of invariable restraint. Both argue implicitly for a direct correspondence between feeling and the occasion for feeling. When such a correspondence exists, as it does for Eloisa, the expression of strong emotion is itself a rational act, since it is based on a clear perception of inherent values. Eloisa, unlike Belinda, knows the difference between losing a lapdog and a lover. In far more difficult circumstances than befell Martha Blount, she remains truly mistress of herself, for she refuses to deny the uniquely developed powers of memory and of imagination which create for her a coherent identity and a fully human self.

Probably the most effective means which Pope employs to stress the remarkable extent of Eloisa's powers is the simple but forceful device of contrast. Both Abelard and the Paraclete itself, linked imagistically throughout the poem, vividly embody the unimpassioned state of forgetfulness which is the polar opposite of Eloisa's condition. Memory for Eloisa inspires feeling, and feeling signifies life, while the walls of religion and the dead calm inflicted upon Abelard enforce an unnatural severance of the knot uniting memory and desire. Addressing the walls which seem to oppress as they enclose her, Eloisa might also be accusing Abelard himself of an inhuman loss of feeling: "Tho' cold like you, unmov'd, and silent grown, / I have not yet forgot my self to stone" (23–24). In truth, Eloisa is far from cold, despite the efforts of "stern religion" to quench the "unwilling flame" of Love (39), and the inseparable warmth and pain she feels become a measure of her sentient humanity. Not to feel, like not to remember, is virtually not to exist. The victory of reason over passion, whether won by confinement, by philosophy, by religion, or by mutilation, leads only to the lifeless virtue of stoicism, an excess Pope rejected outright in *An Essay on Man*:

> In lazy Apathy let Stoics boast
> Their Virtue fix'd; 'tis fix'd as in a frost,
> Contracted all, retiring to the breast;
> But strength of mind is Exercise, not Rest:
> The rising tempest puts in act the soul,
> Parts it may ravage, but preserves the whole.
>   (2. 101–106)

The images of frost and of fixity—recalling the stony coldness repeatedly associated both with Abelard and with the Paraclete—can remind us that Pope normally characterizes Eloisa through imagery of warmth, motion, and light. She can never achieve the serenity which she attributes to the blameless vestal of her imagination. ("The world forgetting, by the world forgot"

[208]) because the price of such composure is oblivion, a denial of the individual identity created and sustained through the lively process of remembering . Eloisa finds herself surrounded by various temptations to rest, to immobility, and to forgetfulness. Together they emphasize her determination not to lapse into a stonelike fixity, contraction, and cold, forgetting state of self-denial.

Pope's attempt "to better mankind" depends not upon the extraction of an all-subsuming ethical precept but upon our willingness to experience through Eloisa the humanizing power of tragic passion, with its oblique testament to the dignity of human nature. In a mind wholly conscious of its division between mighty opposites, Eloisa's rising tempests of passion do indeed "put in act" her soul; and although memory and imagination undeniably "ravage" with the pain of conflict, her struggle itself affirms the value of an active consciousness: "strength of mind is Exercise, not Rest." While recognizing the finality of loss, the inevitability of error, and the perplexity born of chance, of circumstance, and of man's own nature, the poem recognizes beyond these a value in suffering which redeems its pain. If Cato's suicide is the logical consequence of stoic rationality when confronted with the intolerable, Eloisa's struggle asserts the self-sustaining and creative worth of conscious endurance. Not everyone will fall prey to the particular "sad variety of woe" (36) which is Eloisa's lot. But everyone, in Pope's view, shares with her the same fundamental powers of mind, the same exposure to misfortune, the same capacity for self-torment, and the same necessity for struggle. Amelioration for Pope is not restricted to the influence of ethical precepts or of rational morality. "Eloisa to Abelard" instead illustrates one of the subtlest ways in which Augustan generality can be called didactic.

Pope's effort "to better mankind" does not stop with the mere depiction of Eloisa's struggle. Another means, one central to much of his work, involves the attempt to evoke in his readers an emotion which may be termed "redemptive sympathy." Thus, while the poem depicts one kind of intense and painful feeling, it seeks to evoke in the reader, through the depiction, another and considerably less violent species of emotion. Although the two main varieties of feeling are quite distinct, their relationship in "Eloisa to Abelard" is close and complementary: each is enhanced by the presence of the other, and neither alone is sufficient to achieve Pope's intended ends. An effective way of appreciating their difference is to examine the poem's concluding passages, in which Eloisa composes herself for death and (seeming to merge her voice with that of the poet) pleads for remembrance in generations to come.

The disagreement over Eloisa's final state of mind cannot be settled

here. Both those who view her as genuinely repentant and those who find
her merely lapsed into temporary quiet can offer reasonable supporting arguments and evidence. My own opinion is that interpretations of Eloisa's
final state do not significantly affect the main concerns of the poem. Pope
seems less preoccupied with Eloisa's salvation or damnation in a life hereafter
than with her situation of conflict in this life. It might not be too extreme
to suggest that the question of Eloisa's final state of mind is irrelevant to
this main concern, for her composure presupposes her most compelling act
of imagination: the vision of her own death. The new and vivid presence of
death changes utterly the nature of her conflict, just as a quarrel can dissolve
at the introduction of a power which transcends quarreling. Preparing to
die, Eloisa virtually shifts the poem to a higher plane, a shift reflected in the
changed tone of thoughtful resignation. Yet, while this shift brings the
poem neatly to a conclusion, it seems imprecise to call the ending a resolution. Death ends Eloisa's struggle between her love for Abelard and her
love of God, but it does not resolve the conflict. It simply terminates a
struggle which otherwise might continue indefinitely as long as both earthly
and spiritual love assert their justified claims on her emotion. Pope in effect
does not show Eloisa's conflict resolved but instead shows it transcended.

One measure of the drastic shift which occurs at the conclusion of
"Eloisa to Abelard" is Eloisa's changed view of human affection. The once
passionate lover of Abelard now imagines death so vividly present that she
addresses it by name, finding no apparent torment in the thought that even
Abelard is "lov'd no more": "O death all-eloquent! you only prove / What
dust we doat on, when 'tis man we love" (335–36). The importance of
Eloisa's apostrophe to Death is often disregarded because readers interpret
the word "only" in a loose, modern sense, as if Eloisa were saying that death
"just goes to show" the foolishness of loving. Actually, using "only" in a
strict adjectival sense which parallels an earlier usage (173), Eloisa means
that death *alone*—nothing but death—can make human love seem insignificant. Or, to come even nearer Eloisa's meaning: there is no stronger force
than human love, but in the presence of death, love itself appears suddenly
meaningless.

If such a statement accurately expresses Eloisa's meaning, it does not
fully express the meaning of the poem. The apostrophe, despite Eloisa's
emphasis, also implies that to individuals not confronting imminent death
or the vision of death, human affection necessarily assumes its preeminence.
Thus, while from Eloisa's final point of view the power of earthly love can
seem suddenly insignificant, from Pope's station as poet it appears not only
significant but all-important, the single value capable of redeeming the waste

which accompanies tragic passion. Short of the absolution for sin which God alone can offer, human sympathy remains the one redemptive gift within the range of mortal giving. Even Eloisa, caught up by the vision of her own death, cannot resist a final imagined wish:

> From the full quire when loud *Hosanna's* rise,
> And swell the pomp of dreadful sacrifice,
> Amid that scene, if some relenting eye
> Glance on the stone where our cold reliques lie,
> Devotion's self shall steal a thought from heav'n,
> One human tear shall drop, and be forgiv'n.
>
> (353–58)

Amid the celebration of the Eucharist, the major Christian sacrificial rite, which commemorates and perpetuates the mystery of Christ's redeeming love, Eloisa longs for a less exalted but complementary act of redemption. If in good times, as Pope asserts in the conclusion to *An Essay on Man*, the interpenetrating power of charity "Gives thee to make thy neighbour's blessing thine" (4.354), in times of misfortune and tragedy it also breaks the potential isolation of suffering, redeeming man from the most dangerous (because most natural) form of solipsism.

Eloisa's prophetic wish for a "future Bard" (359) to tell her story, a desire (like her vision of the "relenting" worshiper) without source in Hughes's translation, emphasizes Pope's intention that compassionate understanding rather than moralistic judgment ought to be our response to her plight:

> Such if there be, who loves so long, so well;
> Let him our sad, our tender story tell;
> The well-sung woes will sooth my pensive ghost;
> He best can paint 'em, who shall feel 'em most.
>
> (363–66)

In desiring sympathy instead of vindication, Eloisa appeals to one of the defining human attributes, like reason itself, which distinguishes man from the rest of animate creation: "he only knows, / And helps, another creature's wants and woes" (*Essay on Man*, 3.51–52). Further, she is correct, Pope would believe, in assuming that the poet is (or should be) the social custodian of this high power. The walls of religion enforce one kind of judgment; the art of the poet, while not disputing the categorical judgments of religion, offers a different perspective upon human experience. Just as he achieves, through skill in language, a grace beyond the narrow rules of propriety— "Which, without passing thro' the *Judgment*, gains / The *Heart*, and all its

End *at once* attains" (*Essay on Criticism*, 156–57)—the poet also, through his heightened insight and feeling, interprets the experience of mankind in a way consistent with the intuitive immediacy of heartfelt knowledge. If Pope later seems warily conscious that the heart can be as easily mistaken as the head, in "Eloisa to Abelard" he allows full range to the redeeming power of sympathetic awareness.

Eloisa, however, asks for more than sympathy. She previously had linked Fame with Love as the two "best of passions" (40), and, though both may be selfishly abused, fame in Eloisa's final request means something close to simple remembrance. It is quite natural that the possibility of being forgotten should disturb the woman who herself cannot forget, and the poet, as Pope knew, is of all creatures particularly sensitive to this anxiety. Throughout his life, Pope engaged in his own version of the characteristically Romantic quest for pemanence. Abiding and eternal pemanence in his view was not to be achieved within the natural order—as it is for the early Wordsworth— but only within the atemporal structure of Christian redemption. Eloisa's soul is the province of her Maker alone. The earthly permanence with which the poet concerns himself belongs to the circumscribed realm of memory, memory sustained in moving language which, as Milton wrote of his chief aspiration, the world would not willingly let die. On some occasions, the contrast between time's power to destroy and the poet's limited preserving art could evoke the elegiac tone of Pope's lament to the painter Charles Jervas: "Alas! how little from the grave we claim? / Thou but preserv'st a Face and I a Name." Yet in other moods this minimum could become the rock bottom on which to build an ambitious theory of the poet's role. If the poet can indeed preserve a name, he might simultaneously preserve *in* the name the essence of its owner's life. This capacity to preserve through naming may underlie Pope's love for writing epitaphs, a taste otherwise so inexplicable in a great poet that most readers, if acknowledging it at all, usually dismiss it with a shrug. It also helps to explain the extraordinary number of real people whose names he consistently assimilated into the pattern of his verse. Thus in his moments of panegyric and of measured praise Pope labored to infuse the names of his predecessors and contemporaries with significant value, often introducing or concluding a general argument with the portrait of a living person. He also sensed the darker use to which this power might be put. His satirical poems deliberately employ the names of living offenders in ways which tend to empty them of value, fixing and perpetuating them as mere signs of vice and folly. In both instances, the poet virtually creates identity in the future by interpreting and by preserving the memory of past and present. With an appropriateness which betrays

Pope's guiding hand, Eloisa wisely directs her final request toward this aspect of the poet's art.

As the creator and preserver of Eloisa's identity in the future, Pope employs his substantial powers to win her a sympathetic hearing from posterity. "The Epistle of Eloise grows warm," he wrote to Martha Blount of the poem's development, "and begins to have some Breathings of the Heart in it, which may make posterity think I was in love" (*Correspondence*, I). Perhaps he was in love. The final couplets have traditionally been read as a private allusion to Pope's own passion for the absent Lady Mary Wortley Montagu, whom he followed in her travels with an imagination as active as Eloisa's. But the comment to Martha Blount suggests a more important implication. Eloisa's "Breathings of the Heart" by themselves affirm a value basic to Pope's outlook. Art for Pope achieves one of its closest and most essential contacts with life when through the quickening powers of memory and of imagination it restores the dead and forgotten past to feeling presence in the minds of responsive readers. In order to approach "Eloisa to Abelard" in "the same Spirit that its Author *writ*," we must to some degree share Pope's excitement at watching a remarkable woman emerge from the shadows of history as a fully human, complex, and sympathetic individual.

Any favorable reading of "Eloisa to Abelard" ought to consider a discomfiting piece of information supplied by Dr. Johnson. After expressing his admiration for Pope's epistle, he adds: "This piece was, however, not much his favourite in his latter years, though I never heard upon what principle he slighted it" (*Lives of the Poets*, III). Assuming that Johnson's information is correct, and assuming with Johnson that some principle of judgment is involved, it seems proper to speculate upon possible reasons for Pope's disfavor, especially as such speculations may uncover difficulties inherent in the poem which have troubled generations of readers. Their response cannot blithely be written off to misinterpretation, and, added to the generally reliable evidence supplied by Johnson, it suggests that something in the poem prevents it from achieving the unqualified appeal which Pope intended.

One recent explanation of Pope's judgment can be construed from the account of the poem which Thomas R. Edwards, Jr., has given. "For all its brilliance as drama and its attractive sympathy for its heroine," Edwards writes, "*Eloisa to Abelard* lacks the Augustan mediation between opposites that is the great achievement of Pope's early career." Such a lack of mediation may, for some readers, prove troubling, yet a crucial allowance must be added: although the poem does not *depict* a mediating ideal, it nonetheless contains one. Between the poles of Eloisa's tragic passion and Abelard's unimpassioned calm, Pope finds the power of redemptive sympathy a valuable and an acceptable middle way. It offers, as do his other forms of mediation, a practical ideal. Its exercise is a significant way "to better mankind." In this sense, although death and penitence cannot resolve but only transcend the struggle which divides Eloisa between Abelard and God, the extensively developed plea for compassionate understanding, both openly expressed by Eloisa and evoked by the manner of Pope's presentation, creates a well-conceived resolution to the poem itself. From the exploration of related forms of excess, "Eloisa to Abelard" attempts to inspire a corrective synthesis, one rendered persuasive by our experience of the inadequate alternatives. Pope does not wish all men and women to act like Eloisa. He would insist, however, that an intelligent and sympathetic response to her dilemma can refine our powers of feeling and of perception, thus leading to improvements in the way we live. But, of course, an unanswerable reply suggests itself at once. A well-conceived resolution may in fact exist without necessarily creating a wholly convincing and successful poem. The vague unease persists.

A different explanation of this uneasiness is possible through attention to Pope's complex treatment of perspective. The difficulties were twofold. First, he attempted to treat within the framework of tragedy a situation which, to Eloisa's age and to his own, was not necessarily tragic. From a medieval perspective, Eloisa's struggle between earthly and spiritual love is merely a sign of her weakness: the dilemma is easily resolved by affirming the supremacy of sacred love. Viewed in an eighteenth-century or modern perspective, her dilemma is meaningless; there is no inherent contradiction in loving both Abelard and God, while the pathos of Abelard's mutilation and of its consequences for Eloisa hardly rises above the level of severe misfortune. The need to confront this first main difficulty led Pope directly to the second. Unwilling to place Eloisa's experience within a framework either wholly medieval or wholly modern, Pope tried to create a perspective independent of time, where the medieval claim of her higher duty to God and the modern notion of uncontradictory choices no longer apply. This independent perspective locates the poem solely in the autonomous region of Eloisa's mind. As Eloisa perceives them, the claims of earthly and of spiritual love cannot be reconciled. She cannot, as her own experience persuades her, simultaneously love both Abelard and God with equal ardor. In addition, she knows that she cannot love one to the exclusion of the other without suppressing and denying half of her own nature. Reconciliation, without being false to her experience, and choice, without being false to herself, are both impossible. Inside the autonomous region of her own mind,

she faces mutually exclusive, contradictory, and singularly inadequate alternatives. Her dignity becomes tragic because she lives fully what (in her
own mind) are implacable contrarieties. Death, with its transforming perspective on all worldly affairs, brings her the only possible relief.

Pope must eventually have recognized that, however ambitious and
skillful the attempt, "Eloisa to Abelard" cannot survive as he intended once
the conflict is removed from the perspective of Eloisa's mind. If modern readers
interpret her struggle within the context of her own age, her inconstancy
seems at once willful and wrong. If they judge in the context of their own
times, she seems merely pathetic and foolish, if not immoral. Her experience
is tragic and her inconstancy heroic only within the circumscribed region of
her own mind, and, short of writing a different poem, there remains no way
Pope can force readers not to view her struggle from any but the perspective
which he intended to create. It is little wonder that many readers are uneasy.
And, almost as if the poem had taught him a useful lesson, Pope never again
allowed the interpretation of his works to hinge so fatefully upon the acceptance of a less than explicit perspective. In all of Pope's later poetry, the
reader knows exactly where he stands.

Still, an awareness of Pope's intention to place Eloisa within a framework
of tragic experience defined solely by the limits of her own mind, while it
may not dissolve all the uneasiness which readers have felt, does restore to
Eloisa much of the dignity with which Pope meant to invest her, for one
of the strengths of tragedy is that it avoids dividing life into right choices
and wrong. If it recognizes error, weakness, and wrongdoing, it also respects
the process of suffering which allows certain extraordinary individuals to
experience fully the contrarieties of human nature, leading finally to an
awareness that while suffering may have been unavoidable, it was not pointless. Yet at stake is more than a restoration of Eloisa's stature. Only by
placing the poem within a context of tragedy can we understand what "Eloisa
to Abelard" meant to Pope's development as a poet and thereby correct those
who view her story as an abrupt, inexplicable effusion of Romantic feeling
from which Pope hastily retreated into reason and morality. He was not,
whatever his later opinion, simply wandering lost in fancy's maze. The erotic
content is certainly unusual, but the situation of conflict and its location in
the mind are recurrent Popean motifs. In an early letter (dated 11 August
1713) he marveled:

Good God! what an Incongruous Animal is Man? how unsettled
in his best part, his soul; and how changing and variable in his

frame of body? The constancy of the one, shook by every notion, the temperament of the other, affected by every blast of wind. What an April weather in the mind! In a word, what is Man altogether, but one mighty inconsistency.

(Correspondence, I)

Despite his affected Hamlet-like pose, the belief is wholly sincere, recurring more profoundly in the second epistle of *An Essay on Man* (3–18), where it lost none of the calculated universality. Created "half to rise, and half to fall" (2.15), man is for Pope a fabric of potentially conflicting parts. It is essential to notice, however, that man's natural inconstancy does not itself, for Pope, partake of tragedy. The optimism of *An Essay on Man* is sustained by a faith that the wise and virtuous may reconcile the forces of potential contrariety, creating a harmonious paradise within. Eloisa, then, experiences a situation of interior conflict which Pope would have equated with the human condition. But he persuasively represents, within the region of her own mind, the impossibility of reconciling the claims of her divided nature. In Eloisa's psyche, the human condition has become a tragic dilemma. She stands unique among the characters of Pope's verse, not because she is extravagantly impassioned, but because her extravagance is appropriate to her situation. As Pope interprets her experience, there is no exit from suffering except through death and utter resignation. If her soul is finally at peace, earthly solace for Eloisa also requires the "well-sung woes" with which Pope redeems the memory of her tragic struggle.

LAWRENCE LEE DAVIDOW

Pope's Verse Epistles: Friendship and the Private Sphere of Life

Pope's epistolary writings, both prose and verse, constitute a large and extremely significant portion of his literary output. As Swift noted, "you have been a writer of Letters almost from your infancy, and by your own confession had Schemes even then of Epistolary fame." Pope's letters were clearly important to him, for both personal and literary reasons; and while his pronouncements on them may seem a bit clichéd to a modern reader, a more sympathetic view would maintain that Pope, more consistently and sensitively perhaps than any other letter writer, had his finger on the vigorous pulse of a long-lived and fecund epistolary tradition. Frequently he reiterates commonplaces in favor of freedom, naturalness, and sincerity in writing, and following a convention that dates at least from Demetrius Phalareus sees his letters as portraits of his own heart, as extensions of his own being. In a letter to Lady Mary Wortley Montagu, he refers characteristically to "Those Shadows of Me, my Letters," and writes again: "I can say little to recommend the Letters I am beginning to write to you, but that they will be the most impartial Representations of a free heart, and the truest Copies you ever saw, tho' of a very mean Original."

Pope's verse epistles and his most interesting letters have many themes in common, particularly virtue and friendship. Of the latter, Pope makes what George Sherburn has called "almost a cult." For Pope these themes are not philosophical abstractions, like various topics in the *Essay on Man*, nor are they roughly equivalent to the particular themes of the Moral Essays.

Both poetically and ethically, virtue and friendship are ideals far more basic
to him than (say) "taste" or the proper use of riches; and thematically they
underlie not just individual epistles but all of Pope's epistles, and a large
part of his nonepistolary verse as well.

For Pope, the idea of friendship is a rich one, indicative of the whole
range of values associated with the private life. Like Cicero, he connects it
with ideas of honesty, sincerity, and intimacy, and with positive social
feelings generally. The capacity for friendship represents sound ethical principles: the preference for goodness over greatness, happiness over ambition
and worldly success, the public and social spirit over self-interest. It signifies,
as much as any other quality, a distillation of humanistic ideals.

If Pope may be said to modify the Ciceronian tradition on friendship
in any consistent way, he exaggerates the anti-Court implications of the
concept, and the important distinction between public and private life.
Cicero had regarded political glory as a stronger temptation than money in
diverting men from the wholesome pleasures of friendship. To an even greater
extent than Cicero, however, Pope associates the abuse of friendship with
political corruption. Walpole and the Whig party become primary targets
for satire. Hence Pope portrays the Court and the Ministry as insincere
friends:

> With that, a WIZARD OLD his *Cup* extends;
> Which whoso tastes, forgets his former friends,
> Sire, Ancestors, Himself.
> > (*Dunciad* IV. 517–519)

In the same poem, he attacks "ever-listless Loit'rers, that attend / No cause,
no Trust, no Duty, and no Friend."

As portrayed by Pope, the Court typically fails to recognize or reward
genuine worth, and fosters relationships based on servility rather than on
friendship. Pope's own friendship for unrewarded worth puts him very much
in an anti-Court posture:

> But does the Court a worthy Man remove?
> That instant, I declare, he has my Love:
> I shun his Zenith, court his mild Decline;
> Thus SOMMERS once, and HALIFAX were mine. . . .
> Names, which I long have lov'd, nor lov'd in vain,
> Rank'd with their Friends, not number'd with their Train;

And if yet higher the proud List should end,
Still let me say! No Follower, but a Friend.
                    (*Epilogue to the Satires* II.74–93)

It is not surprising, therefore, that the epistle addressed to an incumbent secretary of state, James Craggs, distinguishes sharply between the addressee in his capacity as statesman and in his capacity as a private human being: "Proceed—a Minister, but still a Man." The words "Minister" and "Man" symbolically contrapose two kinds of personal identity, two spheres of human experience, even while the sense of the passage, reinforced by the verbal consonance, suggests that this dichotomy may be fruitfully reconciled. Significantly, friendship serves, in the last eight lines of the epistle, as the source, end, and test of public virtue:

> Then scorn to gain a Friend by servile ways,
> Nor wish to lose a Foe these Virtues raise;
> But candid, free, sincere, as you began,
> Proceed—a Minister, but still a Man;
> Be not (exalted to whate'er degree)
> Asham'd of any Friend, not ev'n of Me,
> The Patriot's plain, but untrod path pursue;
> If not, 'tis I must be ashamed of You.
>   (II.10–17)

In an epistle addressed to another minister of state, Lord Oxford, Pope reiterates the distinction between minister and man which he had raised with regard to Craggs. He describes Oxford as "fond to forget the Statesman in the Friend," as if Oxford's condescension involves a radical transformation from one state of being to another. For the company of Swift and Parnell, Oxford rejects the "Farce of State":

> For him [Parnell], thou oft has bid the World attend,
> Fond to forget the Statesman in the Friend;
> For *Swift* and him, despis'd the Farce of State,
> The sober Follies of the Wise and Great;
> Dextrous, the craving, fawning Crowd to quit,
> And pleas'd to 'scape from Flattery to Wit.
>   (II.7–12)

One of Pope's most frequently used words, "friend" has a strangely adhesive quality, appearing with surprising frequency in pairs and series of terms. While this phenomenon partly results from technical factors, like its metrical convenience and its serviceability as a rhyme word, it may reasonably be argued that the word is semantically colored by the company it keeps. "Friends"has numerous fellow travelers (if one may call them such), comprising several distinct classes of words, a fact indicative of its wide range of meaning and association.

The most prominent class of these fellow travelers consists (perhaps not unexpectedly) of words of family relation. "Come thou, my father, brother, husband, friend!" says Eloisa to Abelard (I.152). and in his "Epistle to Jervas," Pope refers to "The tender sister, daughter, friend and wife" (I.52). Even more than today, when the phrase "friends and relations" still has a kind of tautological cohesion, the denotive distinction between the two terms was not air-tight in the eighteenth century. For "friend" still occasionally signified kinsman. This customary linking helped not only to establish friendship as a fixed, quasi-natural category of human relation, but also to emphasize the association of friendship with the emotions, attitudes, and values proper to the private sphere of life. In addition, the idea of friendship also implied giving moral or spiritual direction, as phrases like "guide, philosopher, and friend," and "Muse's Judge and Friend," indicate.

While Pope thus associates friendship with social roles and human relationships, he also frequently places it among conceptual abstractions, specifically ethical, emotional, or personal qualities which, taken together, constitute the attributes of the good or happy man. The Dunces are loyal to "No cause, no Trust, no Duty, and no Friend," while Pope wishes the addressee of "To Mrs. M. B." "long Health, long Youth, long Pleasure, and a Friend." In the *Essay on Man* Pope connects friendship with "love sincere" and "each home-felt joy that life inherits here" (II.255–256).

Almost osmotically, a kind of moral idealism permeates the concept of friendship. Pope's tendency to place friendship in two dimensions, that of the roles and relationships of private life and that of moral abstractions, suggests (what may not, after all, be very surprising) that these realms qualify and define each other. The role of the friend as moral adviser—as "guide, philosopher," and so on—connects the private life of personal relationships with moral idealism, and this connection is reflected on the purely verbal level as well, perhaps with symbolic import, by the juxtaposition of these two dimensions. In the epitaph of John Knight, the following lines appear only slightly separated:

> The pious Son, fond Husband, faithful Friend.
>
> (I.4)
>
> In Death, by Friendship, Honour, Virtue; mourn'd.
>
> (I.10)

The words "friend" and "friendship" form a semantic "equals sign," equating the two dimensions. Private life becomes, both verbally and conceptually, the locus of real virtue.

As Pope considers it, friendship plays an essential role in many of the professional endeavors associated with poetry. Pope extends the commonplace that only a good man can be a good poet ("And each bad poet is as ill a friend") to include the critic, the patron, and the satirist (as a specific kind of poet) as well. In *Essay on Criticism*, the ideal critic, like Horace or (on a lesser scale) Walsh, is noted for friendship. Horace can "like a friend familiarly convey / The truest notions in the easiest way." In the tribute to Walsh which concludes the poem, Pope describes his late friend in terms that amalgamate criticism and friendship:

> Such late was *Walsh*,—the Muse's Judge and Friend.
> Who justly knew to blame or to commend:
> To Failings *mild*, but *zealous* for Desert;
> The *clearest Head*, and the *sincerest Heart*.
>
> (II.729–732)

Properly, the critic does professionally what the good friend should do privately:

> 'Tis not enough, Taste, Judgment, Learning, join;
> In all you speak, let Truth and Candor shine:
> That not alone what to your *Sense* is due,
> All may allow; but seek your *Friendship* too.
>
> (II.562–565)

Pope reiterates this idea in the epistle to Jervas, where he describes himself and his addressee reviewing each other's work, "each finding like a friend / Something to blame, and something to commend" (21–22).

In "Epistle to Dr. Arbuthnot" Pope carries these associations of friendship over to the role of patron, primarily through negative examples like Bufo and (as far as "moral patronage" is concerned) Atticus. Pope characterizes such patrons as not only fops but selfish men:

> That Fop whose pride affects a Patron's name,
> Yet absent, wounds an Author's honest fame;
> Who can your Merit selfishly approve,
> And show the Sense of it, without the Love;
> Who has the Vanity to call you Friend,
> Yet wants the Honour injur'd to defend.
>
> (291–296)

The notion of selfish approval contrasts with the example of Walsh, who "justly commends," or Jervas, who does so "like a friend," making the self-styled friendship of this patron a grotesque inversion of the ideal Ciceronian concept, with its rejection of flattery and hypocrisy.

Pope extends this requirement of friendship to the office of the satirist, basing his self-justification as a satirist on his being a kind of friend—a friend of virtue and mankind:

> To VIRTUE ONLY and HER FRIENDS, A FRIEND.
> (*Imit. of Horace* Sat. II.i.121)

> No Pow'r the Muse's Friendship can command;
> No Pow'r, when Virtue claims it, can withstand.
> (*Epilogue to the Satires* II.118–119)

Pope relies heavily on this benevolent posture in "Arbuthnot," where he repudiates all poetry that might jeopardize true friendship:

> Curst be the Verse, how well soe'er it flow,
> That tends to make one worthy Man my foe,
> Give Virtue scandal, Innocence a fear,
> Or from the soft-ey'd Virgin steal a tear!
> (II.283–286)

I would emphasize three points with regard to the theme of friendship and its relation in Pope to the epistolary form: first, that friendship plays a role of central importance in Pope's poetry, his letters, and in what one may call his "self-image"; second, that friendship symbolizes, in a virtually synecdochical way, the values which Pope attributes to the private sphere of life; and third, that the verse epistle serves as a natural medium for espousing friendship and the virtues of the private sphere. Hence it is no accident that the theme of friendship plays so important a role in the "Epistle to Dr. Arbuthnot," or (to state the case conversely) that Pope chooses an epistolary format, as in "Arbuthnot," for treating themes related to private virtues.

While the theme of friendship is important in many epistles of the seventeenth and eighteenth centuries, because letter writing represents an act of friendship, Pope finds it especially useful as a kind of touchstone for a whole range of desirable personal qualities. Ben Jonson, it may be noted, connects friendship with specific moral actions; and the performance or recommendation of virtuous actions provides the occasion or focus of many of his epistles. With Pope, whose major epistles are far less occasional, the case is somewhat different. For him friendship represents a more immanent or static quality, suggesting a whole order of experience. As depicted in his epistles, friendship consists primarily of a kind of moral, emotional, and intellectual sympathy between poet and addressee, and of the more or less socially-defined virtues, like "sense," "benevolence," or "temper," that reflect possession of a good head or a good heart.

Pope affirms this moral and emotional condition more in his epistles than anywhere else. In fact, Pope's epistles make up one of the three different "worlds" that correspond roughly to his most productive genres or modes and include the epic and pastoral, as well as the epistle. Pope treats the epic and pastoral as basically symbolic modes, since their settings—the battlefield or sylvan field—significantly predetermine not only certain conventions of theme or subject matter but also our ethical evaluation of the action in the poems. In the epistle, the conventions of the form do not alter our normal evaluations. In other words, the virtues which Pope praises in the epistles have an enduring social utility, whereas the conventional nature of the epic and pastoral forms extends to the ethical values which pervade them. Such values are, one might say, generically contingent; hence the facility with which heroic figures are satirized in mock epics. The greatness of (say) Achilles, Alexander, or Aureng-Zebe appears not simply ridiculous but actually culpable when abstracted from its generic context. Fielding's distinction between greatness and goodness in *Jonathan Wild* and his satiric indictments of Alexander and Caesar reveal how vulnerable to explosion the epic hero and epic values are, once removed from the literary battlefield. On the other hand, the values espoused in the epistles have a legitimate claim to nearly absolute validity.

The epistles may be said to embody domesticated versions of the heroic and pastoral ideals. They transmute Achilles' wrath into the satirist's indignation and domesticate the *Iliad*'s world at war into "the strong antipathy of good to bad." Heroic qualities, like the force of arms and strength of will, become through this translation the force of wit and strength of virtue. And the fulfillment of heroic qualities registers not excess but a "golden mean."

If Aeneas proved a more acceptable heroic model than Achilles because of his superior piety, patriotism, self-possession, and concern for civilization, Pope's epistolary exemplars, Burlington, Bathurst, and Cobham, provide a similar ideal removed from its martial context. While the epistles contain military heroes, like Peterborough, they present them as "chiefs out of war." The grotto and garden at Twickenham, or their counterparts at Stowe and Burlington House, provide a peaceful, reflective substitute for Arcadia that, like their model, symbolizes cosmic order and incorporates aesthetic ideals and principles into a moral landscape. Unlike Arcadia, however, Twickenham is part of, and an active counterpoise to, the larger world of real events. Real problems, like the horde of poetasters in "Arbuthnot," intrude upon it. Moreover, the ideals of Twickenham have specific social and political associations rather than simply ideal meanings. For the eighteenth century, Twickenham represents (rather than symbolizes) an achievable way of life.

Pope's attraction to the idea of semipastoral retirement, contrasted with Swift's skepticism about it, makes for one of the amusing aspects of their correspondence, just as Pope's free acceptance of most Ciceronian commonplaces on friendship often draws witty caveats from the Dean. While Swift maintains that Pope's letters provide "the best system that ever was wrote for the conduct of human life" (IV), and while he adopts some of the same poses that Pope does, he seems a bit uncomfortable with his friend's posturing. When Pope states that he prefers the conversation of fools to that of knaves, a preference which implicitly draws attention to his own moral sensitivity, Swift ironically demurs and when Pope talks favorably about retirement, Swift deflates him:

> I have no very strong Faith in you pretenders to retirement, you are not of an age for it, nor have you gone through either good or bad Fortune enough to go into a Corner and form Conclusions de contemptu mundi et fuga Seculi, unless a Poet grows weary of too much applause as Ministers do with too much Weight of Business.
>
> (II)

In a previous letter Pope had written Swift about changes he had been undergoing:

> The merry vein you knew me in, is sunk into a Turn of Reflexion, that has made the world pretty indifferent to me, & yet I have acquir'd a Quietness of mind which by Fitts improves into a certain degree of chearfulness, enough to make me just so good humourd as to wish that world well.
>
> (II)

While this letter represents one of Pope's finest, its posturing demands tolerant indulgence. The verse epistles are basically more effective than the letters for this reason. Although the epistles are not, generally speaking, as self-centered as the letters, they contain sentiments similar to those in the correspondence. The theme of retirement from the literary arena, expounded by Pope in his letter to Swift, occurs in "Arbuthnot" as well:

Oh let me live my own! and die so too!
('To live and die is all I have to do:')
Maintain a Poet's Dignity and Ease,
And see what friends, and read what books I please. . . .
I was not born for Courts or great Affairs,
I pay my Debts, believe, and say my Pray'rs,
Can sleep without a Poem in my head,
Nor know, if *Dennis* be alive or dead.

(II.261–270)

And Pope's self-conscious modesty, revealed by the reference to himself as a "very mean Original" in his letter to Lady Mary, has an equivalent in the epistle to Craggs: "Be not . . . / Asham'd of any Friend, not ev'n of Me."

If Pope's posturing undermines the success of his letters, it enhances that of his verse epistles. Here the different decorums of the two forms become relevant. Both the letters and the verse epistles are literary forms, providing semiautobiographical, semifictive "masks" through which the writers address their audience; but, to different degrees, audiences tend to associate the epistolizer—the author as he appears in his work—with the epistolographer—the "real" or "historical" author. The earl of Shaftesbury, for example, rejects out of hand the possibility that Cicero and Horace had addressed their epistles to fictive addressees, a possibility which magnifies the fictive aspect of the writers themselves within their works. While Shaftesbury includes Horace and Cicero together, without distinguishing verse epistles from prose letters, it is clear that some distinction between the forms existed for audiences. Swift claimed that his correspondence with Pope consisted of "mere innocent friendship" (III), implying that it was not intended for publication, and, by extension, was not strictly literary—a claim which could hardly have been made for the verse epistle.

In fact, Swift seems to regard Pope's verse epistles in a fundamentally different way from his prose letters, since he pleads with Pope for a public memorial to their friendship in the form of a verse epistle addressed to him. In addition to memorializing friendships, the epistle as a genre constitutes a forum in which poets strive informally with each other to present cogent philosophical systems for considering particular ethical problems. Swift objects to the concluding lines from Congreve's "Epistle to Richard Temple," which contends that people in all ages have been the same (III), implicitly recognizing the epistle as something more ambitious than the "innocent friendship" of his correspondence with Pope.

The more formal or public nature of the verse epistle seems to

accommodate Pope's posturing more easily than the prose letter. In his letter
to Arbuthnot justifying specific satire (III), Pope seems to be shadowboxing
with abstractions; in the epistle to the same man, he actually enters the
ring. It is not simply the use of real or thinly veiled names that makes Pope's
role of censor more effective in verse than in prose, although this technique
is part of his satiric method. As he points out to Swift, his epistles represent
a specific kind of satire: "You call your satires, Libels: I would rather call
my satires, Epistles" (III). The fact that a poem like "Arbuthnot" is a satire
as well as an epistle allows it an intensity of feeling and description not
appropriate to a letter. And since the pose of the censor or moralist in verse
satire is eminently rationalized by English literary precedent (Shaftesbury
objects, however, to Seneca's adoption of this role in prose), he assumes the
role more easily in the satiric verse epistle than in a prose letter.

Not only are Pope's postures more effective in verse than in prose, but
the discipline of the couplet and of verse itself makes Pope more sensitive
to tonal effect, giving him greater artistic control over his self-portrayal.
The description of how he "stooped to Truth" or rejected "mere Description"
for "Sense," his stated reluctance to "give Innocence a Fear," and his contempt
for Gildon and Dennis, might well have seemed self-congratulating, sen-
timental, or petty in prose. But Pope's verse gives these sentiments a coherent
shape and strategic purpose which they otherwise might have lacked. For
example, the stichomythic repartee embodied in the couplets against Dennis
and Gildon conveys a sense of emotional discipline, as well as of precise
technique:

> Yet then did *Gildon* draw his venal quill;
> I wish'd the man a dinner, and sate still:
> Yet then did *Dennis* rave in furious fret;
> I never answer'd, I was not in debt.
> ("Arbuthnot," 151–154)

Pope was not oblivious to his own posturing, although he perceived
himself as growing more serious, and hence more direct, with age. In No-
vember of 1729 he wrote to Swift:

> It is many years ago since I wrote as a wit. How many occurrences
> of informations must one omit, if one determin'd to say nothing
> that one could not say prettily? . . . I ceas'd to be a witty writer;
> as either my experience grew on one hand, or my affection to my
> correspondents on the other.
>
> (III)

Characterizing his verse epistles, Pope tells Swift: "They will consist more of morality than wit, and grow graver, which you will call duller. I shall leave it to my Antagonists to be witty (if they can) and content myself to be useful, and in the right" (III). The pose of the benevolent moralist or philosopher seemed the culmination of Pope's career, and the epistles, in a sense, culminate that culmination. He perceives the epistle as a grave, moral form. In addition to the letter to Swift, cited immediately above, Pope refers in his version of Horace's Satire I.i. to "grave *Epistles*, bringing Vice to light, / Such as a *King* might read, a *Bishop* write" (151–152). In this passage the word "epistle" obviously conveys a greater sense of personal responsibility (i.e., "gravity") on the part of the poet than "satire," which Pope ironically associates with "lampoon." The epistolary form thus serves to define Pope's satire along lines of gravity and moral purpose.

The epistle, then, seems in retrospect to have been an inevitable form for Pope to adopt. It had an advantage over the letter in being able to accommodate his favorite postures, and hence his favorite themes, more effectively; it had an advantage over formal verse satire because the "grave" associations of the epistle testified to his serious moral intentions. In short, the epistle allowed Pope to affirm virtues more convincingly and to attack vices more responsibly than any other form.

Even though Pope seems to identify his epistles with his satires ("I . . . call my satires, Epistles"), scholarly tradition had always distinguished the two forms on the basis of the ultimately affirmative function of the epistle and ultimately destructive function of satire. Scaliger had compared the two genres with two different sorts of medicine: satire he regarded as a purgative, intended to inculcate virtue. The edifying themes of the Moral Essays, or the tributes to the addressees contained in virtually all the epistles, thus may be regarded as essential to the epistolary nature of these poems. In a poem like "Arbuthnot," which can be considered either an epistle or a satire, the theme of friendship serves to highlight the particularly epistolary function of affirming virtue. This point should be kept in mind, because, while "Arbuthnot" is easily the most famous of all Pope's epistles and possibly the most famous epistle in English, its affiliation with that genre has not always been allowed. The stylistic affinity between "Arbuthnot" and the Moral Essays, for example, is tenuous. Warburton's alternate title for the poem, "Prologue to the Satires," and his decision to place it in the volume of Horatian Imitations, may be misguided, but they are not completely illogical.

The arguments for considering "Arbuthnot" as primarily a formal satire are fairly obvious and can be noted briefly. It has a mood far different from that of Pope's other epistles, like the Moral Essays; a mood that is more

Juvenalian than Horatian. Pope responds to the objects of his satire not with wry amusement but with indignation and exasperation. Pope's stance with regard to his addressee approximates that in his dialogue satires. He uses the prudential advice of an interlocutor to elicit his self-justification as a satirist. The formal character sketches of Atticus, Bufo, and Sporus obviously reflect satiric convention, and the piecemeal composition of the poem inhibits to some degree a unified sense of epistolary occasion and structure—a sense that the poem was written for a single correspondent on a single occasion. Pope's Advertisement calls the poem "a Sort of Bill of Complaint," a phrase which certainly suggests satiric intent.

To maintain proper perspective, however, the epistolary qualities of the poem deserve to be noted. Aside from strictly formal considerations, like the address format and the title of the poem, the chief epistolary quality is, as I have said, thematic. At the center of "Arbuthnot" lies the formal relationship between Pope and his addressee. While Arbuthnot is not characterized at length, he emerges in the poem as having substantial presence, a felt identity. The vocabulary of the poem underlines his role as Pope's physician: "What Drop or Nostrum can this plague remove?"; "I cough like Horace"; "Friend to my Life, which did you not prolong." A quasi-biographical reference recalls Arbuthnot's real existence: "I too could write, and I am twice as tall." The figure of Arbuthnot characterizes himself by giving cautionary advice to Pope and by professing friendship with him: "Learn Prudence of a Friend."

No discussion of friendship in "Arbuthnot" can legitimately avoid touching on Arbuthnot himself, the nature of whose poetical "presence" is determined not simply by the qualities which Pope puts into the poem but by those which the contemporary reader brought to it as well. Arbuthnot was a well-known and respected physician, a satirist, a moralist, and, according to opinion, a fine human being. And these biographical associations constitute a second major "epistolary" element (after the thematic) in the poem. Arbuthnot had been physician-in-ordinary to Queen Anne; and after her death he retained as patients respected men like Pulteney and Chesterfield. Praising Arbuthnot both as physician and human being, Chesterfield voiced sentiments typical of those who knew him:

> Dr. Arbuthnot was both my physician and my friend, and in both these capacities I justly placed the utmost confidence in him.
>
> Without any of the craft, he had all the skill of his profession, which he exerted with the most care and pleasure upon those unfortunate patients who could not give him a fee.

His social character was not more amiable than his private character was pure and exemplary; charity, benevolence, and a love of mankind appeared unaffectedly in all he said or did. His letter to Pope against personal satire, published in the works of the latter, breathes, in a most distinguished manner, that amiable spirit of humanity.

Because the profession of medicine served through the Renaissance as a metaphor for the purgative and restorative effects of satire and the epistle respectively, Arbuthnot's profession bears on Pope's self-justification in the epistle. Pope's claim to be a kind of physician to society is emphasized by the presence of a real physician in the role of addressee.

Arbuthnot, however, was a physician in this metaphorical sense as well. He had written a number of satirical pieces, including the *History of John Bull*, the *Art of Political Lying*, and the bulk of the *Memoirs of Martinus Scriblerus*. Nor was satire his only vein, for he was also something of a moralist. His poem "Know Yourself" reflects some of the same ideas and attitudes as Pope's *Essay on Man*. In a treatise on the *Usefulness of Mathematics*, he rebuts the idea that mathematics and religion are inimical. Thus Arbuthnot's literary endeavors made him a physician in both the purgative and restorative senses.

Arbuthnot's Tory sympathies and his involvement with Queen Anne's reign presumably made him amenable to an attack on a Whig partisan like Lord Hervey, and Arbuthnot had himself been attacked without provocation by one of Pope's enemies, Leonard Welsted, in *One Epistle to Mr. Pope*. Hence Pope benefited from association with a figure whose reputation was above injury, though not immune from attack, a figure whose situation in this respect Pope saw as identical with his own.

Although Arbuthnot was a linchpin of Pope's circle, maintaining especially close ties with Swift in Ireland, he also served as a kind of intermediary with "hostile factions." He was a close friend of Lady Mary Wortley Montagu, who asked him to discover the cause of Pope's enmity to her. He could not, therefore, have been regarded as overly partisan in Pope's quarrels. His objective position made his opinion, even if only an attributed one, of great weight in Pope's epistle.

Pope and Arbuthnot had actually discussed the matter of "naming names" in satire in their correspondence, thus anticipating the issues covered in Pope's epistle and his dialogue satires:

And I make it my Last Request, that you continue that noble *Disdain* and *Abhorrence* of Vice, which you seem naturally endu'd

with, but still with a due regard to your own Safety; and study
more to reform than chastise, tho' the one often cannot be effected
without the other.

(III)

But General Satire in Times of General Vice has no force, & is
no Punishment: People have ceas'd to be ashamed of it when so
many are joined with them; and tis only by hunting One or Two
from the Herd that any Examples can be made. If a man writ all
his Life against the Collective Body of the Banditti, or against
Lawyers, would it do the least Good, or lessen the Body? But if
some are hung up, or pilloryed, it may prevent others. And in my
low Station, with no other Power than this, I hope to deter, if not
to reform.

(III)

Pope refers to this exchange in the Advertisement to the epistle, maintaining
that he had eliminated some personal references in deference to Arbuthnot's
objections. The "dialogue" in the poem concerning specific satire (Arbuthnot
urges that Pope "learn Prudence of a Friend") in some sense recreates an
actual correspondence.

While Pope's choice of addressees for his epistles generally perplexed
Dr. Johnson, both men were at one in regarding the nature and reputation
of such addressees as important considerations in the epistles. As physician
and moralist, but especially as a friend not only to Pope himself but to all
mankind, Arbuthnot served perfectly as an embodiment of the private virtues
which Pope chose to inculcate by way of his epistle.

Pope's general strategy for expounding the theme of friendship in "Arbuthnot" is essentially dialectical. True friendship serves as an ethical norm
or mean-point in the poem, and as such implicitly contrasts with the op-
posite-seeming vices of flattery and malignity. In addition, friendship contrasts
(in the "Atticus" section) with a "failed mean"; with a merely mechanical
combination of flattery and malignity that is, if anything, worse than either
quality separately. The motif of failed friendship recurs like a chime throughout the satirical passages of the poem, because the evils which Pope describes—opportunism, envy, malignity, self-conceit, and the like—all involve
a radical failure of the heart. All these evils express a kind of meanness that
makes friendship or any positive emotion, including love, charity, benevolence, or patriotism, impossible.

The dramatic opening of the poem touches primarily on the theme of
flattery, though Pope refers even here to malicious detractors. Pope finds

himself besieged by an army of poetasters trying to exploit his talent, influence, and (worst of all) his friendship:

> Is there a Parson, much be-mus'd in Beer,
> A maudlin Poetess, a ryming Peer,
> A Clerk, foredoom'd his Father's soul to cross,
> Who pens a Stanza when he should *engross*?
> Is there, who lock'd from Ink and Paper, scrawls
> With desp'rate Charcoal round his darken'd walls?
> All fly to *Twit'nàm*, and in humble strain
> Apply to me, to keep them mad or vain.
>
> (II, 15–22)

In his "dire Dilemma" Pope equates false friends with real foes: "If Foes, they write, if Friends, they read me dead" (32). Other references to false friendship occur: "Three things another's modest wishes bound, / My Friendship, and a Prologue, and ten Pound" (47–48).

Pope contrasts this false friendship with genuine friendship, using the word "friend" in positive contexts many times. He calls Arbuthnot "Friend to my Life." His Muse serves "to ease some friend, not Wife." In an affecting autobiographical passage, Pope describes the friendships that he has formed with the poets and statesmen who helped and advised him in his youth:

> But why then publish? *Granville* the polite,
> And knowing *Walsh*, would tell me I could write;
> Well-natur'd *Garth* inflam'd with early praise,
> And *Congreve* lov'd, and *Swift* endur'd my Lays;
> The Courtly *Talbot, Somers, Sheffield* read,
> Ev'n mitred *Rochester* would nod the head,
> And *St. John's* self (great *Dryden's* friend before)
> With open arms receiv'd one Poet more.
>
> (135–142)

The love of such men, Pope states, was more important to him than their patronage: "Happy my Studies, when by these approv'd! / Happier their Author, when by these belov'd!" (143–144).

This affirmation of friendship and benevolence serves as a transitional passage from the evil of flattery to that of malignity. Turning from the self-interested poetasters to the more antagonistic, if not necessarily more annoying, rivals and critics, Pope satirizes Gildon, Dennis, and Theobald. As with the poetasters, their motives lie in their own deficiencies—in poverty, envy, and empty pride. Atticus typifies the ineffectually genteel man who combines the twin evils of flattery and malignity. "A tim'rous foe, and a suspicious friend" (206), he virtually personifies the rhetorical figure of oxymoron. He views fellow writers not as brothers but as rivals, regarding them with "jealous, yet with scornful eyes." His refusal "Alike . . . to blame or to commend" violates the obligations of the true critic and friend which Pope had enunciated in *Essay on Criticism*. The oxymorons not only suggest vividly the discord in Atticus' moral nature, but, captured in Pope's dynamic hemistichs and "hitched into rhyme," they convey a sense of the controlled artistry by means of which Pope shapes and disciplines his indignation for poetic effect.

Although, like Atticus, Bufo perverts the idea of patronage, his very lack of discrimination paradoxically bolsters Pope's friendship with Gay. In claiming independence from such patrons, Pope invokes the idea of friendship, thus associating friendship with retirement from poetic endeavor in a public spotlight: "I was not born for Courts or great Affairs, / I pay my Debts, believe, and say my Pray'rs" (267–268). While he is "above a Patron," he does "condescend / Sometimes to call a Minister my Friend" (265–266). And he sees as part of a poet's "dignity and ease" the freedom to "see what friends . . . I please" (263–264).

Friendship clearly serves throughout the poem as a touchstone for determining the quality of a man's heart, no matter what social or public role he fulfills. In apologetic or self-descriptive passages, the references to friendship become more prominent, often pointing, in satiric or elegiac moods, to false friendship or the loss of true friendship:

> That not for Fame, but Virtue's better end,
> He stood the furious Foe, the timid Friend,
> The damning Critic, half-approving Wit,
> The Coxcomb hit, or fearing to be hit;
> Laugh'd at the loss of Friends he never had,
> The dull, the proud, the wicked, and the mad; . . .
> Abuse on all he lov'd, or lov'd him, spread,
> A Friend in Exile, or a Father, dead.
>
> (342–355)

These lines, while hardly the most celebrated passage in the poem, characterize Pope's ethical position and personal stance more succinctly perhaps than any others. Pope recapitulates the opposition between "Fame" and "Virtue's better end" in the catalog of his enemies and the reference, in the final couplet, to his allies. The word "friend" occurs three times in this short passage, twice ironically, as if to emphasize that true and false friendship

are the two most salient facts in Pope's personal situation. The idea of lost
friendship takes on a paradoxical double meaning. He laughs, albeit bitterly,
at "the loss of Friends he never had," while he regrets the absence of true
friends, like Bolingbroke, who have been denied him through political
malice. The double loss which Pope suffers in the necessarily bitter contem-
plation of false friendship and the absence, by exile or death, of several true
friends, sets up a kind of emotional tension which he only resolves in the
conclusion of the epistle by the effusive tribute to a present (in fact, immediately so) and true friend.

As the idea of friendship is not invoked in the emotionally climactic
sections of the poem, the "Sporus" portrait and Pope's self-description immediately following, one hesitates to call it the central theme of the poem.
It is clear, however, that "the trifling Head, [and] the corrupted Heart,"
which characterize Sporus refer to a moral and psychological state in which
friendship is impossible. If "Arbuthnot" has a central theme or ideal, it
resides in an overall quality of heart that subsumes friendship, benevolence,
love, and virtue. The whole tenor of Pope's self-description suggests qualities
associated with the capacity for friendship. His "manly ways," the Golden
Mean between arrogance and servility, are required qualities in a friend. In
a later passage, Pope cites his benevolence toward the needy Dennis and his
friendly relations (at one time) with men who later became his enemies:

> This dreaded Sat'rist *Dennis* will confess
> Foe to his Pride, but Friend to his Distress:
> So humble, he has knock'd at *Tibbald's* Door,
> Has drunk with *Cibber*, nay has rym'd for *Moor*.
>
> (II.370–373)

The portrait of Pope's parents which completes his apology presents
his father in particular as a composite of virtues proper to the private sphere
of life. The closing lines of the poem, the peroration to Arbuthnot, begin
with the invocation, "O Friend!" Since Arbuthnot represents a counter-
example of the two kinds of lost friendship which Pope has depicted (those
"Friends he never had" and those "in Exile" or dead), the words have a
cumulative power, and seem to contain the emotion implicit in the preceding
passages. The expression is both a formal apostrophe and a seemingly spontaneous gesture in response to his foregoing satire and self-description.

The blessings which Pope wishes for Arbuthnot reinforce the focus on
the private sphere and are explicitly domestic: "May each Domestick Bliss
be thine." Pope's "tender Office" of caring for his aged mother, extended
and generalized by reference to other "Cares like these," has a similar func-

tion. In connection with such domestic obligations, Pope invokes the consoling power of his friendship with Arbuthnot:

> On Cares like these if Length of days attend,
> May Heav'n, to bless those days, preserve my Friend.
>   (414–415)

The couplet, simultaneously a unit of verse and of thought, symbolically
unites domestic cares and friendship. In asking Heaven to preserve Arbuthnot's life, Pope seeks, of course, to repay in kind the service which his friend
has rendered him in his capacity as physician ("Friend to my Life, which
did you not prolong," etc.). Pope's wish for Arbuthnot's health makes the
relationship between them, in this regard, aptly reciprocal. The concluding
tribute to Arbuthnot serves the formal epistolary function of valediction; in
addition, the personal relationship, emphasized by the double use of the
word "friend," and the domestic orientation of the passage as a whole,
recapitulate the thematic concerns of the poem. As a result, the epistolary
relationship between poet and addressee, emphasized by this valediction,
serves as not only the formal but the thematic center of the poem as well.

Hence to undervalue the epistolary quality of "Arbuthnot" is necessarily
to distort the thematic importance not simply of friendship, as embodied
in the relationship between Pope and his addressee, but also the private
sphere of life, as it sustains and enriches that friendship. All of Pope's verse
epistles, in fact, exploit the formal relationship between poet and addressee,
that of friendship, for thematic purposes. Even though the explicit importance of friendship may be far smaller in the other epistles than in "Arbuthnot," they rely for an ethical context on the values associated with
friendship and the private sphere of life. While the specific virtues which
Pope affirms in them—like sense, temper, or taste—may themselves be
entirely conventional, Pope dramatically succeeds (as lesser epistolographers
do not) in displacing the center of value from the public sphere to the private,
thus providing those virtues with a context particularly suited to the form,
one which subsumes and in some sense gives meaning to them.

When a poet fails to invoke this context, his advocacy of specific private
virtues seems perfunctory. Edward Young's satires and epistles, though popular in his own time and perhaps even influential on Pope's epistles, have lost
whatever claim they may once have had to enduring literary value. Why
they should seem now so much more academic than Pope's is a hard question
to answer fully, and the appeal to Pope's superior craftsmanship simply
restates the question in different terms. In his poem, "On Reading Dr.
YOUNG'S SATIRES, called the UNIVERSAL PASSION," Swift sarcastically notes

the inconsistency between the ethical subject-matter of Young's satires, which includes rather conventional complaints against contemporary manners, and the fact that they were addressed as tributes to incumbent ministers of state:

> If there be Truth in what you sing,
> Such Godlike Virtues in the *King*,
> A *Minister* so filled with Zeal,
> And Wisdom for the Common-Weal.
> If *he*, who in the Chair presides,
> So steadily the *Senate* guides. . . .
> If this be Truth, as you attest,
> What *Land* was ever *half* so *blest*?
>
>   OR take it in a diff'rent View;
> I ask, if what you say be *true*,
> If you allow, the present Age
> Deserves your *Satire's* keenest Rage;
> If that same *Universal Passion*
> With ev'ry *Vice* hath fill'd the Nation. . . .
> If these be of all Crimes the worst,
> What *Land* was ever *half* so *curst*?

The significance of Swift's observation for this study is not that Robert Walpole was a more corrupt minister than Pope's ministerial addressees, Bolingbroke, Oxford, and Craggs, nor even that Young was implicitly writing to win patronage while Pope was not, but that Young's tributes to incumbent ministers—in their capacity as ministers—virtually endorses the public sphere in preference to the private. Pope, on the other hand, addresses ministers who are "out of place" (Bolingbroke), in a distinctly private capacity (Oxford), or who uphold private virtues in exercising their public duties (Craggs). Pope's adherence to the private sphere makes his satire more incisive. When a typical eighteenth-century satire attacks an abuse—say, that of patronage—the satiric object is clearly the abuse rather than the institution itself. And it is easy for the audience to identify with the norm rather than the abuse. The dedication of such satire to a wealthy patron or political figure, who serves as an example of wise patronage (see John Gay's epistle to Paul Methuen), underscores the limited scope of such satire, making it more a public exercise on standard themes than an attempt at genuine social commentary.

Pope's satire is more radical. His vaunted independence, both personal and financial, and his indictment of "public life" that is unredeemed by private virtues, put his own satires on Bufo (in "Arbuthnot") or Timon (in "Burlington") in a considerably different light. While Pope does not argue that patronage itself is bad, his own example causes one to impugn any relationship based primarily on differences of rank or wealth. Pope uses the private life as an alternative source of ethical norms to those he satirizes. Thus, while most satire tends finally to reinforce the institutional norms, Pope's does not. Instead of affirming the status quo, he places ultimate value on the rigorous ideals of personal integrity and an open heart.

C. E. NICHOLSON

A *World of Artefacts:* The Rape of the Lock *as Social History*

W hen Geoffrey Tillotson, in the final paragraph of his introduction to the 'Twickenham' edition of *The Rape of the Lock*, comments that 'the second version is inexhaustible,' readers cannot help reflecting upon the fact that generations of commentators on the poem, as well as the detailed annotations offered editorially by Tillotson himself, conspire to undermine his remark. Indeed the wealth of scholarship revealed by those annotations demonstrates conclusively that almost every line in *The Rape* echoes, parodies, adapts or rephrases moments of a literary tradition reaching from the Bible to the reign of Queen Anne. Pope's wholehearted devotion to the formal excellence of his verse is evinced in the poem's marvellous ability to carry within itself both a deep respect for, and also a jester's irreverence towards, patterns of poetry that are normally taken to be standards of Classical elegance. And yet this formal ambivalence of the mock-heroic genre, as Pope manipulates it, has received scant critical attention. Similarly, although a wide range of Pope's work has been examined for the light it sheds upon shifting patterns of social, personal, and political behaviour during the period in which he lived, *The Rape of the Lock* has usually been accepted as a relatively superficial treatment of his society, as 'the mock-epic of a mock-world, the make-believe celebration of a society of play-actors.' Even Geoffrey Tillotson expresses a kind of doubt when he writes that 'though no reader can fail to be "conscious of the rich Brocade" of the 1714 version, the story itself is not so proportionate in 1714 as in 1711.'

What seems to have escaped attention is the possibility that in the

From *Literature and History*. Copyright © 1979 by Thames Polytechnic.

1714 version of *The Rape*, the story itself has changed and that the thin thread of the incident between Lord Petre and Arabella Fermor is woven into a complex design in which the youthful poet undertakes a light-hearted but nonetheless profound and far-reaching examination of what was happening to a particular section of his England. He felt able, in a letter to the Marriot ladies, to describe the five-canto version as 'a pretty complete picture of the life of our modern ladies in this idle town,' and the nature of the expansions upon the earlier version registers much more than simply a desire to produce a more polished and sophisticated example of a mock-epic poem. One literary critic has paid serious attention to the underlying themes explored by Pope: Ralph Cohen rightly insists that 'in *The Rape of the Lock* change must be interpreted in terms of natural or normal change and unnatural or artificial and grotesque change.' Social and economic historians of the period offer convincing evidence in support of such an approach to the poem, and it will be useful to glance briefly at what some of them have to say about the social milieu from which the poem sprang, as well as to glance at literary parallels to provide a context and a sense of contemporary consciousness wider than the immediate issues that gave the poem its first birth.

In his book *The Financial Revolution*, P. G. M. Dickson describes the effects of what he calls the process of 'building up the [financial] infrastructure of the industrial revolution,' a process whereby an entirely new system of finance rapidly changed the basis upon which government organised both itself and its national responsibilities. 'The economic effects of government borrowing on the landed interest were discussed primarily in terms of social prejudice . . . On the other hand, the effects of the Financial Revolution were discussed in largely economic terms, for trade was increasingly accepted as the motor that drove the whole economy.' To a student of the literature of the period such a remark might appear to have more relevance to the writings of Swift or Defoe, or perhaps to Pope's 'Epistle to Bathurst' with its hilarious attack upon the notion of paper credit. But if such a student is prepared to listen to other historians, then Pope's interior design in *The Rape of the Lock* might begin to reveal itself. And in this respect, J. G. A. Pocock's *The Machiavellian Moment* is a work that should form part of any bibliography seeking to assist students of Augustan literature. It should, for example, make no unwarrantable demand upon such readers to accept that 'the half-century following the revolution of 1688 . . . was the era in which political thought became engrossed with the conscious recognition of change in the economic and social foundations of politics and the political personality, so that the *zoon politikon* took on his modern character of participant observer in processes of material and historical change fundamentally affecting his nature.' But Pope's affectionately indulgent attitude towards the 'beau-monde' of Queen Anne's reign together with his sheer delight in satirizing London's fashionable society might continue to persuade some that *The Rape* is nothing more than a piece of light-hearted raillery. So perhaps another remark made by Pocock might provide the necessary corrective: 'an anatomy of the great debate between the "landed" and "monied" interests, conducted by the journalists and publicists of Queen Anne's reign, reveals that there were no pure dogmas or simple antitheses, and few assumptions that were not shared and employed to differing purposes by the writers of either side.' The ambivalence of comic surface and the deeper implications of Pope's poem suggests a ready poetic analogy for Pocock's comment.

From the wealth of possibilities that the period presents, one literary parallel should prove helpful. If we remember that five years after the complete version of *The Rape* appeared, *Robinson Crusoe* was first published, and, three years after that *Moll Flanders* was for sale, a common factor (and perhaps the pun is in this instance permissible) begins to emerge. Dorothy Van Ghent, in her study *The English Novel: form and function*, makes the following observation,

> We notice, for instance, that Moll's world contains many things—
> tangible things such as watches and wigs and yardage and goods
> and necklaces and dresses and barrels and bales and bottles and
> trunks. . . . In *Moll* there is a relatively great frequency in the
> naming of that kind of object which constitutes material
> wealth. . . . Schematically what has been happening here is the
> conversion of all subjective, emotional and moral experience—
> implicit in the fact of Moll's five years of marriage and moth-
> erhood—into pocket and bank money, into the materially
> measurable.

Compare that with Tillotson's acknowledgement that 'the epic is thing-less beside Pope's poem with its close-packed material objects'; and a literary-historical link suggests itself.

Of course a gulf of social class separates Moll from Belinda, but in a more abiding sense they both inhabit a world whose values are fundamentally similar, and it can even be argued that an apparent social separation had, anyway, a topographical foundation since 'London was a double town. One end was a royal and parliamentary capital, governed, so far as it had a government, by an obscure condominium of palace officials and nominees of the Dean and chapter of Westminster. The other was virtually a mercantile republic.' And when Pope, in the letter to the Marriot ladies quoted earlier, reflects upon the fact that 'people who would rather [*The Rape*] were let alone laugh at it, and seem heartily merrily, at the same time that they are uneasy,' we are tempted to wonder whether the cause of that uneasy laughter might not be rooted in an unwilling recognition that the Molls and the Belindas of the period differed not at all in kind but only in degree. The degree, of course, is crucial. It accounts for the wit and grace with which Pope embellishes his perception of the times. Though even here it might be worth suggesting that his 'rich Brocade,' as well as his superb parody of epic style, are themselves indications of ambivalent yearnings for what Pocock calls 'a classically cognizable history and a classically cognizable society, neither of which is to be expected in a universe of mobile credit and expectation.' So, when Dorothy Van Ghent notices that 'these tangible, material objects with which Moll is so deeply concerned, are not at all vivid in texture,' she is indicating the different styles which present these two archetypes of fictive women, since the opposite is true of the luminous, vibrant things that compose Belinda's universe.

If, then, 'in both his career and his writings Defoe embodied the projecting spirit of self-interest, avarice, and individualism,' Pope can, with equal accuracy be seen to reach more deeply into the psychological effects of such motivation. For although Moll Flanders expends her spirit in a materialist pursuit, she does at least possess a combative kind of initiative. In contrast, Belinda has receded into a relative passivity. Moll's vigorous scramble for commodities is transformed, in Belinda's couplet-world of ease and elegance into a fetishised sexuality, so that the 'thinghood' which Moll sees as the index of success enters Belinda's soul and recreates that soul in its own image. Belinda, recognizable as the classic portrait of woman in the new rentier class, becomes an object of voyeurism not only for others, but in her own eyes also.

The very title of *The Rape of the Lock* registers the remoteness of authentic human relationships from the fetishised consciousness of Belinda's existence, and practically every couplet in the poem infers unnatural connections between social life and the world of objects, systematically and ingeniously suggesting the ways in which human life is 'lived' by means of an extension into the objects that gradually form the subject of the poem. It is the 'trivial Things' which operate in the world Pope creates, and human capacities are correspondingly diminished. The famous line from the equally famous toilet scene, 'Puffs, Powders, Patches, Bibles, Billet-doux' (I. 138) is only the most obvious example of the pervasive displacement of values explored by

the poem; for if, as Pocock suggests, 'money and credit had indeed dissolved
the social frame into a shifting mobility of objects that were desired and
fictions that were fantasized about,' then such a collapse of traditional religious significance is appropriate. And the same point can be made about
the couplet, 'On her white Breast a sparkling *Cross* she wore, / Which *Jews*
might kiss and Infidels adore' (II. 7–8), where the italics are only the first
sign of dislocated values, but also where the epithet 'sparkling,' harking
back as it does to the 'glitt'ring Spoil' with which Belinda has just been
decked, further suppresses any specifically Christian connotations adhering
to the image of crucifixion, reducing the cross to an item of jewellery and
equating its power with Belinda's breast, after either of which Jew or Infidel
may 'legitimately' lust.

In this giddy world of gilded chariots, garters and stars, it is hardly
surprising that a deep-rooted reaction should take place:

> With Varying Vanities, from ev'ry Part,
> They shift the moving Toyshop of their Heart;
> Where Wigs with Wigs, with Sword-knots Sword-knots strive,
> Beaus banish Beaus, and Coaches Coaches drive.
>
> (I. 99–102)

The heart itself has become the production centre of a kind of puppet-life.
But what is happening here is more than simply the proliferation of objects.
Rather it is the expropriation by the objects of human motivation, the
assumption by the non-human of human characteristics, so that the human
residue, the beaus, and the aural pun is emphatic, becomes inseparable from,
because identified through, the objects which clutter not only their physical
universe but also their spiritual being. The difficulty of actually reading the
third line quoted is apt, and the interpenetration of human and non-human
is consistently developed so that by the time we read 'But now secure the
painted Vessel glides' (II. 47), we have little idea whether Belinda or her
boat is being described.

II

What is being suggested is that *The Rape of the Lock* provides a poetic grammar
for the process whereby relations between people acquire the characteristics
of being relations between things, a process during which commodities
acquire an autonomy which conceals their true nature. More than a hundred
years later, Karl Marx found it difficult to express the theory of this movement
towards reification, and it is a tribute to the extraordinary perceptiveness

displayed by Pope that a comment by Marx can be adapted to account for the function of the sylphs. Marx writes,

> A commodity appears, at first sight, a very trivial thing, and easily understood. Its analysis shows that it is, in reality, a very queer thing, abounding in metaphysical subtleties and theological niceties . . . In order that these objects may enter into relation with each other . . . their guardians must place themselves in relation to one another, as persons whose will resides in those objects, and must behave in such a way that each does not appropriate the commodity of the other, and part with his own, except by means of an act done by mutual consent.

Accordingly, in Pope's scheme of things, the deities of the poem are named after objects, they attend to the objects which name them and, at the moment of appropriation, they are as ineffectual in their task 'in air,' as the notion of honour is inoperative in the mundane realm. Certainly the sylphs, as object-spirits in an object-world, cannot protect Belinda herself. The elaborate fiction of their particularised domain collapses when she succumbs, 'in spite of all her Art,' to the natural occurrence of sexual desire (III. 143). Until that point, sexuality is repressed, attenuated, fetishised—a surrogate performance as in the game of Ombre, or a fantasy of erotic substitutionism, as in the Baron's need for the trophy of the lock of hair itself.

The famous toilet scene which closes the first Canto can be seen to derive its significance from the dehumanising process that characterizes the poem as a whole, for when Belinda 'intent adores / With Head uncover'd, the *Cosmetic* Pow'rs' (I. 123–4), she is in fact idolizing herself through the medium of the objects which will tranform her appearance, which will 'create' her public image. There is only one Belinda, but the mirror reflexion conveys to the reader precisely the reified image that is the object of all her devotions. And again the cosmetic paraphernalia surrounding Belinda rises to an active presence, as she surrenders herself to them; a casket 'unlocks' its jewels, perfume 'breathes,' and 'Files of Pins' transitively extend themselves. Finally an abstraction, 'awful Beauty,' assumes command and presides over the contrived dawn of Belinda's attractions. And in the second Canto, Pope's precise use of reificatory zeugma reveals his own awareness of the radical dislocations embodied in Belinda:

> Whether the Nymph shall break Diana's Law,
> Or some frail *China* Jar receive a Flaw,
> Or stain her Honour, or her new Brocade,

> Forget her Pray'rs, or miss a Masquerade,
> Or lose her Heart, or Necklace, at a Ball;
>
> (II. 105–9)

It has already been seen that the heart, in this poem, reproduces the values of objects, and Pope's placing of these lines immediately before the naming of the deities points to his awareness. For beneath its fluently contrived surface-structure, *The Rape of the Lock* charts with hilarious accuracy the historical advent of a form of social organisation of men wherein, as Marx comments, 'their own social action takes the form of the action of objects, which rule the producers instead of being ruled by them,' so that human behaviour, and the values it constructs appear to be not the productions of human activity at all, but 'laws of nature' imposed from outside. Or, as the poem slyly puts it, ' 'Tis but their *Sylph*, the wise Celestials know, / Though *Honour* is the Word with Men below' (I. 77–8).

Pope is at pains to indicate the pervasiveness of this quality of life, and the third Canto opens with just such an extension of the area of the poem's concern, introducing statesmanship as the equivalent of sexual horse trading, and regard for monarchy as the equivalent of admiration for filigree wood-work. But more significantly, there follow the lines that for one critic of the poem represent a 'momentary glimpse of the world of serious affairs, of the world of business and law . . . an echo of the "real" world':

> Meanwhile declining from the Noon of Day,
> The Sun obliquely shoots his burning Ray;
> The hungry Judges soon the Sentence sign,
> And Wretches hang that Jury-men may Dine;
> The Merchant from th' *Exchange* returns in Peace,
> And the long Labours of the *Toilette* cease—
>
> (III. 19–24)

It may seem odd to seek a separation at this juncture between Belinda's world, and another, 'glimpsed' here, which somehow exists outside it—and the comic perversion of values is in any case characteristic. But the essential unity of vision, the underlying link between the apparent brutality here and the seeming frivolity everywhere else, is again suggested by Pope's conflating use of italics.

The scramble for commodities which defines a Moll Flanders as 'economic woman' is strictly equated with Belinda's adoration for the objects of her dressing-table, and Pope's earliest readers would have had little difficulty in recognising the equation being made, since the architectural design of the Royal Exchange gave immediate point to the couplet. A contemporary description runs, 'Above stairs there are *Walks*, with near 200 Shops, full of choice Commodities, especially for Mens and Womens Apparel, besides other *Shops* below the portico.' There is, in fact, further evidence to suggest that Pope was perfectly aware of the correspondence being made in these two lines. Twelve months before the first version of *The Rape* appeared in Lintot's *Miscellany*, Addison published an essay as *Spectator* 69 in which he confessed himself ravished by the prospect of a busy day at the Royal Exchange, and which provides a useful gloss for significant elements in *The Rape of the Lock*—indeed, at certain points in the poem Pope appears to have had Addison's eulogy consciously in mind:

> Almost every *degree* [of traffic] among mankind produces something peculiar to it. The Food often grows in one Country, and the Sauce in another. The Fruits of Portugal are corrected by the Products of *Barbadoes*; the Infusion of a *China* Plant sweetned with the Pith of an *Indian* Cane; the Phillipick Islands give a Flavour to our *European* Bowls. The single Dress of a Woman of Quality is often the Product of an hundred Climates. The Muff and the Fan come together from the different Ends of the Earth. The Scarf is sent from the Torrid Zone, and the Tippet from beneath the Pole. The Brocade Petticoat rises out of the mines of *Peru*, and the Diamond Necklace out of the Bowels of *Indostan*.

Belinda springs irrepressibly to mind, as what Addison calls 'a kind of Additional Empire' lands in profusion upon her dressing-table. And the series of transparent verbal and thematic similarities is continued:

> Nor has Traffic more enriched our Vegetable World, than it has improved the whole Face of Nature among us . . . Our Tables are stored with Spices, and oils, and Wines: Our Rooms are filled with Pyramids of *China*, and adorned with the Workmanship of *Japan* . . . We repair our Bodies by the Drugs of *America*, and repose ourselves under *Indian* Canopies . . . Traffick . . . supplies us with everything that is Convenient and Ornamental.

What Addison considers to be an improvement, Pope treats more ambivalently as a process of glittering, though nonetheless grotesque, transformations. And in the same essay, Addison blandly asserts what Pope, in the opening lines of the third Canto, chooses to leave at the level of satiric suggestion, 'Factors in the Trading World are what Ambassadors are in the Politick World: they negotiate Affairs, conclude Treaties, and maintain a good Correspondence between those wealthy Societies of Men that are divided from one another by Seas and Oceans.' Pope similarly collapses the distinctions between these two worlds but in high comic spirit:

> Here Britain's Statesmen oft the Fall foredoom
> Of Foreign Tyrants, and of Nymphs at home;
> Here Thou, Great *Anna!* whom three Realms obey,
> Dost sometimes Counsel take—and sometimes *Tea*.
> (III. 5–8)

The trader and the politician are one, and the historical accuracy underpinning the satire is now accepted. Carswell, for example, comments that it was 'undoubtedly the case that the new class of business men were finding it worth their while to find and occupy seats in Parliament. By 1702 there were at least sixty of them in the Commons.'

A glance at Pope's treatment of the new riches celebrated by Addison reveals his more ambiguous attitude, and the comically inflated description of the coffee ritual in Canto three is to the point:

> For lo! the Board with Cups and Spoons is crown'd,
> The Berries crackle, and the Mill turns round.
> On Shining Altars of *Japan* they Raise
> The silver Lamp; the fiery spirits blaze.
> From silver Spouts the grateful Liquors glide,
> While *China's* Earth receives the smoking Tyde.
> At once they gratify their Scent and Taste,
> And frequent Cups prolong the rich Repast.
> (III. 105–12)

A sense of the marvellous is richly maintained, while subtle ambiguities in grammar are left to make their mark. In a letter to Arbuthnot, dated July 1714, Pope records a scene in which there was 'likewise a Side Board of Coffee which the Dean roasted with his own hands in an Engine for the purpose, his landlady attending, all the while that office was performing.' The human control over the making of coffee expressed here tends to vanish when the same ritual enters *The Rape*, for what is occurring in the poetic version is the inference of partial autonomy for the objects under view, blurring the issue of who or what is in control. It is the berries which crackle, the mill which turns round. Liquors which, by transferred epithet, can be described as grateful, glide, while the cups, with equal stress on their performing abilities, both receive and prolong.

Parallel to this technique is the treatment of the Baron's actual assault upon Belinda, where Pope's resources in revitalising stock notions of poetic diction succeed in directing attention to the instrument itself with which the Baron carries out his designs. The 'two-edged Weapon,' the 'little Engine,' the 'glitt'ring *Forfex*' and the 'fatal Engine' all serve to maintain the sense of object predominance until the grammar suggests that the 'Instruments of Ill,' a pair of scissors, complete the assault on their own; 'The meeting Points the Sacred Hair dissever / From the fair Head, for ever and for ever!' (III. 153–4). Such examples provide instances of the ways in which the grammar of the poem carries this sustained pattern of meaning; inanimate noun-phrases repeatedly cast in an agentive role, or human activity finding its strict equivalent in non-human activity ('Nymph shall break . . . Jar [shall] receive,' or, more ambiguously perhaps, 'the nice Conduct of a *clouded Cane*'). And Belinda's own words indicate the extreme lengths to which this transfer of power has been carried: 'Thrice from my trembling hand the *Patch-box* fell; / The tott'ring *China* shook without a Wind' (IV. 153–4), where the first of these lines suggests wilful action on the part of the patch-box (it was not dropped, it fell), and the second, picking up an image which forms part of the total pattern, confronts us directly with the automatic drama of object-life.

III

It is this ambience which helps to explain Belinda's complaint at the end of the Fourth Canto, 'Oh hadst thou, Cruel! been content to seize / Hairs less in sight, or any Hairs but these!' (IV. 175–6). In desperation, Belinda voices her preference for real, but concealed, as opposed to attenuated, but evident, rape. Her assaulted coiffure is in visible disarray; retrospectively, actual rape at least offers the protection of an invisible discomposure. For it is in this Fourth Canto that Pope enacts most fully the reification that is at the heart of the poem. The comic descent into the particular grotesquerie of this hell is carefully designed to tell the truth of the preceding Cantos, to reveal nakedly what has hitherto been artfully suggested:

> Unnumber'd Throngs on ev'ry side are seen
> Of Bodies chang'd to various Forms by *Spleen*.
> Here living *Teapots* stand, one Arm held out,
> One bent; the Handle this, and that the Spout;
> A Pipkin there like *Homer's Tripod* walks;
> Here sighs a Jar, and there a Goose-pye talks;

Men prove with Child, as pow'rful Fancy works,
And Maids turn'd Bottels, call aloud for Corks.
                                                                    (IV. 47–54)

One hardly needs the benefit of a Freudian method to discern how the
previously repressed and fetishised sexuality is now producing its own pan-
tomime of perverted psychology. But again it is the mode of this production
that is interesting. Earlier the world of objects has challenged human sway,
threatening to displace it; here, at a deeper level of psychological farce, the
non-human assumes total control of once-human vessels. Objects perform
their 'danse macabre' at will.

      And if it is true that in this Fourth Canto Pope is revealing more openly
the underlying concerns of the poem as a whole, he is also revealing something
of 'the truth' about the origins of Belinda's coquettish nature, and in this
respect J. G. A. Pocock makes an illuminating observation. 'The personi-
fication of Credit as an inconstant female figure, it is startling to discover,
is a device of Whig rather than Tory writers, and in particular of Defoe and
Addison at the time when they were undergoing the assaults which Swift,
in the *Examiner*, had launched against all forms of property except land as
"only what is transient or imaginary." Taking up one of the writers mentioned, it is doubly interesting that Dickson chose to include as a frontispiece
to *The Financial Revolution* a lengthy excerpt from Addison's third *Spectator*
paper, 'The Bank of England: vision of "Public Credit"; her friends and
enemies.' In a dream Addison sees in the great hall of the Bank of England
'a beautiful Virgin seated on a Throne of Gold. Her name (as they told me)
was *Publick Credit* . . . with the Act of uniformity on the right Hand, and
the Act of Toleration on the Left.' The dreaming spectator sees heaps of bags
of gold behind the throne, piled to the ceiling, and learns that the lady in
question 'could convert whatever she pleased into that precious Metal.' However, at the approach of 'Tyranny,' 'Anarchy,' 'Bigotry,' and 'Atheism,' the
virgin 'fainted and died away.' There are already connections between Pope's
'Goddess with a discontented Air,' and Addison's 'troubled with Vapours.'
But then, in lines not included by Dickson, Addison goes on to describe
further effects of this invasion:

      There was as great a change in the Hill of Money Bags, and the
      Heaps of Money; the former shrinking and falling into so many
      empty Bags, that I now would have found not above a tenth part
      of them had been filled with Money. The rest that took up the
      same Space and made the same Figure as the Bags that were really
      filled with Money, had been blown up with Air, and called into

my Memory the Bags full of Wind, Which Homer tells us his
Hero received as a present from Aeolus. The great heaps of Gold
on either side the Throne now appeared to be only heaps of Paper,
or like little piles of Notched Sticks, bound up together in bun-
dles, like Bath Faggots.

Again the echoes are clear as Pope describes his own Goddess of Spleen:

> A wondrous Bag with both her Hands she binds,
> Like that where once *Ulysses* held the Winds;
> There she collects the Force of Female Lungs,
> Sighs, Sobs, and Passions, and the War of Tongues.
>
> (IV. 81–4)

Both writers are expressing kinds of transformation, and the source of Addison's imagery suggests a more immediate monetary correlative for the
social and psychological mutations explored by Pope. The point at issue here
is not whether Pope is actively satirising Addison's essay, but rather that
revolutionary forms of finance become a literary subject for Addison in ways
that show definite affinities with the methods employed by Pope for his own
more ambivalent purposes.

It is perfectly fitting then, that as the farce returns to the by now
splintering elegance of the mundane realm in the final Canto, Pope should
make his final addition to *The Rape of the Lock*; Clarissa's classic statement
of Augustan 'good sense.' But the significance of this inclusion reaches further
than the simple assertion that 'Pope obviously agrees with Clarissa.' Pope,
after all, controls the shape of the whole poem, and he has earlier (III. 127–
30) placed Clarissa in the invidious position of having unwittingly provided
the Baron with the weapon for his assault. More important, though, is the
fact that the net result of her calm reasoning is action which first ignores
and then noisily contradicts what she has to say. It is a way of acknowledging
that the world constructed in *The Rape* is one that has moved beyond the
bounds of Augustan rationalism and can no longer be naturally contained
by it, given that its characters themselves are unnaturally 'contained.' And
the poetic heaven which provides the final resting place for Belinda's much-
abused hair offers one of the last images of the human contained within the
inanimate. 'There Heroes' Wits are kept in pondrous Vases, / And Beaus'
in *Snuff-boxes* and *Tweezer-cases*' (V. 115–116). The pessimistic gloom that
settled upon Pope in his later years might paradoxically be traced to the
exuberant perceptions playing beneath the surface of his mock-epic. In his
mid-twenties he felt able to end the poem with a celebration of the breadth

of his poetic vision. Indeed, he still felt able to revel in the proclamation of his own 'quick Poetic eyes' as the only possible container for this disjointed world. Since the deeper meaning of Belinda's personal and social life is an insight necessarily denied to her, the structure of the five Cantos brings it into focus for us.

MELINDA ALLIKER RABB

Lost in a House of Mirrors: Pope's Imitations of Horace

In *To Fortescue*, during one of the passages that depart radically from the original text in Horace, Pope says that his poem is a kind of mirror: "In this impartial Glass, my Muse intends / Fair to expose myself, my Foes, my Friends" (58–59). Here and elsewhere in the Horatian poems, the "Glass"— either as mirror, lens, or window—and ideas associated with the "Glass," particularly reflection and perspective, suggest certain relationships between Pope and his text and his readers. Certain interpretive implications emerge when one views the relationships as a means of satiric entrapment.

The mirror is not Pope's only metaphor for satire in the *Imitations*. The others, at first, sound more heroic, more forceful, more dangerous. Satire is a "sacred weapon," virtue's "armor," a stinging nettle ("touch me and no Minister so sore"), a purifying corrosive ("yet let me strip"). The glass, on the other hand, is simply "impartial" and "fair." But the seeming indifference of the mirror, its apparent passivity and ambivalence, activate responses that are painfully, sardonically, sometimes passionately, "fair." "Many will know their own Pictures in it," Pope said of the *Epistle to Dr. Arbuthnot*. Although criticism of the Horatian poems has stressed *hearing* their varied tones and dramatic interchanges, Pope asks the reader, in several senses, to *see* these poems, to be aware of their visual and spatial dimensions, to situate them in "the non-place of language." Studies of reflection and perspective, from the Renaissance on, had put space more firmly in the grasp of the imagination; both concepts become cognitive metaphors for self-knowledge and knowledge

From *Papers on Language and Literature*. Copyright © 1982 by The Board of Trustees, Southern Illinois University.

of the world. In Pope's poems, the general problems of how and what the reader can know surround Pope's more specific satiric purposes. As images reflect from line to line, there is more than the reader can easily reconcile; ultimately, the reader sees himself.

Swift also spoke of a mirror of satire: it is "a sort of Glass, wherein beholders do generally discover everybody's Face but their Own." According to this definition, it is not surprising to learn, in the *Epilogue to the Satires*, that when a new work of Pope's appears, "the Court sees nothing in't" (Dialogue 2.2). How and why, then, does the self-conscious satirist proceed? What can he make "beholders" discover? Pope's answers to these questions lead him to even broader questions about the nature of representation and perception. The reflecting and perspective glass, to put the matter in more contemporary terms, express metaphorically both certain dynamics of reader-response and certain dimensions of the written text.

In the Horatian poems, the "Glass" stands as a paradigm metaphor with fourfold significance: satire, imitation, autobiography, and self-reflexivity. When Pope holds a glass up to his own "times of general Vice," he simultaneously holds mirrors up to Horace, to himself, and even to the process of illusion-making: "Mirror on mirror mirrored is all the show." Locke defined *reflection* as "the mind's perception of its own operations." It seems fitting that Pope should have conceived of his most mature, most introspective poems as reflecting surfaces. It seems equally fitting that he make his farewell to satire while he watches men who are "wise and great," "noble" and "generous," gradually diminishing in "the still, clear Mirror of Retreat" (Dia. 2. 78). The end of Pope's career marks, as well, the end of an era of satire. The last lines of the *Epilogue* create one of the mirror-effects discussed below. At present, it is enough to note that the two great Augustan satirists share the metaphor of the glass. Swift's youthful definition and the image of refracted lights in the "Digression on Madness" culminate in *Gulliver's Travels*, book 4. Gulliver, in the madness of his self-loathing, prefers to see the reflection of a common Yahoo in the water, rather than see his own face there. He does not understand that he, the Yahoo, and the two reflections are all mirror-images of one another. The mirrors of Pope's *Imitations* are a culmination, too, of all four distinct meanings of the metaphor: satire, imitation, autobiography, reflexivity. The purpose of this essay is to describe the ways in which they produce an experience of readjustment and doubt and evoke a world of perceptual ambiguity and flux. The first step is to gain a perspective on the poems by looking at some mirrors from earlier in Pope's career.

II

In *Windsor Forest* (1713) nature provides mirrors for lovesick nymphs and shepherds, and Pope describes them from a relatively simple—certainly a less self-conscious—point of view. Optical illusions in an innocent world may be lovely:

> Oft in her Glass the musing Shepherd spies
> The headlong Mountains and the downward Skies,
> The Wat'ry Landskip of the pendant Woods,
> And absent Trees that tremble in the Floods;
> In the clear azure Gleam the Flocks are seen,
> And floating Forests paint the Waves with Green,
> Thro' the fair Scene rowl slow the ling'ring Streams,
> Then foaming pour along, and rush into the Thames.
>
> (211–18)

These lines are filled with undercurrents that grow stronger in later poems. The most famous pastoral encounter with a reflection is Narcissus', the emblem of self-love and self-scrutiny, themes that Pope explores with ever-increasing zeal. Narcissus also represents the artist, "for what else can you call painting but a similar embracing with art of what is presented on the surface of the water in the fountain?" The Ovidian "Landskip" is endowed with latent powers that "tremble" beneath the shimmering surface of the water. The water/glass exists only because the nymph Lodona, fleeing Pan, has been transformed into a stream. Her allegiance, of course, is to Cynthia, moon-goddess of reflected light. In her, the dreamy swain sees the world turned upside-down, "headlong," "pendant," for mirrors reverse their images. The mirror becomes both a product of and an agent of metamorphosis. In it, illusions begin to create illusions, making it difficult to distinguish between real and unreal. At first, the reflected woods, hanging and shimmering in the "Floods," are called "absent Trees"; but the "absent Trees" assume their own reciprocal creative powers: "floating Forests paint the Waves with Green." The "fair Scene" also meshes stasis and motion. The "Ling'ring" stream would stay beneath the apparently stable yet transient beauty of the reflection, but reverts to foam and rushes "into the Thames."

The potential for the "Glass" to become an agent of transformation develops further in *The Rape of the Lock* (1714), a poem in which Pope's use of mirrors begins to multiply. Canto 1 opens with a clear mirror (Pope identifies it as "Platonic" in his notes) reliably reflecting truth. Ariel "rang'd the Crystal Wilds of Air" and sees "in the clear Mirror of [Belinda's] ruling

Star" the impending "dread Event." But Belinda is no Platonist; she, all the while, has her eyes closed in sleep. When they open on a billet-doux, "all the Vision vanish'd," and she moves to a second mirror, the one on her dressing-table. This glass is flattering, magical, the scene of a mystic rite and an area of metamorphosis. In it, unveiling, exposing, reflecting, and transforming merge:

> And now, unveiled, the Toilet stands display'd,
> Each silver Vase in mystic Order laid.
> First rob'd in White, the Nymph intent adores
> With Head uncover'd, the Cosmetic Pow'rs.
> A heav'nly Image in the Glass appears,
> To that, she bends, to that her Eyes she rears;
>
> Unnumber'd Treasures ope at once, and here
> The various Off'rings of the World appear.
>   (1. 121–30)

The perspective on the whole "glitt'ring" Ovidian scene is *into* the mirror: the reader watches Belinda watching herself, decking her Goddess/reflection/self while "Tortoise . . . and Elephant unite, / Transform'd to Combs."

The mock-heroic mode (in which Belinda's reflection "put[s] on all its Arms") is itself a two-way mirror reflecting a heroic past and an unheroic present. The imitative mode, in general, is frequently described with the same metaphor. Pope translated Achilles' arming scene ("arms that reflect a radiance" and "beamy light," "reflecting Blaze on Blaze against the Skies") in which the hero becomes a mirror of the sun, almost becomes a sun as he lights the world with a "radiance through the Skies." As Belinda prepares to meet, not Hector, but the Baron, her reflected glory is kept one step further removed: it is literally seen in a mirror. Only her bright eyes, in canto 2, rival the sun's beams.

Pope continues, from these natural, Platonic, and artificial mirrors, to the mirror of art. In the often-quoted passage from the *Epistle to Jervas* (1716), he calls the twin "Sister Arts" mirror-images of one another: "images reflect from Art to Art" and "each from each contract new strength and light." Pope here seems confident that the mirrors will be "lasting," that both "stroke" and "line" will "shine" from them. Despite Pope's polite humility about the immortality he and Jervas will share ("Alas! how little from the grave we claim? / Thou but preserv'st a Face and I a Name.") he can speak of the reflecting mirrors as means of preservation. If art is a mirror, the golden age of classical art is the brightest one. Appropriately, the *Dunciad Variorum* (1728) heralds an unreflective "age of Lead" whose goddess has a name, Dulness, that describes—

in addition to her power to foster boredom and stupidity—her lack of brightness, that is, her inability to serve as a mirror. She is the symbol of anti-art. She also is unreflective in the Lockean sense. The dunces are hollow men who cannot scrutinize the operations of their own vacant brains.

In this more pessimistic mood, Pope turns to the metaphoric possibilities of the perspective glass. (Swift used an actual one to amuse himself by burning holes in paper.) Prudence clairvoyantly sees "th'approaching jayl" through hers (1.49). (The emblem tradition typically depicts Prudence as a woman looking into or holding a perspective glass.) The goddess Dulness "beholds through Fogs that magnify the Scene." The mists that surround her face function like the distorting lenses of trick spectacles. They also symbolize the general inversion of the poem as an un-Creation story. According to St. Paul, Christian Platonists, and others, God's bright face emits light that is reflected in the natural world and in the human mind and soul. Dulness' face is covered; the natural world ends in universal darkness; the dunces' hearts and minds are black voids in which her "image [is] full exprest." Nothing can be mirrored back but darkness.

Natural, metaphysical, magical, and artificial mirrors persist, although Pope becomes increasingly interested in the human "Glass," a warped apparatus full of cracks, flaws, and stains. "Remembrance and Reflection how ally'd," he says in the *Essay on Man* (1734). He becomes interested in the "opticks giv'n" man for reflecting and remembering, in what "no Eye can see" and "no Glass can reach." Following the borrowed optimism of the *Essay on Man*, Pope, in *To Cobham* (1734), discusses human perception as if it were a perspective glass or prism. This differs greatly from the glass of imitation, which confirms, as it reflects, an external reality. The glass of perception confirms only an inner reality that is subjective and individualistic, that stands between the perceiver and his object:

> [T]he diff'rence is as great between
> The Opticks seeing, as the Objects seen.
> All manners take a Tincture from our own,
> Or come discolour'd thro' our Passions shown.
> Or fancy's beam enlarges, multiplies,
> Contracts, inverts, and gives ten thousand Dyes.
> (23–28)

With such delusive powers of perception, not even "the Sage . . . would from th'apparent What conclude the Why." These epistemological problems underlie the doubts and self-consciousness of the Horatian poems. Pope proposes an "impartial Glass," but how impartial can a glass be? Its ambiguities and limitations, its ability to symbolize contradictory pairs of concepts (honesty/ deceit, self-knowledge/vanity, rational understanding/delusory materiality, and so on) make it an ideal image to find in a work of entrapment.

It is the image Swift and Pope both use for morally corrective satire. Yet it is also the image they use for the futility of satire: "How fade and insipid do all Objects accost us that are not conveyed in the vehicle of Delusion. How shrunk is everything, as it appears in the Glass of Nature?" The mirror has symbolized artistic representation from Socrates and Plato on. Velasquez' *Las Meninas* is perhaps the most famous example of an artist mirroring his own art in a mirror, although many other examples exist. Picasso's parody of *Las Meninas*—in which he holds a mirror up to Velasquez' mirror—is like Pope's treatment of Horace. The perspective glass equally evokes ambiguities. "[I]f it were not for the Assistance of Artificial Mediums, false Lights, refracted Angles, Varnish, and Tinsel; there would be a mighty Level in the Felicity and Enjoyments of Mortal Men," wrote Swift. The study of optics, which at first encouraged confidence in human rationality and in the orderly proceedings of natural phenomena, gradually revealed a "more complex and ambiguous relationship between the knower and the knowable." In the recent background of Pope's poems is the English fascination with "optical ingenuity of all kinds—in anamorphic images, perspective boxes, mirrors and lenses, telescopes and prisms" which found its way into many other fields, including verse, "not only through importation of optical imagery but through a deeply felt concern with the way we look at the world." Holbein's *The Ambassadors* forces the viewer into an unconventional stance in order to understand its anamorphic image. In *All Fools*, Chapman writes of a "couzening Picture, which one way / Shows like a crow, another like a Swan" (1. 1. 47). It is a picture that forces its viewer to regard it from different angles, a device similar to Pope's strategy in the *Imitations*.

III

We turn first to these poems as imitations. The imitator, as distinct from the translator, assumes the freedom of "full imaginative remaking" of an original; yet his work owes its existence to, reflects, that original. Pope printed his imitations next to Horace's text, visualizing the dependence and the difference—"so Latin, yet so English all the while." Seeing Horace in an English mirror is no simple experience. As in the mirrors of the earlier poems, things merge, transform, and create optical illusions. Readers have looked and seen Juvenal, Perseus, Dryden, and other faces as well. Indeed, the reader's powers of recognition figure strategically in the poems. His fictive adversaries are incorrigible misreaders. Fr., in the *Epilogue*, mistakenly protests, "Don't I see you steal? / 'Tis all from Horace." Pope goes to some pains to encourage this misperception some of the time. He announces, for example, that "[t]he occasion of publishing these Imitations was the Clamour raised on some of my Epistles. An Answer from Horace was both more full, and of more Dignity, than any I could have made in my own Person." This disclaimer hardly prepares the reader for the original and self-conscious poems that follow. As an imitator, Pope dramatically extends the possible uses of an original text as grounds for personal license, to distract or mislead the reader, and to inform the reader of ironic similarities or contrasts.

With the mirror of imitation, Pope can make himself both a presence and an absence in the poem. He creates a poetic 'self' that cannot be fully accepted as the 'real' Pope, nor fully rejected because of the poem's classical sanction. Instead of being a form disciplined and limited by an original, the mirror of imitation becomes liberating and coercive. Fr. and Pope both claim that he merely reflects Horatian glory, that he is not really there "in [his] own Person." But, like those "absent Trees" in *Windsor Forest*—passive reflections in water with the power to 'paint' the water—Pope has it both ways. He and his adversary agree that it is all from Horace. Yet one seems sincere, the other wrongheaded; perhaps neither can be completely wrong.

To Fortescue, the poem that calls itself a "Glass," allows us to see Pope and Horace acting as mirrors of one another. This dialogue between the satirist and his legal counselor ostensibly invokes Horace's theory and defense of satire, but, as G. K. Hunter and others have shown, actually alters the original theory drastically. The mirror images clearly do not match. A widely applicable, abstract theory of satire interests Pope less than his own particular reflection, which he shows to be complex and multi-faceted. The contradictory alternatives that the poem offers to resolve for the reader, but does not, form themselves in various ways. They have always frustrated critics, beginning with Johnson, with a strong yen for consistency and organic form. Pope says that the reader will see him, his foes and friends as reflections of Horace. Images seen in a mirror—dependent on the play of light, on the angle of perspective—differ from images of painted portraits or sculptured figures in important, if subtle, ways. The painted or sculpted image is fixed; mirrored faces rarely stand still, for even during the most rapt self-scrutiny, there must be at least the batting of an eye. In *To Fortescue*, which has been called a subjective, romantic, self-centered poem, Pope often turns the mirror toward himself and is not too shy to strike different poses and make a number of faces in it. And yet, it is impossible to say that the poem is a self-portrait. Pope does not furnish us with a finished picture to be carried away from the end of the poem like a souvenir.

By playing conflicting and fragmentary roles, Pope insures that the process of reading the poem (watching in the "Glass") will supersede any end-product or neat theory of satire or simple impression of a complex man. He shows us much, yet he shows us little of how to integrate glimpses of 'Pope' into a coherent, believable whole. The Horatian modulations of tone that move Pope's satiric muse through the roles of ingenu, *vir bonus*, and hero, are disjunctive and dislocating. Like Horace, Pope knows that, as *poeta* and *rhetor*, the reliability of his speaker is crucial to his ability to persuade. Pope seems to want more than to persuade the reader; he wants him to think for himself. Like the viewer of an anamorphic painting, the reader must be willing to consider him from different angles.

In *To Fortescue*, generally, the inadequacy of explicitly stated alternatives is always pressing the poem to open out into new options. In this way, it resists closure. For example, the doubling of the mirror of imitation increases Pope's authority as moralist. Horace is always there to back him up. But the mirror also suggests a more ambiguous configuration of authority, for the poem alludes not only to Horace, but to a series of increasingly vague historical precedents. Pope looks in a mirror and sees Horace, who is looking in a mirror at Lucilius, who looks, in turn, at Ennius and Pacuvius, all Roman satirists who, in Horace's stated view, "depend on writers of Greek Old Comedy such as Cratinus and Aristophanes." Does this ancient genealogy give weight to a poem about satire and about Pope as writer and man? Or does it simply imply that the ever-receding, ever more distant past is like an endless series of mirrors within mirrors? Do the grounds for writing satire drop endlessly away? Dunces and fools, too, are an ancient race. Lord Fanny descends with undiminished vigor from Fannius and presumably from his forebears. Dunce the second reigns like Dunce the first, as will Dunce the third, and so on. What comfort or conclusion is to be drawn from past precedents in a seemingly endless "warfare upon earth"? The imitation's evocation of mirrors into the past may be seen as a Popean variation of the idea of infinite regression, or boxes within boxes, that Rawson applies to Swift's satire.

As autobiography, the *Imitations* have provoked critical disagreement, often because Pope seems so "careless how ill I with myself agree." He brings to light more details of his private life than Horace ever did, yet these details may be blatantly contradictory: "And for my Soul, I cannot sleep a Wink," he says at first. "Know, all the distant Din that World can keep / Rolls o'er my Grotto and but soothes my Sleep," he says later. More subtly, the imagery transforms him into passive or empty vessels—dependent upon or responsive to forces from outside (Sat. 2. 1. 14, 51–58, 62–63, 92)—yet elsewhere grants him the strength of Achilles and the power of God (67–71, 118–20). Pope often describes himself as liquid, a substance that suggests the flux, the shifting identity of the speaker. More important, liquid (from Latin *liquid-us*: clear, transparent) means capable of either clarity or opacity, of either reflecting back at the reader or allowing the reader to see within. When Pope wishes to play the role of private citizen and friend, he treats the physical space of his text (and his textual self) as if it were the surface of a linear perspective painting. It is imagined as a transparent plane, an open window. His personal letters contain many images of transparency and clear water: "I cannot be *Sub-Persona* before a man I love," he writes (Corr. I.) He even uses the same metaphor as the theorists of perspective painting when he confides, "The old project of a Window in the Bosom, to render the Soul of Man visible, is what every honest friend has manifold reason to wish for." Images of clearness represent idealized friendship, trust, understanding in the *Imitations*, too: "I love to pour out all myself as plain / As downright Shippen, or old Montagne / In them . . . / The soul stood forth, nor kept a Thought within." Even his "Spots" will "prove at least the Medium must be clear." But as a public figure, he assumes qualities of the mirror or lens. He must be "plain" (from Latin *plan-us*, flat) and full of "candor," a word he changes from Horace's *fortim* (stealthy) and which means "white and shining." Horace may appear as a "Screen," but Pope as satirist will be a "Glass." Non-satiric writers are dismissed as honey, dew, and cream.

The properties of the imitative/satiric/autobiographical mirror remain ambiguous and contribute to the "visual irony" of the poems. Earlier, *To a Lady* compliments Martha Blount at the close with an implicit image of a mirror, in which spiritual beauty results from divine rays reflected in the natural world:

> Ah Friend! to dazzle let the Vain design,
>
> [W]hen the Sun's broad beam has tir'd the sight,
> All mild ascends the Moon's more sober light,
> Serene . . . she shines,
> And unobserv'd the glaring Orb declines.
>
> (249–56)

Here the indirect light of the moon glows steadily and will not "dazzle" and "tire the sight." Similarly, Virtue, in Dialogue 2, "points" and "shines" and "casts a Glory" on her followers. But mirrors, if positioned correctly, can dazzle, too, and in the *Imitations* they may blind or confuse the beholder.

To Bethel (Sat. 2. 2) opens with a mirror image of a "gilt Buffet's reflected Pride" which "turns you from sound Philosophy aside" (5–6). Facing this symbol of vanity and materiality, the "brain dances" and the "eyeballs roll." Like the "beaming diamonds" and "reflected plate" in the *Imitation of Epistle 1.6*, they create confusing optical illusions that "double the surprise" of a beholder who has been "struck with bright Brocade" (29–32). At the end of *To Bethel*, Pope offers another kind of mirror: "His equal mind I copy what I can, / And as I love would imitate the Man" (131–32). Within an imitation of Horace is an imitation of Bethel. In the autobiographical con- clusion ("[I]n five acres now of rented land. / Content with little, I can piddle here / On Broccoli and mutton, round the year . . . ") Pope imitates Bethel by holding a mirror up to himself, by trying to make the two images agree. This desire to make diverse reflections match one another figures else- where in the *Imitations*, often in relation to Pope's fractured images of himself ("how ill I with myself agree"), with his desire for self-knowledge and self- scrutiny when he worries that nothing "is half so incoherent as my Mind" (166). Thus, in *To Bathurst*, he expands Horace's lines on a pair of twins. They appear to be mirror images of one another, but really are entirely different men: "[Y]ou'll find, / Two of a Face, as soon as of a Mind" (268– 69). The wish for coherence is frustrated on all sides. Pope reminds the reader of Dulness' self-deluding fogs when his attempt to paint a glowing image of himself is clouded by "a Fit of Vapours."

The belief that one man can serve as a mirror of another informs the "admiring" poems *To Bethel, To Bolingbroke* (Ep. 1. 1), *To Murray* (Ep. 2.6), and *To Bathurst* (Ep. 2. 2). Ep. 1.6., for example, contains only a few specific mirror images. But its language diffuses the process of mirroring throughout the first half of the poem: "Not to admire is all the Art I know" (1), "Admire we then" (11), "In either case, believe me, we admire" (21), "not to admire, but be admir'd" (41), and so on through eight examples. Because *admire* and *mirror* come from the same Latin world (*mirari*: to wonder), the principal verb of the poem performs a kind of mirroring, sometimes active, sometimes passive. If only, Pope seems to say, men could admire—and mirror in themselves—worthy originals, but instead they "admire whate'er the mad- dest can admire" (68).

But, perhaps more significantly, the idea of one man as mirror of another works itself out in the dialogue form of some of the imitations, especially in the *Epilogue to the Satires*. It is as if the idea of the human mirror, latent in the Horatian satires and epistles, develops more fully when Pope is freest with the imitative mode. P. keeps trying to act as a mirror in which Fr. can see himself and his corrupted morality (Dia. 1. 113ff., for example, or Dia. 2. 14ff.). That the reader can see himself most clearly in the mirror of others is an insight shared by art and psychology. In yet another sense, the confrontations between the poet and his adversary function in this way. Pope projects these fictive selves, as Griffin and Edwards have argued, to gain a better view of himself. "Both Fr. and P. are versions of Pope himself, or of any man aware of the conflict between his social identity and his secret image of himself as autonomous moral hero." As Swift observes, nature holds forth two mirrors, one flattering and delightful, the other grotesquely distorted. So Pope can see himself at his best, and as his own worst enemy. The dialogue form, which Pope develops far beyond anything in Horace, has further relevance to the idea of the perspective-glass.

There is yet another way in which the texts of the Horatian poems function as mirrors: they reverse images. A statement, for example, made in the beginning of a poem may, by the end, have reversed itself. In the beginning of Satire 2. 1, to recall one instance, Pope says he cannot sleep but, before the poem closes, says that nothing can disturb his slumber. Similarly, his adversary neatly reverses "write no more" to "you may then proceed." In fact, the legal case cited as evidence in Fortescue's prosecution is taken from *A Mirror for Magistrates*. He literally holds up a copy of *A Mirrour* for the poet to look at: "here you have it—read" (149). Elsewhere, images reflect back and forth not within a poem but between poems. The two triumphs that end Dialogues 1 and 2 are mirror images of one another. Virtue is first "pendant" and "headlong" like the "absent Trees," but then is righted and ascendant. Throughout the *Imitations*, Pope reflects back on his earlier work as he alludes to and quotes from himself. The last lines of the *Epilogue*, for example ("Alas! alas! pray end what you began, / And write next winter more *Essays on Man.*"), recall, somewhat sardonically, the *Essay's* philosophical seriousness. Should Pope take Fr.'s advice and pick up at the end of Epistle 4, he would return to an image of a mirror: "For Wit's false Mirror held up Nature's Light; / Shew'd erring Pride, WHATEVER IS, IS RIGHT: / That Reason, Passion, answer one great Aim; / That Virtue only makes our Bliss below; / And all our knowledge is, OURSELVES TO KNOW." In the mirror that closes the *Essay*, resolution is possible: six abstractions are described as mirror-images of each other. Self-scrutiny, the final wisdom, seems an obtainable goal. Further, one of the frequent comments about the form of the *Essay* is that it ends where it began. That is, the last lines of Epistle 4 recapture the first lines of Epistle 1. They are about vantage point, scope of vision, perspective—where should we look and what can we see?

In the *Imitations*, especially in *To Fortescue* and the *Epilogue*, Pope talks about his art in what contemporary criticism calls a "self-reflexive" mode. The problems of writing satire form the principal subject of the poems. They seem less satires on society or learning or politics than they are satires about satire, mirrors of mirrors. One self-reflexive technique is to refer directly to Pope's already published work. Another is to refer to the work in progress. Pope often reminds the reader of the artifice of the text, often breaks his own illusions. For example, the attention-getting rhymes on abbreviations force the reader to see the text as text. Or, Pope may wrench our attention away from the action—the triumph of Vice, for example—to remind the reader of the physical reality of the text and of his own controlling artistic consciousness: "Yet may this Verse (if such a Verse remain) / Show there was one who held it in Disdain." Whenever Pope startles us out of his own illusions, whenever he works only "partial magic," he asks us to readjust our responses as readers. To forget the artifice for the illusion, to mistake the mirror for the reality, is to be deceived.

IV

By the time Pope concluded the *Epilogue* with the facetious suggestion that he "write more *Essays on Man*," he presumably viewed that earlier poem from a different perspective. The later imitative poems, generally, evoke a world in which perspective shifts inevitably, which cannot be understood from a single perspective. Pope reminds the reader of his dual roles as reflector and creator. Just as often, he reminds the reader of the roles spectators and responders can play. The reader looks in vain for a single vantage point that will control and focus his experience of the poem, but light is not reflected simply in this world and every perspective proves incomplete. Instead, we are forced to accept surroundings that can "dupe and play the wag" with the understanding. Appropriately, a questioning atmosphere pervades these poems. Pope asks thirteen questions in Dialogue 1 alone.

Pope cites dozens of different points of view on his satire during the *Imitations* as a group. Their sources include Fortescue, Paxton, the Town, the Court, P., Fr., Walpole, Swift, Peter, Bolingbroke, Judges, Whigs, Tories, the King, Shylock and his wife, Directors, Peers, patriots, pamphleteers, fools, friends, and foes. These are quoted, remembered, anticipated, alluded to. The responses of Pope's readers are part of the poem that the reader responds to. Pope's view of himself as a "bundle of incongruities" is matched by the incongruous opinions of him (they are all inadequate) held by others.

The most sustained play with shifting perspective is acted out dramatically in the dialogues of *To Fortescue* and the *Epilogue*. Pope begins *Fortescue* with a perspective on his own work that differs from his own: "There are (I scarce can think it but am told) / There are to whom my Satire seems too bold." This view comes from a vaguely identified public who doesn't understand or approve of satire. The perspective of this faceless conglomerate is contradictory, although it is consistently wrong. Some say his lines are "much too rough," but "another's pleas'd to say" they are too "weak." In this state of feigned confusion, P. turns to "Council learned in the Law" for clarification. One of the ironies of the poem is that the law proves to be equally liable to differing perspectives, equally subjective, for, as Fortescue admits, "Laws are explain'd by Men—so have a Care" (144). P. and F. alternate points of view and cite others' points of view, until P. exclaims that no one can see him rightly: "Verse-Man or Prose-man, term me what you will, / Papist or Protestant, or both between, / . . . Tories call me Whig, and Whigs a Tory" (64–68); "The world may murmur, or commend." The imagery of the rather wistful comparison to Montaigne ("I love to pour out all myself, as plain / . . . as old Montagne") recalls the ideal of the clear glass, the transparent window in the bosom: Montaigne, a luckier man, may be viewed from a simple perspective about which there is no disagreement. He is "as certain to be lov'd as seen."

To Fortescue, however, offers little hope for the fulfillment of Pope's wish to be, like Montaigne, simply seen and loved. The process of reading the poem, to the contrary, is one of perceptual uncertainty. Analyses of it frequently contend with its subjectivism, with Pope's reliance on feeling as a basis of judgment. A position of absolute moral authority, an external structure of value, an ultimate perspective seems to be missing from the poem. The satirist's motive—"The Strong antipathy of Good to Bad," Pope would later describe it—is affective rather than effective; his perspective on the world, filtered through feeling, must be individualistic and not authoritarian. The 'romanticism' of Pope's Horace and the epistemological question of perspective become interrelated.

Shifting perspective also prevents closure in *To Fortescue*. In the concluding lines, Fortescue has completely, almost too casually, changed his point of view about P.'s future as a satirist. He also has the last words of response to Pope's initial questions: should he write satire or not? Should satire be general or specific? Does satire disturb or entertain? Fortescue, with a subtle but important departure from Horace, replies:

> The case is alter'd—you may then proceed.
> In such a Cause the Plaintiff will be hiss'd,
> My Lords the Judges laugh, and you're dismiss'd.
>
> (154–56)

Like Chapman's "couzening Picture," these lines read two ways. One possible reading is that Pope's cause will be dismissed because his satire will be recognized as virtuous. But the sound of dismissive laughter at the end reminds us that Pope has not successfully pleaded his cause before "my Lords the Judges," that he is untried and unheard by them. The ambiguity of the central phrase of the final sentence leaves the end open. The hissing is clearly directed at the Plaintiff, the dismissal clearly pertains to the defendant, but the laughter with which the judges distance themselves from and disregard the matter pertains equally to both. It is difficult to think of Pope seriously maintaining his high heroic stance in a courtroom filled by a hissing mob and laughing magistrates. The dialogue form reinforces the sense of unfinished business and varied perspective. The reader drops into an ongoing conversation that breaks off before it has quite finished. The poem stops while Pope has not yet completed the sentence that Fortescue interrupts. One has the dramatic sense that more follows, that the matter is not settled.

Even more disturbing to P. (in *To Fortescue* and the *Epilogue*) than incorrect responses to the reflection of Pope in his past publications are incorrect responses to the work in progress, to its immediate artistic and moral intention. The *Epilogue* grows increasingly exasperated and preoccupied with the poet's inability to control the perspective of his readers; it urges the reader to be aware of the limitations of his point of view. In Dialogue 1 Fr. has a very skewed notion of Pope as an imitator of Horace. He has grown "correct that once with rapture writ." "Decay of parts, alas!" sighs Fr. By making the character of Fr. specifically into the character of a sample reader, Pope demonstrates how thoroughly different is Fr.'s understanding of both Pope and Horace. Horace, from this skewed point of view, is prolific, witty, creative, delicate, sly, insinuating, "a kind of screen"; Pope is meager, stiffly moral, unoriginal, violent, heavy-handed, an exposing "Glass." Faced with his adversary's misperception of himself and of satire in general, Pope attempts to dislocate this point of view. Instead of debating subtle points of satiric strategy, P. makes a wild swing of perspective: "So—Satire is no more"; it dies and disappears. But P. finds that Fr. idealizes a state of total unresponsiveness (93–104) where all is "silent and soft," "lull'd," "where no Passion, Pride, or Shame transport." It is a condition of stupor and death: "All tears are wip'd forever from all Eyes; / No Cheek is known to blush, no Heart to throb." To counteract and correct this view, P. takes drastic measures. In the second half of the poem, P. inverts the normal ways of looking at vice and virtue: "Virtue, I grant you, is an empty Boast; / But shall the Dignity of Vice be lost?" The long passage describing the triumph of Vice is passionately, angrily designed to startle us, even as it tempts us to enjoy it. The reader sees words associated on the page in a manner to which he is not accustomed: "The Wit of Cheats, the Courage of a Whore"; "Not to be corrupted is the Shame."

The reader never knows, in Dialogue 1, if P. has succeeded in changing Fr.'s perspective on Pope, Horace, and satire. The strategy is daring—to view Vice in the heroic mode and thereby force the viewer to reconsider. But the reader never hears Fr.'s response. P. breaks off at the end with a frustrated withdrawal into his own point of view: "there was one who held it in disdain."

In Dialogue 2, P. resumes his efforts to make Fr. see things his way. As these efforts collapse, P. grows more desperate. First, he sarcastically assumes Fr.'s point of view: "Come then, I'll comply—/ Spirit of Arnall, aid me while I lye." But his attempt to show Fr. a mirror of himself evokes only "Hold Sir!" At this point, P. resorts to the "filthy Simile" of the hogs "in Huts of Westphaly" (172–80). He prolongs a nearly intolerable excremental vision until Fr. cries out, "This filthy simile, this beastly Line, / Quite turns my Stomach." When all intellectual and moral argument fails, in other words, P. elicits a 'gut reaction' that, for the first and only time, is the appropriate response to a passage of Pope's poetry.

The self-reflective irony of the *Imitations* brings a quixotic quality to the end of Pope's career. In these poems, an older writer begins to meet himself—and mistaken notions of himself—in his own work. After years of debating about satire and his own society, Pope writes poems in which a poet and a friend debate about his satire and society. Both fictive characters have read his former work. Both are projections of him who pass judgment on him, and are themselves judged. Fr. blithely misunderstands and misinterprets; P. complains that he must write or perish. In a sense, *To Fortescue* and the *Epilogue* are about writing and reading. Borges said of *Don Quixote*: "[I]f the characters of a fictional work can be readers or spectators, we, its readers or spectators, can be fictitious." Borges probably carries the matter too far for Pope. Yet the late poems implicate the reader in the multiple uncertainties of experience.

The ambiguity of mirrors and perspective could have no resolution. These metaphors serve to confirm a reality outside the self, of which there is only limited, faulty perception. As symbols of entrapment, the metaphors have appealed to many besides Pope. One thinks, for example, of Alice's adventures through the looking-glass (mirror) and in Wonderland (perspective). These worlds distort rational principles; they insist upon two realities. In them, to be confined to a single point of view is one trap, yet to step outside that point of view is another:

> "But I don't want to go among mad people," Alice remarked. "Oh, you can't help that," said the Cat: "we're all mad here. I'm mad. You're mad." "How do you know that I'm mad?" said Alice. "You must be," said the Cat, "or you wouldn't have come here."

Pope's "impartial Glass," in all four applications of the metaphor, "sums up all our epistemological terrors," even as it is a means for seeing him and the self more clearly.

ROBERT GRIFFIN

Pope, the Prophets, and The Dunciad

"*I really wish myself something more, that is, a Prophet.*"
—POPE in a letter to Edward Blount, 3 October 1721

"*When the enemy shall come in like a flood, the Spirit of the
Lord shall lift up a standard against him.*"
—Isa. 59:19

The inseparability of classical and Christian elements in Pope's poetry is so obvious that it would seem to require no further comment. Yet, with few exceptions, Pope scholarship has focused almost exclusively on the classical heritage and, taking Pope's Christianity as a given, has overlooked the significance of biblical influence on his poetry. In particular, the number and range of allusions to the Old Testament in *The Dunciad* has, I believe, been seriously underestimated by its critics. Hence there is an entire dimension of meaning to the poem which has been recognized only intermittently. The argument which follows hopes to reorient our sense of Pope by attempting to revivify the force of only some of the prophetic allusions in *The Dunciad* and, therefore, hopes to restore the Bible as a significant context of allusion for Pope's poetry.

No reading of *The Dunciad* can proceed without reference to Aubrey Williams's early book on the poem. Williams identified several layers to the "action" which brings the Smithfield Muses to Court. There is the parody of the Lord Mayor's Day procession, the parody of Aeneas bringing his household gods to Latium, the parody of the *translatio studii*, and the parody of the return-of-the-Golden-Age motif which appeared in the contemporary verses of flatterers of the King. There is also what Williams identified as the "anagogic" sense of the poem, or its theological significance. On that level, Dulness, as nonbeing, is presented as a blasphemous, satanic version of the Christian God. The network of prophetic allusions discoverable in the poem essentially reinforces the theological significance articulated by Williams, while it offers yet another level of meaning created by Pope's art. On that level the duces are presented in Old Testament terms as either rebellious Israelites who have forgotten their Lord, or as false prophets who, without vocations, prostitute the Word.

The general approach to the poem I am advocating is one already widely accepted, but, as it has been the object of recent criticism, it requires a few words of defense. Donald T. Siebert has argued that Williams's view of *The Dunciad* (along with that of such distinguished critics as Battestin, Brower, Fussell, Price, Sutherland, and Spacks, among others) leads us into "too solemn a reading of the poem." Williams's book, in Siebert's view, "gives authority to the opinion that the duces are truly evil and threatening," whereas Siebert, not denying "the theological metaphor associating the duces with the forces of darkness," claims that Pope's vision is "essentially comic, not tragic," and that "the consistent attitude of Pope towards the duces is one of laughter." The value of Siebert's article is in reminding readers of the lighter side of Pope's irony. However, the conclusion that laughter precludes seriousness seems to me untenable. Irony and serious vision are not by necessity mutually exclusive. There is no compelling reason to choose between comic "dunciad" and tragic "jeremiad" ("the two impulses obviously do not harmonize") when it is precisely the presence of irony which allows for their fusion. Maynard Mack, for one, recognized this possibility when, in a discussion of the complexities of the mock-epic vehicle of *The Dunciad*, he observed "the tension between all these creatures as comic and ridiculous, and their destructive potentiality in being so." Furthermore, the representation of Cibber as an evil man is quite explicit in the section, *"Richard Aristarchus of the Hero of the Poem,"* which, for all its being a takeoff on Bentley's style, juxtaposes in a straightforward manner the qualities of *"Wisdom, Bravery,* and *Love"* requisite in the hero of the *"Greater Epic"* with the qualities of *"Vanity, Impudence,* and *Debauchery"* required in the hero of its opposite, the *"little Epic"* or *"Satyric Tragedy."* Illustrations of Cibber's preeminent qualifications for the latter role are drawn from his own self-characterizations.

Turning for a moment to the poem, the Argument of Book III is a good example of the way mock-epic irony is compatible with the moral indignation of the prophets. In an ironic typology, "A Scene, of which the present Action of the Dunciad is but a Type or Foretaste," Cibber is cast in a role which conflates Aeneas in Hades, Adam's vision in *Paradise Lost* XI (itself adapted by Milton from Ezekiel), and Moses on Mt. Pisgah. In the underworld Cibber is taken to a "Mount of Vision," from which he will view the past and present of Dulness's Empire, and will be given a "glimpse, or Pisgah-sight of the future Fulness of her Glory, the accomplishment whereof is the subject of the fourth and last book." Rome's future greatness and the growth of its civilization as foreseen by Aeneas, the New Jerusalem as seen by Ezekiel when he is taken up into the visions of God and set upon "a very high mountain" (Ezek. 40:2), the future glory of Israel as seen by Moses, and Adam's vision of history finally redeemed by the Son, are all conflated and subjected to the ironic inversions of a mock-epic in which Cibber, as "Bedlam's Prophet" (Book III.6), foresees the triumph of Dulness. The Argument thus sets up this mock-epic structure as an explicit context for Books III and IV. Given this structure, the vision of future glory and salvation, in being subjected to irony, results in a prediction of future shame and damnation. The ironic inversions of mock-epic are, therefore, actually parallel to the other half of the prophet's vision, the denunciation of evil through the vision of its destruction. By means of allusion, Cibber is set ironically against true prophecy, and is therefore seen within the evoked context of Scripture as a false prophet and usurper of the Word. Through irony Pope can make a joke of Cibber, and yet, without explicitly placing himself in the role of true prophet and poet, can draw upon all of the force of righteous scorn for evil available in his tradition. What transpires in *The Dunciad*, therefore, lends itself to interpretation in terms of the vision in the prophetic song Moses gave to his people *before* ascending Pisgah. Knowing he was to die, Moses depicted a grim future for the Israelites should they forget the Lord, giving them the song as a warning, saying: "For I know that after my death ye will utterly corrupt yourselves" (Deut. 31:29).

The general connection between satire and the prophets' denunciation of evil has not gone unnoticed. With Pope's late poetry in view, however, the affinity between satirist and prophet needs to be stressed. To clarify, the root meaning of prophecy is "speaking forth," or a speaking out of one's mind under the pressure of moral vision. In its biblical sense, prophecy does not primarily mean "clairvoyance," although clear-sightedness into the causes of unwitting destruction abounds in the prophetic books. Essentially, prophecy recalls the past, or depicts a future, as either warning or consolation to the present, for its primary concern is direct moral reformation. The prophetic books of the Bible thus evidence two alternating visions: the vision of an ideal, a New Jerusalem projected into the future; and the vision which responds to the reality of corruption by foretelling widespread destruction, from which only a few, a saving remnant, will survive. Scholars such as Battestin and Paulson have discussed the arc of Pope's career in terms of the ideal of a Golden Age. Paulson, in particular, anticipates my point by identifying a "Pollio" and an "anti-Pollio" vision, drawing his terms from the Virgilian half of *Messiah*. But if, recalling Isaiah as the other half of that early poem, we transpose this structure into a biblical key, then *The Dunciad*, as anti-Pollio nightmare, is seen as presenting a parallel to the prophets' negative vision.

    Messiah (1712) reminds us that the prophetic books were a constitutive factor in Pope's verse from an early date. In the Advertisement to that poem we learn of Pope's intention to annotate the poem "since it was written with this particular view, that the reader by comparing the several thoughts might see how far the images and descriptions of the Prophet are superior to those of the Poet." Naturally, *Messiah* offers excellent examples of the way Pope fused classical and biblical elements. Lines 81 and 82, for example, describe how, with the return of the Golden Age, "The smiling Infant in his Hand shall take / The crested Basilisk and speckled snake." Pope's footnote cites Isaiah 11:8: "And the sucking child shall play on the hole of the asp, and the weaned child shall put his hand on the cockatrice' den." Pope's image, obviously, is not identical to Isaiah's, nor is there an analogue in Virgil's eclogue. It evokes, for me at least, the baby Hercules holding a strangled snake in either hand, the same image, in fact, Milton had used to portray his Infant at the close of the Nativity Ode. Pope appears to be conflating a classical image of strength and courage with an image of strength of a different order, the Messiah who renders evil harmless. With Milton's procedures in mind, the classical element is transformed as it is subordinated and assimilated to religious ideals.

    Messiah therefore conflates Virgil's Fourth Eclogue and Isaiah in the humanist mode, subsuming pagan poetry in terms of revelation. *The Dunciad*, though, involves a more complicated fusion of figures and moral principles drawn from biblical writings with satiric forms based on the inversion of epic models. The components of meaning in this fusion can be briefly identified with reference to Horace and Isaiah. The fundamental procedure of *The Dunciad*, Williams has said, is "the use of artistic deterioration as the metaphor by which bigger deteriorations are revealed." The breach of artistic decorum censured in the famous opening lines of *Ars Poetica* results from a violation of Nature. If we saw a painting, Horace conjectures, joining a human head with a horse's neck and feathered limbs, we would laugh and consider it the empty dream of a feverish man. Pope describes a similar artistic confusion in Book I when he portrays Dulness peering into a Chaos where "Realms shift their place, and Ocean turns to land" (line 72), going on to describe scenes which incongruously mix places and seasons. In Book III, the biblical context to such confusion is added when Cibber, on the Mount of Vision, foresees a new world emerging from "one wide conflagration":

> Thence a new world to Nature's law unknown,
> Breaks out refulgent, with a heav'n all its own.
>
> (lines 241–42)

This, of course, alludes ironically to Isaiah 65:17: "For, behold, I create new heavens and a new earth: and the former shall not be remembered, nor come into mind." But, in this new and better creation of Dulness,

> The forests dance, the rivers upwards rise,
> Whales sport in woods, and dolphins in the skies.
>
> (lines 245–46)

If the aesthetic judgment of Horace controls our reading of these passages, the moral judgment of Isaiah supplies its complement:

> Surely your turning of things upside down shall be esteemed as the potter's clay: for shall the work say of him that made it, He made me not? or shall the thing framed say of him that framed it, He had no understanding? Is it not yet a very little while, and Lebanon shall be turned into a fruitful field, and the fruitful field be esteemed as a forest?
>
> (Isa. 29:16f.)

The artistic confusion that Horace cautions against has, thus, its counterpart in the moral confusion of the atheistic solipsism Isaiah denounces. In fusing the two, Pope measures beauty and truth by a single standard. When beauty is inverted, the result is grotesque. When truth is inverted, the result is demonic. I must therefore repeat what so many of *The Dunciad*'s critics have long known: bad art, for Pope, implies a moral failure, which begins in the arrogance of presuming a function beyond one's abilities. Dulness, we recall, is only ridiculed "when he sets up for a Wit." Pope's own wit, directed at the dunces, supplies the comedy of the poem, but that wit is fueled by moral indignation.

The biblical context is present in key incidents throughout the poem. Tuvia Block, for instance, established the connection between the altar sacrifice in Book I and Elijah's altar in I Kings 18:24f. Both altars are composed of twelve units, stones in one case and volumes in the other. But, whereas the Lord consumes Elijah's sacrifice as a sign to the priests of Baal (whose God, Elijah taunts, must be sleeping), Dulness, alarmed by the light given off by the blaze, rushes to rescue the worthless books by putting out the fire. Part of the significance of the allusion to Elijah is spelled out when, in lines 185–86, Dunce Cibber states:

> Me Emptiness, and Dulness could inspire,
> And were my Elasticity, and Fire.

Cibber apes Elijah, but the meaning we infer is not simply a function of the irony of mock-epic. The Bible provides models for true prophets and false, so that, in portraying Cibber as the opposite of Elijah, Pope locates him among the worshippers of Baal.

In Book II, the celebration of the Lord Mayor's Day, which includes diving into the sewage of Fleet-ditch, is, of course, set against the epic games tableaux in Homer and Virgil. Emrys Jones has judged the playful tone of these festivities to be at odds with the sublime ending of Book IV, reviving Ian Jack's criticism of the poem's unity. The serious undercurrent of Book II, however, is probably drawn from several passages in the prophets which refer to dung, the most apt being Mal. 2:3: "Behold, I will corrupt your seed, and spread dung upon your faces, even the dung of your solemn feasts; and one shall take you away with it." If I am correct, the dunces' activities can be interpreted both in terms of the mock-epic inversion of contests for honor, and in terms of the imagery by which the prophets decried the pollution of evil. The image of a dirty flood, we recall, occurs in the *Epistle to Bathurst*, "Corruption, like a gen'ral flood" (line 135). And, in a letter of 1723, Pope refers to the "Generation who are doomed to be swallowd up and drownd in their own Dulness and Dirtiness." This figurative turn on the Flood has several parallels in the prophetic books, one of which I have used as an epigraph. The flood has become here not simply the destructive agent of the Lord's wrath, but a symptom of the problem. A further example, though slightly different, can be adduced: "But the wicked are like the troubled sea, when it cannot rest, whose waters cast up mire and dirt" (Isa. 57:20). Once again, the ridicule that results from comparing the dunces to Greek and Roman heroes is reinforced and given, though in subtle ways, more ominous nuances of meaning through biblical images.

Once Cibber is compared to Elijah, and then dubbed "Bedlam's Prophet" and set upon a visionary mountain, it is not surprising to find the figures of harlot and wizard in Book IV. Aside from Hosea, the *locus classicus* for the figure of Jerusalem, or the daughter of Zion, as a bride who becomes an adulterous wife, is probably Ezek. 16, where it is developed extensively. There we read that Jerusalem was of humble birth, was cast out into a field and pitied by none. The Lord took her up, and gave her life. In return, as she waxed great, she grew proud in her jewels and costly raiment, and forgot the source of her greatness. So she committed abominations with the gods of the Assyrians, the Babylonians, and the Egyptians. And, having "played the harlot," the Lord will return her to humility. Isaiah, similarly, describes the daughters of Zion who "are haughty, and walk with stretched forth necks and wanton eyes, walking and *mincing* as they go, and make a tinkling with their feet" (Isa. 3:16, my emphasis). I suggest that Pope had these passages, or similar ones, in mind when he thought to portray the Italian opera in Book IV:45f.:

> When lo! a Harlot form soft sliding by,
> With mincing step, small voice, and languid eye;
> Foreign her air, her robe's discordant pride.

The word "mincing" suggests a direct echoing of Isaiah. Other similar elements are the haughtiness and the focus on the eyes. Mock-epic generally juxtaposes two contexts, an ancient paradigm and a modern reality. In this case, the modern opera and a biblical text are joined by describing the gait used in the opera by means of details drawn from the prophet's portrayal of the degenerate daughters of Zion. Aesthetic and moral are fused here by presenting Opera in terms of unfaithful "wives" taking up strange gods. Moreover, Pope seems to suggest that Opera herself is a false god, whose appearance mirrors the cultural, and implicitly moral, degeneration of her admirers.

The prophets thought worshipping false gods a peculiarly duncelike activity. Isaiah asks us to consider a man who cuts down a cedar, a cypress, or an oak; perhaps one he had planted himself and the rain had watered. He burns the wood to roast his food, and "the residue thereof he maketh a god . . . he falleth down unto it, and worshippeth it, and prayeth unto it, and saith, Deliver me; for thou art my god. . . . And none considereth in his heart, neither is there knowledge nor understanding to say, I have burned part of it in the fire; . . . shall I fall down to the stock of a tree? (Isa. 44:14f.; cf. Jer. 2:26). Furthermore, the degradation of human values involved in this duncelike forgetting of the Lord includes the perversion of justice, the seeking after lucre and the taking of bribes (cf. 1 Sam. 8:3), the oppression of the stranger and the fatherless, and the shedding of blood (cf. Jer. 7:6). The leaders of society are particularly at fault, and are often figured as shepherds who fatten themselves on their flocks (e.g., Ezek. 34). Also at fault are the false prophets whose divinations flatter their patrons, and the sorcerers who seduce the people into abandoning the true God.

By bringing "The Festival of the Golden Rump" to light, Maynard Mack has demonstrated how virtually any reference to sorcery or wizardry may involve Robert Walpole. In that print Walpole wears a robe embroidered with dragons (cf. Jer. 9:11: "And I will make Jerusalem heaps, and a den of dragons"). The explanation of that print as it appeared in *Common Sense*, 19 March 1738, identifies the Walpole-figure as the Pharaoh's Chief Magician, the power of whose wand can be overcome only by Aaron's rod. It is thus relevant to note in passing that Pope was not alone in presenting a view of the contemporary scene through the satiric use of biblical imagery. Note further that Isaiah speaks disparagingly of the "wizards that peep and mutter" (Isa. 8:19), and that, in Rev. 21:8, sorcerers are consigned to the burning lake. *Dunciad* IV. 517–19, reads:

> With that, a Wizard old his *Cup* extends;
> Which whoso tastes, forgets his former friends,
> Sire, Ancestors, Himself.

One thinks of Circe, and perhaps also of the wizard son Milton had attributed to her, Comus. Yet one also thinks of the cup of the Whore of Babylon, the figure Pope had used to personify Vice at the close of his *Epilogue to the Satires, Dialogue I*. The relevant passages from Scripture are as follows: "Babylon hath been a golden cup in the Lord's hand, that made all the earth drunken: the nations have drunken of her wine; therefore the nations are mad" (Jer. 51:7); "And there followed another angel saying, Babylon is fallen, is fallen, that great city, because she made all nations drink of the wine of the wrath of her fornication" (Rev. 14:8); "And the woman was arrayed in purple and scarlet colour, and decked with gold and precious stones and pearls, having a golden cup in her hand" (Rev. 17:4). Here there is no ironic inversion of epic material. Walpole as Wizard-Circe-Whore of Babylon proffering a cup of nepenthe-wine of Babylon is simply a powerfully compressed image of evil as beast-like unconsciousness.

Towards the end of the poem, in lines 606–26, Dulness yawns the yawn whose effects permeate the entire society from the churches and the schools to the armies, navies, and houses of government. Pope's footnote to this section suggests the mock-epic once again: "This verse is truly Homerical; as is the conclusion of the Action, where the Great Mother composes all, in the same manner as Minerva at the period of the Odyssey." But there is also a biblical passage, part of the continuation of the prophecy against

Babylon in Jeremiah, which mirrors Pope's action: "And I will make drunk her princes, and her wise men, her captains, and her rulers, and her mighty men; and they shall sleep a perpetual sleep, and not wake, saith the King, whose name is the Lord of hosts" (Jer. 51:57). Or one may cite Isa. 29:10: "For the Lord hath poured out upon you the spirit of deep sleep, and hath closed your eyes." The prophets accuse the ruling powers of their nation for relaxing their moral vigilance, and for ignoring the warnings of their watchmen. Their slothful sleep will lead to the nation's destruction. So too, Pope's wizard extends his cup, the moral judgment of the rulers of England is put to sleep, and primordial Darkness returns.

The ending of *The Dunciad* is often read as a simple inversion of the *fiat lux* of Genesis. Battestin, for example, observes that Pope replaces the *fiat lux* with a *fiat nox*. There are many examples in the Bible, however, of visions of impending darkness which have nothing to do with irony. In his footnote to line 85 of *Messiah* Pope cites a chapter of Isaiah, part of which reads: "For, behold, the darkness shall cover the earth, and gross darkness the people" (Isa. 60:2). There are other examples: "and if one look unto the land, behold darkness and sorrow, and the light is darkened in the heavens thereof" (Isa. 5:30); "For the stars of heaven and the constellations thereof shall not give light: the sun shall be darkened in his going forth, and the moon shall not cause her light to shine" (Isa. 13:10); "That day is a day of wrath, a day of trouble and distress, a day of wasteness and desolation, a day of darkness and gloominess, a day of clouds and thick darkness" (Zeph. 1:15).

The figure of darkness serves a dual purpose. It describes, appropriately enough, the wickedness of those who have turned away from the Lord, and it is simultaneously the sign that, since man has broken the covenant with God, God is released from the original promise he made to Noah whose signature was the rainbow (Gen. 9:8f.). In fact, in an allusion to that covenant (noticed by both Siebert and Knuth), Pope typically conflates Jove's rainbow and Jehovah's in Book II.173–74:

> So Jove's bright bow displays its wat'ry round,
> (Sure sign, that no spectator shall be drown'd).

Typically also for this poem, the biblical reference is elided, while Pope's footnote refers to the *Iliad* and Dacier's translation. This is understandable since the rainbow is caused in this instance by an arc of urine. Responding to the biblical allusion, Siebert argues that "it seems something of an overreaction to regard them [i.e. the dunces] as a threat to the divine plan" since their efforts anyway are "always self-defeating." Yet a reading of the prophets makes clear that the "divine plan" includes both destruction and renewal. And secondly, is it not possible that Pope thought it was precisely the ineffectuality of growing numbers of dunces which was undermining his conception of civilization?

In any case, the usual pattern of prophecy, as I have mentioned, is that the righteous will be spared destruction, and with them, the saving remnant, the Lord will renew his covenant. The instrument of destruction, often figured as fire or flood, is also figured, as I have indicated by the quotations above, in terms of the negation of the light that was created in Genesis. The explicit allusion to Genesis, which can be taken as the paradigm for the numerous evocations of darkness in the prophetic books, is made in Jer. 4:23: "I beheld the earth, and, lo, it was without form, and void; and the heavens, and they had no light." Consider, then, the often-quoted closing lines of *The Dunciad* once more:

> Lo! thy dread Empire, CHAOS! is restor'd;
> Light dies before thy uncreating word:
> Thy hand, great Anarch! lets the curtain fall;
> And Universal Darkness buries All.

To read this as a *fiat nox* is certainly not wrong. The "restoration" of Chaos is an inversion of both Genesis and Hesiod's Theogony, and recalls, as Williams suggested, Satan's extension of Chaos's realm in *Paradise Lost.* Dulness's "uncreating word," moreover, parodies the Word at the opening of the Gospel of St. John, while the theatrical metaphor tempers the final line by hinting that Dulness produces bad theater. Yet Jeremiah's un-ironic vision cannot be discounted as either irrelevant or out of place. On that level an empire of Dulness is not simply a sign of impending doom, but is also the instrument of destruction. The prophet sees that evil causes its own destruction, a sequence which he reads in terms of God, looking upon his creation and finding it no longer good, revoking the light that He had created. Darkness is caused by the dunces, and darkness is sent to them as a scourge. Pope integrates both of these prophetic insights and masks the serious vision with the lighter touch of mock-epic comedy. The comic aspect implies the prophet's vision of renewal and his faith in an ultimate victory. Ironic inversion and serious vision are inseparably fused.

In conclusion, it may be appropriate to remember that Pope lived in a country and in an age in which contemporary poetry had power enough to alter men's thinking. As with Dryden's *Absalom and Achitophel*, political events could be portrayed persuasively through the use of biblical typology. Pope's own question, "Who counsels best?", has been used to describe the collective impulse behind his late satires. That question, it should be noted, is also at the heart of the prophet's sense of crisis, for the nation is "void of counsel" (Deut. 32:28). *The Dunciad* cannot be seen separately from its political context, nor from the conception of the poet as a guardian of his culture's values. There is sufficient reason to conclude that Pope's poem conceives of itself as fulfilling for its time what the Lord told of Moses' song in that time: "And it shall come to pass, when many evils and troubles are befallen them, that this poem shall testify against them as a witness" (Deut. 31:21).

DAVID B. MORRIS

Civilized Reading: The Act of Judgment in An Essay on Criticism

Men must be taught *as if you taught them* not;
And Things unknown *propos'd as Things* forgot.
—POPE

Pope's earliest didactic poem, *An Essay on Criticism*, published in 1711, extends his debt to Dryden by consolidating ideas from Dryden's scattered prefaces and essays within a unified critical theory. It is also, however, a poem which has proved so successful in disguising the unfamiliar as the forgotten that its claims to originality and importance are today automatically dismissed. De Quincey encouraged this fashion in subsequent commentators with his picturesque description of the poem in the seventh edition of the *Encyclopedia Britannica* (1842): "It is a collection of independent maxims, tied together into a fasciculus by the printer, but having no natural order or logical dependency: generally so vague as to mean nothing." For more than one hundred years docile scholars have repeated this opinion. One standard modern history of criticism summarizes Pope's poem with routine nonchalance: "There are repetitions and inconsistencies, some conventional pronouncements along with injunctions of lasting value; but nowhere (and this should be emphasized) are the principles organized into a coherent whole, and no cut-and-dried theory therefore emerges." Even readers alert to Pope's technique of inventive borrowing—the repayment of the past through the refining of what it provides—find it easy to regard the *Essay* as merely an urbane collection of platitudes: "What oft was *Thought*" (I. 298). The poem's

From *Alexander Pope: The Genius of Sense.* Copyright © 1984 by the President and Fellows of Harvard College. Harvard University Press, 1984.

ostensible subject evokes so little serious attention that it is regarded as a screen for loftier ambitions. "Pope's object in the *Essay on Criticism*," we are told, "is not to say something original about criticism, but to announce himself as a poet." Almost no one believes that the twenty-three-year-old prodigy capable of composing such a learned and skillful poem could have thought seriously or cared deeply about the nature of literary criticism. Particularly because modern studies have focused on its treatment of wit, the *Essay* is commonly discussed as a poem about poetry with an unfortunately misleading title. I wish to propose a very different view: that *An Essay on Criticism* is an original and significant contribution to the history of critical theory.

AUTHORITY AND TASTE

Some of Pope's distinguished contemporaries would seem to support the claim of originality and significance. Addison in *The Spectator* (no. 253) lauded the poem as a "Master-piece." Joseph Warton, adept in the labyrinth of ancient and modern critical tradition, ranked the youthful poet among "the first of critics." Samuel Johnson grew even warmer in his praise, calling the poem one of Pope's "greatest" works. If Pope had written nothing else, he claimed, *An Essay on Criticism* "would have placed him among the first criticks and the first poets." When we recall Johnson's stature as a critic and his contempt for versified platitudes, we might begin to suspect that Pope offered his contemporaries more than a slick cento of traditional lore. Both Johnson and Warton elevated Pope, as a critic, to the level of Horace, Longinus, and Aristotle. Their harsh treatment of other poems by Pope suggests that they had no reason to exaggerate the merits of an early work which one representative modern scholar dismisses as simply "a mosaic of scraps." Clearly they found something in the poem of great value. What they found, I believe, is a stimulating and original (if submerged) theory of literary criticism.

The theory takes some finding—for it is one of the ironies of Pope's discourse on method that it appears casually unmethodical, as if directed mainly by a loose association of ideas. "The Observations follow one another," writes Addison, "like those in *Horace's Art of Poetry*, without that Methodical Regularity which would have been requisite in a Prose Author" (*The Spectator* no. 253). The appearance of irregularity, however, is not equivalent to actual disorder—and we should recall Pope's assertion that he had "digested all the matter in prose" before composing his poem. Prosaic method and rigorous argument may simply be disguised for the purpose of instructing readers "as if you taught them *not.*" Yet, its substructure of well-grounded method is not all that the *Essay* conceals. Pope also disguises his originality, preferring the deceptive method of "anamnesis" which had been a strategy of the new science from Galileo to Newton. As an interested student of Newtonian physics, which he encountered in the popular lectures of William Whiston, Pope understood how the method of "anamnesis" avoided controversy by disguising innovative concepts in the language of traditional thought. Then, too, concealment was always Pope's favored mode of disclosure. We should not expect him to make a show of his originality. The unmethodical order of *An Essay on Criticism* imitates (as Addison noted) Horace's prestigious *Ars Poetica*, and this continuing allusion to Horace is a strategic way of transferring to criticism (which Swift depicted as a dwarfish parody of its ancient stature) the dignity and authority of a classical model. It suggested that criticism, like tragedy or epic, possessed its own poetics, and it reflected Pope's attempt to establish English criticism, as Horace had established Roman poetry and drama, on the foundations of a coherent art. The Herculean difficulty of this labor may help explain why Pope considered his *Essay* a work which "not one gentleman in three score even of a liberal education can understand." They would not understand the poem because it proposed a theory of criticism unprecedented in their experience.

The originality of Pope's *Essay*, in its mixture of tradition and innovation, becomes more apparent when we compare his theory with the established critical positions. *An Essay on Criticism* offers a clear alternative to the two main theories prominent in his early years—theories defining the extremes which Pope felt compelled to reject. Simplified, these extremes can be described by the terms *authority* and *taste*. Authority in criticism, for Pope, implied that critics maintain a reverent adherence to a set of doctrines derived from Renaissance interpretations of Aristotle and of Horace. These so-called "rules" were further incrusted with accumulations of critical dogmatism, issuing in such petrified constructions as Corneille's treatment of the three dramatic Unities. With deliberate imprecision, Pope patriotically associated the principle of authority in criticism with the political tyranny of absolutist France (II. 711–714). While France erred at the extreme of slavish authority, England, in Pope's view, failed by indulging the opposite extreme of anarchic taste. Taste as a critical position licensed more than the passing fashions in wit, such as the modish indecency and skepticism that Pope criticized in the reigns of Charles II and William III (II. 534–553). It also encouraged an idle critical dalliance with secluded "beauties" of poetry, invoked in a vague jargon of *je-ne-sais-quoi* or ecstatic cries, permitting the mystery of individual responsiveness to free a critic from accountability to any principle beyond the self-illuminated ego. This boneless criticism was a form of cant which Pope branded "the perpetual Rapture of such Commentators, who are always giving us Exclamations instead of Criticisms" (note to *Iliad* XV.890). Taste licenses a total freedom from reasons; authority shackles criticism to a set of iron rules. Pope, of course, does not take the foolish position that all insights of taste are vacuous or all rules false. (In refining the past, he did not mean to reject its strengths but only its errors.) He objects instead to accepting either authority or taste as controlling principles of criticism. It is only when wrongly hardened into principles that taste degenerates into exclamatory rapture and authority repeats the mechanical rules that Pope parodies in "A Receit to make an Epick Poem" (*The Guardian* no. 78). Although readers sometimes claim that his compromise with taste and with authority is equivocal or confused, Pope consistently adheres to the clear distinction he makes between practice and principle. In practice, critics can learn much from the personal insights of taste and from the public edicts of authority. Pope does not recommend a merely hybrid criticism, combining in the name of moderation two contradictory principles. Rather, once deprived of their status as absolute laws, authority and taste serve a changed function within Pope's theory. In effect, *An Essay on Criticism* re-employs in a changed role the concepts which it rejects as principles, subordinating them to a new theory that provides an alternative to the past. This alternative might be called the criticism of judgment.

The criticism of judgment, as an alternative to past approaches, provides both the theoretical foundations and the practical principles for a new kind of literary discourse. One might argue, of course, that references to the term "judgment" are commonplace in earlier critical writing, especially because the word "criticism" derives from the Greek *krinein*, "to judge." Certainly Dryden (the most distinguished English critic before Pope) liberally sprinkles his prefaces and essays with references to judgment, which for him embraces at least three distinct but overlapping senses. In Dryden's usage, the main technical senses of *judgment* appropriate to neoclassical criticism are: (1) the mental faculty which discerns differences, controls the operations of wit, and comprehends the elements of poetic design; (2) discretion, reasonableness, good sense; and (3) the faculty which distinguishes excellence in literary works and, hence, an opinion of the quality of any work. It is clear that Pope understands and exploits the earlier associations which link criticism with judgment, for his language, in its repetitions, gradually surrounds criticism with an idiom of judging that is not present in his other poems. *An Essay on Criticism*, for example, uses the word *judgment* thirteen times, and *reason* only four. By contrast, *An Essay on Man* uses *reason* forty-four times, and *judgment* none. Yet the traditional associations between criticism and judgment do not require Pope to use the idiom of judging traditionally. (Pope's art of refinement frequently invests familiar words such as *dullness* and *wit* with new meaning.) In reading *An Essay on Criticism*, we should understand that Pope's references to *judgment* (and to other words which share the same etymology) invoke a familiar, quasi-technical term. We should also understand, however, that *judgment* had never referred to a coherent theory. It belonged more to the casual vocabulary than to the conceptual framework of criticism. This central, conceptual, defining position is the innovative place that *judgment* occupies in Pope's *Essay*. In effect, he captures a term having traditional but casual associations with criticism and transforms it into the primary force behind an original and coherent critical theory, an alternative to the personal mysticism of taste and to the fiats of authority.

THEORETICAL FOUNDATIONS: THE SEARCH FOR UNIVERSALS

Before Pope could develop the practical principles of a criticism of judgment, he faced the task of explaining how valid judgments are *possible*. A practical criticism of judgment demands a theory capable of making clear its sources of validity. Otherwise, differing judgments about a single work (like differing tastes or conflicting rules) would be indisputable and indefensible. Thus within his first ten lines Pope confronts the fundamental dilemma that could overturn his whole enterprise:

> 'Tis with our *Judgments* as our *Watches*, none
> Go just *alike*, yet each believes his own.
> (II. 9–10)

This basic human fact, the inconsistency and fallibility of our understandings, might suggest that judgment is wholly relative and impossible to verify. A second observation, applying specifically to critics, compounds the problem of validity:

> *Authors* are partial to their *Wit*, 'tis true,
> But are not *Criticks* to their *Judgment* too?
> (II. 17–18)

The self-love which inclines all people to trust their own judgments is especially well developed among critics, for whom the exercise of judgment is a characteristic function. These inherent flaws or weaknesses in judgment would seem enough to stop Pope cold. The case *against* judgment could hardly be stronger. The cogency of Pope's fundamental questions about the validity of judgment is what creates his agenda for the entire first section of the poem. (The three sections—indicated by blank spaces in the text—I will call "parts.") With allowance for its tangential pursuits, part I of *An Essay on Criticism* may be read as an extended, theoretical defense of the very possibility of valid judgment.

For Pope, valid judgment depends not on repairing the inherent weaknesses of human understanding but on defining fixed, theoretical standards outside the individual that allow us to reason accurately about literature. The weakness and variance of human understanding are facts which, as Locke argued persuasively, do not necessarily preclude the possibility of knowledge. Although individual judgments are likely to differ, the existence of fixed, theoretical standards establishes a norm against which personal variance can be measured and corrected. For example, the minor differences from clock to clock do not preclude the possibility of accurate timekeeping. In Pope's day, the newfangled pocketwatches which adorned the gentry could be corrected against the tolling church bells, just as a century later official clocks could be regulated by the standard of Greenwich time. The possibility of correct time is thus established by the existence of a fixed standard outside the individual, so that we accept minor variations as inevitable and inconsequential. If your watch says ten and mine twelve, we can resolve our dispute by appealing to the outside standard which creates the possibility that one of us is correct. Pope's attitude toward judgment is implicit in the simile of clockwork which he introduces. Minor variances prove acceptable and major differences can be adjudicated once criticism has established the possibility of valid judgment by articulating the fixed theoretical standards that govern literary analysis.

Pope's description of the unshakable standards governing literary criticism occupy two parallel passages which mark the rhetorical peaks of part I. Symmetrically placed and stylistically linked, the passages are far more than fragments of practical advice, which is how they are usually construed. Their task, rather, is to define the norms or standards which make valid judgment possible. Pope's initial standard of validity in criticism is an unsurprising choice:

> First follow NATURE, and your Judgment frame
> By her just Standard, which is still the same:
> *Unerring Nature*, still divinely bright,
> One *clear, unchang'd*, and *Universal* Light,

> Life, Force, and Beauty, must to all impart,
> At once the *Source*, and *End*, and *Test* of *Art*.
>
>   (II. 68–73)

Almost a set piece, the passage is so familiar that readers easily ignore its specific purpose in the *Essay*. Thus, we must remind ourselves that Pope's subject is not the praise of nature but how to "frame" one's judgment. (*To frame:* "To regulate; to adjust," Johnson's *Dictionary*.) Nature is praised specifically because it provides a "just" and changeless "Standard" for ensuring that an individual's judgment can be accurate. The somewhat general or abstract language of Pope's description, for which he is sometimes censured, is perfectly suited to this articulation of a theoretical norm. The fixity and universality of nature provide an indispensable criterion of measurement: all practical exercises of individual judgment derive their validity from its presence and power. Nor does nature's power as a "just" standard derive merely from human choice or arbitrary convention, like Greenwich time or the metric system. As Pope's dominant metaphor implies, the theoretical standard which nature provides for criticism is "just" because its potency, like the sun's, belongs to the inherent order of the world. It is "divinely" ordained.

The second theoretical standard validating the possibility of individual judgment shifts the locus of permanence from nature to art. Here Pope justifies, on theoretical grounds, the commerce with the past that is a continuing resource for his work. Art offers its more limited permanence in the figure of the ancients, an informal designation which for Pope evokes the entire classical tradition from Homer to the Latin poets of the Silver Age. Like his earlier praise of nature, Pope's celebration of the ancients is so familiar—the subject so traditional—that readers often fail to notice its specific function within the *Essay*. The purpose is not merely to praise the virtue of past writers but, as befits a poem about criticism, to advise critics how to "steer," or direct, or regulate their literary judgment:

> *You* then whose Judgment the right Course wou'd steer,
> Know well each Ancient's proper *Character*,
> His *Fable, Subject, Scope* in ev'ry Page,
> *Religion, Country, Genius* of his *Age:*
> Without all these at once before your Eyes,
> *Cavil* you may, but never *Criticize*.
>
>   (II. 118–123)

If criticism is to become an art—not unresolvable wrangling based upon authority or taste—it requires a firm theoretical foundation, and Pope's purpose in praising the ancients is directly related to the needs of a coherent critical theory. True, other writers had advised reading the ancients, just as they had advised following nature. What matters most is not the source of Pope's ideas, since familiar ideas are always subject to refinement. What matters is the *use* Pope makes of traditional materials, which he often employs in nontraditional ways. Although clearly he did not invent the concepts of nature or the ancients, he employs them to original purpose in defining fixed, universal standards which create the possibility of valid judgment in criticism. "Before the use of the loadstone, or knowledge of the compass," wrote Dryden, reflecting upon his early efforts in criticism, "I was sailing in a vast ocean, without other help than the pole-star of the Ancients, and the rules of the French stage amongst the Moderns." Criticism, despite Dryden's strenuous practice, had not advanced in England to the status of a reliable, self-conscious art, established on firm and clear principles. It was an activity which relied more on precedent than on theory. The province mainly of idle aristocrats or professional hacks, English criticism had as yet failed to reflect upon its character as an art of knowing. In isolating nature and the classics as universal standards for validating the possibility of individual judgment, Pope offered readers something beyond Dryden's tentative explorations as a practicing critic. He offered English criticism the theoretical foundations of an authentic art. His next step, logically, was to sketch the practical principles and methods that would guide the critic's day-to-day encounter with literary texts.

JUDGMENT AS CRITICAL METHOD: THE LOGIC OF PROBABILITY

What distinguishes Pope's *Essay* from earlier English discourses on criticism is not only its attention to theory but also its concern with a specific method of reasoning. The rejection of authority and taste involves for Pope the rejection of an entire way of thinking about literature. Authority and taste deal equally in certainties: they do not invite doubt and conflict because they impose an absolute power, personal or impersonal. Pope, as we have seen, is not afraid of proclaiming certainties when he announces nature and the ancients as providing fixed theoretical standards for validating the possibility of judgment. Part I consistently treats the act of judgment within a context of universal, certain, permanent, theoretical values. In parts 2 and 3, however, Pope moves from establishing theoretical absolutes to exploring particular, variable, practical aspects of critical activity. This movement from theoretical to practical, from universal to particular, from permanent to variable is reflected in his new concern with a world of mutability and limitation. Although the theoretical standards for criticism are presented as universal and unchanging and certain, the actual texts to be judged and the daily practice of judgment belong to the fluctuating realm of time and change, where abilities differ, customs vary, creeds lapse, and languages decay. The tone of parts 2 and 3 is set decisively by the extended comparison (II. 219–232)—rare in Pope's work—which contrasts the unknown vastness of human knowledge with the frailty of our individual understandings. Expanded horizons do not so much dispel uncertainty as reveal new vistas of ignorance:

> Th' *increasing* Prospect *tires* our wandring Eyes,
> Hills peep o'er Hills, and *Alps* on *Alps* arise!
>   (II. 231–232)

Pope's disheartening image, which so deeply impressed Johnson, is especially appropriate at the beginning of part 2, where certainties are left behind. It creates an implicit contrast with the hymnlike celebration of the *"Immortal"* ancients (I. 190) that had closed part 1, leading the reader artfully from the realm of timelessness to time, from past clarity to present complexities and doubt. Pope's couplets still carry a crisply authoritative tone when defining terms or giving direct advice, but their assurance flows from observation, experience, logic, and tradition—not from indisputable authority. Even his most confident assertions are subtly modified by their placement within a context where certainty has vanished.

The disappearance of certainty—the dominant fact underlying the final two sections of the *Essay*—creates the context for Pope's association between criticism and a method of reasoning appropriate to a science of uncertainties. This is the method of probable reasoning, the method which becomes a distinguishing mark of the period. The pre-eminence which earlier ages awarded to syllogism, to paradox, and to the varieties of rhetorical persuasion yields in Pope's lifetime to a reasoning based, formally or informally, on the concept of probability. Locke in *An Essay Concerning Human Understanding* (1690) had provided a highly influential account of such probabilistic knowledge, but it was not simply the contemporary importance of probable reasoning which attracted Pope. Pope understood that the method of probable reasoning was also indistinguishable from the act of judgment which defines literary criticism. In fact, he viewed probable reasoning as fundamental not only to criticism but also to all forms of literary composition, where it finds its most prominent place in the practice of revision. Thus Pope would describe his later addition of the sylphs to *The Rape of the Lock* as "one of the greatest proofs of judgement of anything I ever did." Judgment, as an activity poets shared with critics, held great significance for Pope precisely because, unlike invention or imagination, it was not a private and unsummoned power but a human capacity which might be cultivated, improved, and refined.

The importance of probable reasoning extended far beyond the boundaries of polite letters. As a means of analysis, probabilistic thought was understood during the eighteenth century as "the most legitimate and valid method—for Locke, in fact, the only possible method—in most of the arts and sciences and in the everyday thinking of rational people." Yet, its influence upon literary criticism proved especially decisive. In 1764 the young Edward Gibbon could write: "Geometry is employed only in demonstrations peculiar to itself: criticism deliberates between the different degrees of probability." Criticism is thus characterized for Gibbon (as for more experienced critics) by its use of a particular method of reasoning, and his distinction between geometric demonstrations and degrees of probability echoes Locke's discussion. In *An Essay Concerning Human Understanding* Locke distinguishes between two fundamentally different kinds of knowledge: the "clear and certain" knowledge which he imagistically associates with the broad daylight of truth; and a lesser, uncertain, tentative kind of knowing, which he describes as "the twilight . . . of *Probability*." The twilight of probability serves as Locke's metaphor for the normal state of human intelligence, since he believed (as Pope stated in "The Design" prefixed to *An Essay on Man*) that there "are not *many certain truths* in this world." Probable reasoning, in Locke's view, is divine recompense for the absence of certainty. Limited and fallible, it nonetheless guides us through the doubtful twilight realms where demonstrations, proofs, and certainties are chimerical.

Nowhere in *An Essay on Criticism* does Pope argue explicitly that English criticism must henceforth be characterized by the method of probable reasoning. His language conveys such an argument indirectly and implicitly. The final two sections, for example, suffuse an awareness of the human limitation and temporal change that defy certainties and encourage a probabilistic spirit of inquiry. Further, Pope's practical principles of criticism require for their application a spirit and method of probable reasoning. The practicing critic, however informally, constantly assesses degrees of probability and constructs hypotheses about intention or design. But Pope's association of criticism with probabilistic reasoning needed no explicit statement because it was also implicit in his choice of terms. Locke's famous distinction between certain and probable knowledge occurs in the chapter entitled "Of Judgment." There Locke clearly states that the mental power of judgment holds full sway over the operations of probable reasoning. As he declares unequivocally, "the Faculty, which God has given Man to supply the want of clear and certain Knowledge in Cases where that cannot be had, is *Judgment*." In using *judgment* as the key term for his new theory of criticism, Pope gained more than the sum of its traditional meanings. The prestige of Locke's *Essay* had endowed *judgment* with the connotations of an entire method of thought—probabilistic reasoning—which conformed exactly with the spirit and demands of Pope's critical enterprise. Probable reasoning, whether Pope derived its tenets from Locke or from his own thought and reading, underlies his entire approach to the practice of criticism.

The strategic association between criticism and probable reasoning helps considerably to explain the extravagant praise of Pope's *Essay* by eighteenth-century critics such as Johnson, for whom (like Gibbon) the methods of probabilistic thought were inseparable from the methods of criticism. The substitution of probability for the dogmatic certainties of authority and of taste had a profoundly liberating effect. "To judge therefore of Shakespeare by Aristotle's rules," Pope wrote in the spirit of independent, probabilistic inquiry, "is like trying a man by the laws of one country who acted under those of another." The submerged legal metaphor of judging is almost always present, if faintly, in Pope's vocabulary of judgment. Its presence, whether concealed or open, suggests an additional benefit from the emphasis on probabilistic thought, for the English judicial system provides reassurance that uncertainty need not induce a skeptical indifference or relativism, as if all judgments were equally doubtful. Far from clouding critical inquiry in irresolution, probable reasoning grants to critics the same discriminating powers which characterize English law. Most important, the metaphoric equivalence of critic and judge helps to illuminate the final goal of all critical activity. For Pope, the ultimate function of criticism is evaluation. Indeed, no aspect of Pope's critical theory so clearly separates him from modern academic critics as his emphasis upon evaluation as the chief end of criticism.

For most modern critics, interpretation—not evaluation—is what commands their greatest interest. Evaluation is purposely ignored or practiced unknowingly. Often it is openly condemned, especially by science-minded writers who argue that value judgments are an impediment, an impurity, something to be removed from critical writing at all costs. Pope, like most of his contemporaries, considered interpretation the tedious business of commentary, relegated (as in his translations of Homer) to the status of notes. Criticism, as distinguished from mere commentary, rose above detailed inquiry into meaning—a drab, pedantic chore—which (he wrote) only "puzzles the text." Pope has short patience for meanings which seem so deeply hidden as to require intricate labors of excavation. "We care not to Study, or

Anatomize a Poem," he wrote, "but only to read it for our entertainment."
Yet, Pope's breezy contempt for editorial scholarship and textual commentary—even though he edited the plays of Shakespeare and wrote long com-
mentaries in his notes on Homer—not only reveals a widely-shared prejudice
but also emphasizes how essential he felt evaluation was. The worthy critic,
in Pope's view, must accept the responsibility of making evaluative judgments, even as judges do. It is no accident that the portraits of exemplary
ancient critics in *An Essay on Criticism* conclude with Longinus gowned in
legality as an "ardent *Judge*" (I. 677). As a judge, the critic necessarily
evaluates what is good and bad. Certainly English criticism had often performed this function, although not with notable understanding or distinction. (Thomas Rymer's condemnation of *Othello* as "the tragedy of a
handkerchief" is a classic instance.) Where Pope departs from his predecessors
and contemporaries is in emphasizing the responsibility of critics to seek a
method of evaluation which would make criticism less biased, less arbitrary,
less whimsical, and less wrongheaded.

Evaluation for Pope must issue from a responsible method. Thus a
crucial function of probabilistic reasoning is to impart the fairness and consistency required when the critic-judge, as a final act, delivers the "Sentence"
(I. 678) which evaluation demands. Evaluation as the final purpose of criticism gives the critic not only a personal goal but also a larger social role.
The critic's rigorous separation of good writing from bad serves the world
of letters in the same way that a wise judge serves a social community, with
the added boon that wise critics reward as well as punish. The judge is not
Pope's only image of the critic, but the implications of this role are far-
reaching, especially because judges and poets were not (as they seem now)
almost incompatible figures, who belong to separate realms. They were
instead allies in judgment:

> But how severely with themselves proceed
> The Men, who write such Verse as we can read?
> Their own *strict Judges*, not a word they spare.

The good poet internalizes the figure of the judge whom the critic outwardly
personifies. Precisely because criticism ends in decisions on value, for poets
as well as for critics, Pope must stress the methods by which just evaluations
proceed. As a native of twilight uncertainties, his ideal critic endows the
act of judgment with a spirit of deliberative reasoning, judiciously weighing
the various degrees of probability, and it is this probabilistic thinking—
with its frank evaluations of good and bad—which characterizes the best
English criticism for the rest of the century.

PRACTICAL PRINCIPLES OF JUDGMENT: PROPRIETY

The association between criticism and reasoning based on probability exerts a powerful influence not only over the general spirit of Pope's enterprise but also over the practical principles of judgment, which he sparingly defines. Despite the swirl of specific maxims, sententious learning, examples, portraits, and anecdotes that pack the last two sections of the *Essay*, Pope subsumes the entire practice of criticism under two all-embracing principles, propriety and generosity, to which almost every precept or fragmentary insight after part I pertains. Like most of the resonant concepts in *An Essay on Criticism*—nature, judgment, wit, the ancients—propriety and generosity assemble, under deceptively plain terms, a complex series of related ideas. Propriety, for example, evokes in modern usage a simple and limited notion of correctness, the counterpart of etiquette in manners. But for Pope the term had very different connotations. "There is hardly any laying down particular rules for writing in our language," he told Spence. "Even Dean Swift's, which seemed to be the best I ever heard, were three or four of them not thoroughly well considered." Propriety, for Pope, is not a set of specific rules but an abstraction filled with a constantly shifting content. Appropriateness consists solely in a flexible harmony among parts, and on differing literary occasions the content of propriety necessarily differs. The changing shapes of propriety, however, despite their variations, all share one thing. They contribute toward a goal which Pope defines as the ideal condition of every literary work. This is the state of poetic "wholeness."

Pope's idea of poetic wholeness does not imply either symmetrical form or hidden unities. Especially when compared with earlier neo-Aristotelian treatments of "the Unities" in drama and epic, his approach has a flexibility that frees criticism from narrow, rigid obsession with the details of "correct" composition, where everything is done by the rules. Poetic wholeness, for Pope, involves a harmonious relationship between the two major elements of composition, which he calls (although not with absolute consistency) conception and execution. Conception, which is close in meaning to the classical term *invention*, denotes the preliminary and essential creative work of the poet which governs the subject, form, and purposes of a text. It includes authorial intention, choice of genre, establishment of an underlying moral, disposition of the structural design, and discovery of plot, characters, argument, and incidents. Execution, on the other hand, involves the actual process of writing. It compasses the lesser details of what Pope calls "the Thoughts, the Expression, and the Numbers." The poet's movement from conception to execution is a descent from the pure ideas of poetry into the materials of language, versification, and statement. Both, of course, are crucial to a finished work. The actual history of composition may not follow a clear sequence from conception to execution, as if the poet worked from blueprints. But, as opposed to most Romantic and modern theories of composition, which imply a necessary fusion between language and thought, for Pope it is the *separability* of conception and execution that creates the precondition for unity.

For Pope, a poet's knowledge of propriety is crucial because the materials of poetry may take so many different shapes. Propriety—not an organic or linguistic determinism—is what selects the final shape that the poem will assume. Thus even a work as fragmented in its form as *The Dunciad* may, where execution and conception coincide, attain a propriety which embraces or supersedes its apparent, satirical improprieties. Despite a discontinuous or extended history of composition, despite changing plans or unplanned changes, the finished poem for Pope always reaches a state in which the harmonious relation between conception and execution creates an appropriate wholeness. Such wholeness does not rule out future revisions; it is not synonymous with completion, finality, or permanence; it is, simply, the point at which a literary work attains the crucial state where we may distinguish poetry from mere verse.

In the formula which determines propriety, the essential and primary term is conception. For Pope, no matter how intricate the meter or how polished the style, no matter how vivid the imagery or how witty the language, a work lacking the support of an underlying conception fails to attain wholeness. This idea of poetic wholeness was meant specifically to repudiate the literary amateurs, hacks, and dilettantes who confused genuine poetry with isolated, fragmentary felicities of execution: "pretty conceptions [that is, witty thoughts], fine metaphors, glitt'ring expressions, and something of a neat cast of Verse." In offering a more comprehensive vision of poetry, Pope in the *Essay* equally repudiates the pedants and scribblers in criticism who ignore a poet's governing conception and simply cavil at minor faults of execution—hence Pope's harsh censure of critics who distort their judgment through a "Love to Parts" (I. 288). True criticism, for Pope, requires a knowledge of poetic wholeness. Only by understanding the intimate marriage of execution and conception can critics render the valid judgments of propriety that Pope's *Essay* expects.

As a principle of criticism, propriety applies not only to the relation between conception and execution; it extends also to judgments concerning the specific parts of execution: the thoughts, words, and metrical patterns that must be judged in relation to lesser, local harmonies. For example,

Pope argues that true wit exists in the harmonious relationship among idea, image, and expression. This argument, in making wit accountable to a standard of propriety, helps to deflect the charge that wit was by nature lawless, excessive, and indecent. It also recognizes the function which context serves in distinguishing true wit from false. Thus, for Pope, the critic judges true wit not by predetermined codes of decency (with their various taboos) but by the demands of a specific context or occasion: even obscene or offensive passages, he would argue, may be perfectly appropriate to their surroundings. A similar, uncramped respect for context also underlies Pope's attitude toward diction, where propriety again supplies a practical standard of judgment. Words must suit both subject and genre. As for versification, which Pope illustrates with famous examples such as his snakelike alexandrine dragging its slow extra syllables, propriety reveals itself in the echoing relationship between sound and sense. In effect, Pope applies to the judgment of particular parts the same subsuming principle of propriety he applies to the judgment of poetic wholeness. The value of propriety, for Pope, lies in its freedom from the absolute and fixed laws of criticism which constrain both poets and critics alike. Propriety gives access to the *varieties* of justness not encompassed by "Aristotle's rules."

Variety, of course, is an aesthetic principle honored in the English and Italian Renaissance, as well as in ancient Greece and Rome, and its meaning has not always remained constant. When Pope told Joseph Spence that "all the beauties of gardening might be comprehended in one word, variety," he imagined variety in gardening very differently than did his Renaissance predecessors. The English landscape garden, which Pope at Twickenham helped to create and to popularize, calls for a fluid mixing of elements—trees, lawn, flowers, water, light, shade—in uneven patterns which break the formal geometry of French gardens, where each distinct part is balanced by a counterpart, where "Grove nods at grove, each Alley has a brother, / And half the platform just reflects the other" (*To Burlington*, ll. 117–118). Variety in gardening demands for Pope the pleasing intricacies and artful wildness which defeat rigid boundaries. So, too, as critic Pope recommends a variety that differs from the bounded and balanced harmonies preferred by earlier writers who emphasized generic purity, symmetrical form, and unities of time, place, and action. In this older tradition, still influential in Pope's day, mixing comedy with tragedy was strictly forbidden; epics contained either twelve or twenty-four books; Rome and Athens were unimaginable on the same stage. Pope's distance from that tradition is noticeable even in the apparently casual metaphors of dress (I. 318) and fashion (I. 333) which he associates with poetic diction. Like his extended lament for the mutability of language (II. 476–493), such metaphors acknowledge that literature cannot exclude the change and variety intrinsic to social life. Criticism for Pope quickly turns moribund if it fails to incorporate in its most basic principles of judgment the provision for change.

It is not merely the changeable nature of language and of occasion which makes variety an important concept for Pope. All poems, in his view, observe proprieties which are to some degree historical and personal, thus subject to change. For example, he argues that in certain poems we can trace the distinctive proprieties fostered by a particular age, country, and poetic character: "*Homer* hurries and transports us with a commanding impetuosity, *Virgil* leads us with an attractive Majesty: *Homer* scatters with a generous Profusion, *Virgil* bestows with a careful Magnificence: *Homer* like the *Nile*, pours out his Riches with a sudden Overflow; *Virgil* like a River in its Banks, with a gentle and constant Stream." Each writer, in other words, creates a different form of propriety. This view of variety—implicit in the concept of appropriateness—means that, unlike some of his contemporaries and predecessors, Pope does not feel forced to choose *between* different forms of literary merit: Homer *or* Virgil, Pindar *or* Horace, Shakespeare *or* Jonson. Propriety recognizes and encourages diverse individual possibilities of justness. Only such an elastic and inclusive principle could be appropriate, in Pope's view, to a criticism locked within the world of change, uncertainty, and human limitation. With its generous endorsement of variety, it offers critics an unprecedented freedom to admire the unique proprieties of even the most irregular works in which conception and execution attain a plausible and pleasing harmony. "I had some thoughts of writing a Persian Fable," Pope confessed to Spence, "in which I should have given a full loose to description and imagination. It would have been a very wild thing if I had executed it"—wild, doubtless, and appropriately so.

PRACTICAL PRINCIPLES OF JUDGMENT: GENEROSITY

The undogmatic flexibility implicit in Pope's criticism finds its clearest expression in his treatment of generosity. Generosity is not a concept we would expect to encounter in modern discussions of critical theory. For Pope, however, a person—not a theory or method—is the ultimate source of literary judgment, and no program for criticism would be complete if it failed to discuss the personal, ethical aspects of critical activity. As the opening couplet of part 3 proclaims, the critic's knowledge of propriety must be complemented by equal achievements of character:

> LEARN then what MORALS Criticks ought to show,
> For 'tis but *half* a *Judge's Task*, to *Know*.
>
> (II. 560–561)

Even in an age of moralists, Pope's emphasis upon the ethics of criticism is extraordinary. He is not demanding, like John Dennis and earlier English critics, that criticism stress the moral qualities of art, as expressed in such critical doctrines as poetic justice (the good triumph, the bad repent or die). He is demanding that critics themselves exemplify and embody individual virtue. Moral character, in fact, comprises fully *"half"* of the critic's equipment and identity. This requirement alone argues for the prominence of Pope's *Essay* in the history of critical theory. It also suggests a strong personal bias, exemplified in Pope's later turn to explicitly ethical verse and his lifelong combat with dunce-critics whose characters, as well as criticism, he attacked. Valid criticism, for Pope, is always an expression of virtuous character. Why is generosity, however, more prominent than other virtues which critics might possess? If we wish to understand Pope's emphasis on generosity, we need to see how generosity was a virtue particularly relevant and timely in addressing the problems he confronted in *An Essay on Criticism*.

One reason for Pope's stress on generosity is historical. At the turn of the century, two stereotypes dominated the portraits of contemporary critics: the coffeehouse fop and the ill-tempered crank. The critical fops and butterflies so often satirized in Augustan literature personified for Pope the shallowness and ignorance of modern criticism. The parade of Ned Softleys and Dick Minims who mumbled platitudes and flaunted banalities suggests how far English criticism had degenerated from the noble line of Aristotle, Horace, and Longinus. But even more degrading than the coffeehouse fop was a contrary image of the critic as a carping, ill-natured, irascible, cantankerous crank—an outlaw from polite society. Thus Swift was merely alluding to a stock figure when he described criticism in *A Tale of a Tub* (1704) as the allegorical offspring of Pride and Ridicule. For Pope, a surly character seemed (along with unsound judgment) the inevitable source of all bad criticism. "Sure upon the whole," he wrote in 1717, "a bad Author deserves better usage than a bad Critic; a man may be the former merely thro' the misfortune of an ill judgment, but he cannot be the latter without both that [that is, ill judgment] and an ill temper." While a knowledge of propriety rescued criticism from foppish ignorance, the principle of generosity promised to correct the ill nature that equally disfigured modern criticism. The generous critic, for Pope, has resources of character which ensure that sound judgment will operate with temperance and humanity. Generosity transforms the Den-nis-like crank into a fossil from the less-refined past.

A second reason for Pope's emphasis on generosity of character is, strangely, epistemological. Generosity is indispensable to criticism because valid judgment requires that critics face their own uncertainties and imperfect knowledge. "To err is human" remains among the best-known quotations from world literature, but how many readers know that its source is *An Essay on Criticism*? The compression of Pope's thought suggests not simply that human creatures are prone to error but that error is a distinguishing mark of our humanity. Despite its aphoristic sweep, this idea has specific relevance to Pope's ideas about criticism. Generosity, with its forgiving spirit, implicitly recognizes the human limitations and natural tendency to error which all critics and poets share. As a poet as well as critic, Pope understood that no poem completely satisfies its author: "We grasp some more beautifull Idea in our Brain, than our Endeavors to express it can set to the view of others; & still do but labour to fall short of our first Imagi-nation. The gay Colouring which Fancy gave to our Design at the first transient glance we had of it, goes off in the Execution; like those various Figures in the gilded Clouds, which while we gaze long upon, to seperate [sic] the Parts of each imaginary Image, the whole faints before the Eye, & decays into Confusion. Pope's complaint here echoes his extended lament in the *Essay* at how time damages the poem, blurring its diction and effacing its design (II. 476–493). Betrayal is the extreme image which he chooses to suggest how far a poem may falsify or contradict the poet's purity of vision and thought. Execution always falls short of conception. Some residue of flaw necessarily accompanies even the most polished work. Time, human weakness, and the nature of poetry—not hostile critics alone—help to ac-count for Pope's plea that readers hasten to "befriend" true merit (I.74). The metaphor is not entirely conventional. Just as propriety finds figurative expression in the image of the judge, generosity for Pope also calls forth its representative figure: the critic as friend.

Friendship—he called it "the sacred Idea" of friendship—is a concept of unusual significance throughout Pope's work. "There is nothing meri-torious," he said on his deathbed, "but Virtue, & Friendship." As his linking of these two terms suggests, Pope understands friendship to pass beyond simple emotion. He shares Aristotle's view that, although affection resembles an emotion, friendship resembles a moral state, implying purpose, choice, and knowledge (*Nicomachean Ethics,* VIII.vii). Further, while providing a source of social pleasure and literary alliance, friendship also offered Pope an ideal of complete protection or guardedness combined with free disclosure, promising a state in which human character is simultaneously accessible and shielded. The nature of friendship, we should recognize, was considerably redefined during Pope's lifetime. No longer the Aristotelian alter ego or mirror of the self, the friend for Pope assumes the new, unclassical, domestic offices of consolation and understanding, and the role which Pope assigns to critics is curiously similar. The critic, like the friend, is understanding, consoling, sympathetic. Further, critics and friends share the responsibility (in Pope's view) to tell us our faults, which foes are likely to exaggerate or conceal. While generosity in critics acknowledges the inescapable presence of error, friendship thus permits and encourages correction. The friendship which Pope imagines linking poets with critics is not a device for withholding or for disarming judgment but for making it more effective. Together friendship and generosity create the means for reviving an ancient ideal in which criticism served as a civilizing power, encouraging poets and enlightening readers in a community of knowledge:

> The gen'rous Critick *fann'd* the *Poet's Fire*,
> And taught the World, *with Reason* to *Admire*.
> (II. 100–101)

Here, two apparent opposites—emotional admiration and analytical reason— are reconciled, even as traditional antagonists—poet and critic—become collaborators. This belief in the reconciliation of traditional opposites reappears in one of the most personal moments of the *Essay*, when Pope directly praises his own mentor, the critic, poet, and statesman William Walsh, as "the Muse's Judge and Friend" (I. 729). Judge and friend together reconcile the potentially conflicting roles that the ideal critic must embody.

Friendship, with its consoling, corrective, and reconciling powers, does not exhaust the benefits from the critic's generosity. In criticism, generosity achieves finally the exalted status of an ethical opposite to pride. Pride—as represented in *An Essay on Man* and *The Dunciad*—is not only the intellectual sin accounting for mankind's basic failures in living. It is also especially relevant to criticism, as the source of a great many errors in critical judgment (II. 201–204). The effect of pride, within the context of Pope's *Essay*, is always a pressure toward partiality and fragmentation, blocking comprehensiveness of vision. In its pressure against wholeness, pride radically constricts understanding by attaching us to cherished opinions and to favored fragments. The principle of propriety, in demanding a knowledge of poetic wholeness, had offered one means of counteracting the misjudgments of pride expressed in bad critics as a "*Love to Parts*." But partiality takes another threatening form in *An Essay on Criticism*. This mode of fragmentation, rooted in pride, is prejudice.

Prejudice in criticism makes its appearance in two main areas: in the political disputes that divided Augustan writers into Whigs and Tories, and in the equally divisive and prolific literary quarrels. Like the Little-Endians and Big-Endians of *Gulliver's Travels*, Pope's contemporaries seemed capable of transforming almost any human activity into an argument, from saying prayers to cracking eggshells. Writing usually meant taking sides. Such widespread factionalism is what Pope lamented in the 1717 preface to his *Works* when he described the poet's life as a "warfare upon earth." Thus, while *An Essay on Criticism* censures obsessive fondness for specific "parts" of execution (II. 289–383), it also attacks at almost equal length partiality, expressed as prejudice, toward writers from one historical period, one political party, one country, or one school of wit (II. 384–473). What Mr. Spectator condemned as the "Malice of Party" was a pressing threat to sound judgment, in literature as in politics. "If this Party Spirit has so ill an Effect on our Morals," wrote Addison, "it has likewise a very great one on our Judgments. We often hear a poor insipid Paper or Pamphlet cryed up, and sometimes a noble Piece depretiated by those who are of a different Principle from the Author. One who is actuated by this Spirit is almost under an Incapacity of discerning either real Blemishes or Beauties" (*The Spectator* no. 125). Prejudice is regarded by Addison and by Pope as a defect of character which inevitably erodes literary judgment, and for Pope the ethical corrective to prejudice is generosity. Generosity permits the critic to approach an equitable judgment by consciously rejecting whatever is incomplete and partisan. It seeks to move criticism from a warfare of factions to civilized discourse among persons too large-spirited for parties or partiality or prejudice of any kind.

It should be clear that generosity is not for Pope a simple or common-place virtue like thrift. (Its history as an ethical concept runs back at least to Cicero's *De Officiis*.) Pope's critical theory holds, as we have seen, that judgment consider the "*Whole*" (I. 235). This idea of wholeness also requires us to understand the unstated intentions of the author that contribute to the work's conception. Thus Pope insists that criticism must always regard the writer's purposes (I. 255), judging the performance in the light of intentions. But there is an old problem lurking in this good advice. Readers discover every day that not all authorial intentions and purposes can be clearly reconstructed from an impartial study of the text. How, then, can the critic gain access to the author's mental processes and undeclared purposes which are required for understanding the "*Whole*" work? Pope's answer to this difficult question is the power of sympathy. Sympathy, like friendship and virtue, is a necessary characteristic of the generous critic. As an aspect of generosity, it permits the critic to achieve a close emotional and intellectual kinship with the author under study: "No Longer his *Interpreter*, but *He*." The generous critic reads with a sympathetic understanding, which, when perfectly attuned, allows a presumptive reconstruction of authorial plans and purposes and processes that complement a judicious study of the text:

> A perfect Judge will *read* each Work of Wit
> With the same Spirit that its Author *writ*,
> Survey the *Whole*, nor seek slight Faults to find,
> Where *Nature moves*, and *Rapture warms* the Mind.
>
> (II. 233–236)

The "perfect Judge" whom Pope depicts is no ordinary critic. His generous character allows him insights which judgment alone cannot attain. Rather than spend itself in the pointless exclamations of taste, emotion in the ideal critic proves a source of otherwise inaccessible knowledge.

It is not my purpose to debate the soundness of Pope's position, for although generosity solves some critical problems, it also introduces new ones. (How can critics judge or understand a writer with whom they are unsympathetic?) More important, Pope's emphasis upon generosity allows us to reconsider the surprising and neglected prominence which he assigns to emotion in criticism. Judgment alone is not enough. Just as poetry contains "nameless Graces" which gain the heart "without passing thro' the *Judgment*" (I. 156), so, too, criticism cannot rely solely on method but must enlist the powers of feeling without which it proves sterile and mechanical. Such emotional powers are most evident in Pope's portrait of Longinus:

> An ardent *Judge*, who Zealous in his Trust,
> With *Warmth* gives Sentence, yet is always *Just*;
> Whose *own Example* strengthens all his Laws.
> And *Is himself* that great *Sublime* he draws.
>
> (II. 677–680)

Sublimity, Longinus had said, was the echo of a great soul, and the emotional ardor of Longinus stands in stark contrast to the stifled feeling which Pope depicts in his portrait of Atticus: "Alike reserv'd to blame, or to commend." Atticus, in his unwavering reserve, is an antitype of the generous critic. Generosity, for Pope, always retains its etymological link with noble and spirited character, with a magnanimous soul capable of the ardor, warmth, and zeal Atticus denies. Among its other functions, generosity assures that the final judgments of criticism, whether resting in praise or blame, will not be inhuman and unfeeling.

POPE AS METACRITIC

"Criticism," wrote Samuel Johnson in 1751, "reduces those regions of literature under the dominion of science, which have hitherto known only the anarchy of ignorance, the caprices of fancy, and the tyranny of prescription." Johnson's statement is a short history as well as a definition of criticism. It charts the progress in criticism away from the "prescriptions" of authority and the "caprices" of taste—a progress which Pope's *Essay* helped to initiate and secure. Johnson's inclusion of criticism within the "dominion of science" does not imply that criticism now belonged to the disciplines of the new natural philosophy, like chemistry or physics, but that it had established the principles and procedures required of useful knowledge. It was Dryden, in Johnson's view, who deserved credit as "the father of English criticism": "the writer who first taught us to determine *upon principles* the merit of composition." Dryden's primacy is indisputable, for he did more than any writer of his age to free English criticism from the confusions and ignorance in which he found it. But Dryden was most successful as a practicing critic, not as a theorist of criticism. Modern scholars still have trouble making his principles consistent and clear, for his work as a critic ranges from occasional pronouncements to speculative dialogues. With the death of Dryden in 1700, a new generation of writers needed to consolidate his advances and to reflect upon the nature of criticism, to think of it as a coherent discipline conscious of its own aims and methods. John Dennis, with his meaty tracts *The Advancement and Reformation of Modern Poetry* (1701) and *The Grounds of Criticism in Poetry* (1704), had already begun the task of establishing theoretical foundations for English criticism—in what Pope could only regard as a dogmatic and misguided effort to flood England with swollen imitations of *Paradise Lost. An Essay on Criticism* in effect reclaims and refines the example of Dryden for English critics, endorsing his main principles, backing his often speculative and exploratory spirit, and providing a secure, compact, flexible theory of criticism to stabilize the practice of his English successors

Historians of criticism and of critical theory should take a fresh look at *An Essay on Criticism*, for it possesses a coherence (despite its unmethodical form) and originality (despite its use of traditional materials) which deserve reappraisal. Some of the apparent familiarity of Pope's ideas derives, like the "clichés" of *An Essay on Man*, from their subsequent absorption into the language of English thought, where they proved powerfully influential. The strength of his poem, contrary to general opinion, is not in its free-floating couplets of specific advice but its consolidation of traditional wisdom and of native sense within a full (if brief) theory of criticism. Specific couplets, however self-contained they *sound*, reverberate in the larger, surrounding system that endows them with additional meaning, as in this example:

> In ev'ry Work regard the *Writer's End*,
> Since none can compass more than they *Intend*;
> And if the *Means* be just, the *Conduct* true,
> Applause, in spite of trivial Faults, is due.
>   (II. 255–258)

In this instance, the highly compressed language does more than defend an idea of poetic wholeness achieved by understanding the interdependence of execution (*"Means," "Conduct"*) and conception (*"End"*). It entails an entire sequence of theoretical and practical steps. It is embedded in a theory which defines criticism as an act of judgment; which places this definition within its historical context as an alternative to criticism governed wholly by authority or by taste; which indentifies and links, in nature and in the ancients, fixed standards that create the possibility of valid judgment; which associates criticism with the method and spirit of probabilistic reasoning appropriate to a realm of limitation and uncertainty; which articulates, in propriety and in generosity, comprehensive practical principles of criticism embracing both knowledge and ethics; which directs practical criticism toward the goal of fair evaluation; and which justifies such verdicts as helping to revive a true community of discourse, with critics both judges and friends, mediating between writers and readers in a model of ancient civility. Pope's theory may not be "cut-and-dried" (if that is a virtue), but it certainly possesses the rigor and coherence that a useful theory of criticism requires. Where in the previous history of English criticism does one find a more fully integrated model of theory and practice?

It is true that readers must perceive the organization of Pope's critical system without the aid of such prose crutches as statements of purpose, chapter headings, mathematical subdivisons, detailed logical argument, and plain, utilitarian language. These devices, so dear to an age of treatises, encyclopedias, and dictionaries, were too straightforward for Pope. Pope, as Johnson accurately observed, "had great delight in artifice, and endeavoured to attain all his purposes by indirect and unsuspected methods." A writer who advised instructing people "as if you taught them *not*" understood that indirection is a means for overcoming the normal human resistances to instruction. Further, he knew that we are likelier to value knowledge which by our own labors we have helped to discover:

> To Observations which ourselves we make,
> We grow more partial for th' observer's sake;
> To written Wisdom, as another's, less.

If partiality could not be banished from human behavior, at least it could be put to educational uses. Perhaps this explanation accounts for Pope's preference to discuss propriety, for example, mainly through the oblique method of examining various improprieties and errors. Despite its indirections, his treatment gains strength from respecting a basic, even rudimentary, logic of exposition. Part I treats the universal standards validating the possibility of judgment. Part 2 treats the principle of propriety. Part 3 treats the principle of generosity. Within this less-than-cunning framework, however, Pope allowed himself the many excursions or informal digressions sanctioned by the term *essay*, and no doubt he hoped that a loose informality might help deflect charges of youthful presumptuousness. (Accusations, hurled like weapons by the wounded Dennis, came anyway.) But finally we should not miss the obvious point. Like his predecessors Horace and Boileau, Pope chose to write a poem, not a prose treatise. *An Essay on Criticism* is a supple, allusive, complex, sometimes dazzling work in which the reader's participation is crucial. In form and in method, it constitutes a test of the specific critical power it celebrates. We must read by constantly exercising our judgment—or find, like De Quincey, merely a heap of fragments.

Pope, I believe, cared deeply and thought seriously about the nature of literary criticism. He was a skillful practicing critic, as his essays, notes, and prefaces amply demonstrate. He was a connoisseur of critical responses to his own poems—and even reviewed his own Pastorals (favorably) when he thought critics had failed to understand their merit. Before the age of twenty, with virtually no formal schooling, he mastered the tradition of classical, Renaissance, and contemporary criticism in at least three languages. There are no grounds for considering him a shallow opportunist looking for an untried, easy field in which to demonstrate his knack of rhyme. *An Essay on Criticism* is a major attempt to place English literary analysis on the foundation of a coherent theory. Like all his works, it is a labor of refinement—both a commerce with the past and an original engagement with the present, viewed in the light of traditional knowledge. In his own time Pope viewed English criticism as a history of darkness and error, punctuated by the ineffectual efforts of a *"Few"* (I. 719) sound minds. The names William Walsh, Wentworth Dillon (Earl of Roscommon), and John Sheffield (Earl of Mulgrave and Duke of Buckingham and Normandy)—Pope's "*sounder Few*"—hardly define a flourishing native criticism. Although his failure to mention Dryden is surely significant, for the immediate past was less dark than Pope in his rhetorical conclusion needed to claim, yet, naming Dryden would not have invalidated Pope's point. While France derived some benefit from the imported rules its writers (in Pope's view) slavishly obeyed, England, by asserting its independence from French and Roman influence, unfortunately decreed its isolation from the improvements of polite learning:

> But *we*, brave *Britons, Foreign Laws* despis'd,
> And kept *unconquer'd*, and *unciviliz'd*.
>   (II. 715–716)

The phrase "brave *Britons*" contains both a touch of irony and a trace of pride. Pope's task in *An Essay on Criticism* was to civilize an uncivil discipline. Preserving still the spirit of independence basic to British liberty, he wished, by identifying the values which British writers shared with their great predecessors in various nations and times, to define the literary principles which would advance criticism from ignorance and incivility to knowledge. The ideal is to be both unconquered *and* civilized. The criticism of judgment represented Pope's first explicit effort, which continued indirectly throughout his lifetime, to civilize the act of reading. Not coincidentally, it provided England with a workable theory of criticism befitting an era that had begun to imagine emulating the achievements of ancient Greece and Rome.

Chronology

1688   Alexander Pope born in London on May 21, son of a Roman Catholic linen merchant and his second wife.

1696   Pope enters school in a seminary at Twyford, near Winchester.

1697   Pope is withdrawn from Twyford and enrolled in Thomas Deane's school in London.

?1698   Pope's family moves to Binfield, in Windsor Forest.

1703   Pope resides briefly in London, where he learns French and Italian.

1704   Friendship with Sir William Trumbull begins.

?1705   Pope suffers his first attack of the tubercular infection that will severely deform him. With a spine curved in two directions, he grew finally to only four and one-half feet. Headaches and a generally weak constitution plagued him for the rest of his life.

1705   Pope meets Wycherley, Walsh, and other London writers.

1709   The "Pastorals," Pope's first published poetry, appear in Tonson's *Poetical Miscellanies* (May).

?1710   Friendship with John Caryll begins.

1711   *An Essay on Criticism* published in May. Pope meets Addison and his coffeehouse companions, as well as Martha and Teresa Blount, Gay, and Steele.

1712   The "Messiah" is published by Steele in *The Spectator* (number 378). The first version of *The Rape of the Lock* (two cantos) appears in Lintot's *Miscellany*. Pope becomes acquainted with a Tory group that includes Swift and Arbuthnot, Parnell, Gay, and Lord Oxford. Together they form the Martinus Scriblerus Club.

1713   *Windsor Forest* is published in March, celebrating the Tory Peace Treaty signed at Utrecht. Pope is translating and seeking subscriptions for his *Iliad*. He is also studying painting under Charles Jervas.

?1714   Pope meets Henry St. John, Viscount Bolingbroke.

1714   The revised, five-canto *Rape of the Lock* appears in March. The Scriblerus Club is dissolved.

1715   The first four books (volume I) of *The Iliad* are published in February. Pope meets Lady Mary Wortley Montague.

1716   Second volume of *The Iliad* appears in March; Pope probably meets Lord Burlington this year.

1717   *Three Hours after Marriage*, a collaborative dramatic effort by Pope, Gay, and Arbuthnot, is performed at the Drury Lane Theatre. Volume III of *The Iliad* appears in June, as does the poet's first collected *Works*, which include "Verses to the Memory of an Unfortunate Lady" and "Eloisa to Abelard." Pope probably meets Atterbury and Lord Bathurst during this year. Pope's father dies on October 23.

1718   *The Iliad*, volume IV, published in June.

?1719   Pope leases Twickenham on the Thames, and moves there with his mother.

1720   The last two volumes of *The Iliad* are published in May. Pope becomes friends with William Fortescue.

1721   "Epistle to Addison" and "Epistle to Lord Oxford" are published as prefaces to editions of Addison's *Works* and Parnell's *Works* respectively. Pope begins work on his edition of Shakespeare.

1723   Pope's edition of the *Works* of John Sheffield, Duke of Buckinghamshire, is published but immediately suppressed by the government because of the poet's alleged Jacobite sympathies.

1725   Pope's edition of Shakespeare (six volumes) appears in March; volumes I-III of his translation of *The Odyssey* follow in April.

1726   The final two volumes of *The Odyssey* are published in June. Swift visits Pope at Twickenham. Friendship with Joseph Spence begins.

1727   The Pope-Swift *Miscellanies*, volumes I and II, are issued. Swift pays a second visit to Pope. Pope's estrangement from Lady Montague may have occurred in this year.

1728   Last volume of *Miscellanies* published in March, including *Peri Bathous*. In May appears *The Dunciad*, which engenders great hostility among its victims.

1729   The *Dunciad Variorum* is published in April.

1731   The "Epistle to Burlington, Of Taste"—the first "Moral Essay" in a projected series on ethical issues—is published in December. Public reception unfavorable.

1732   Pope-Swift *Miscellanies*, volume IV, are published.

1733   "Epistle to Bathurst" is published in January, followed in February by Pope's first *Imitation of Horace*, "Satire II.i.: To Fortescue." *An Essay on Man* (Epistles I–III) is published anonymously at the same time, and enthusiastically praised. Pope's mother dies.

1734   The January release of "Epistle to Cobham" is followed by Epistle IV of *An Essay on Man*, which is still anonymous. Two Horatian satires published (II.ii and I.ii).

1735   "Epistle to Arbuthnot," a tribute to Pope's dying friend, is published in January; Arbuthnot dies in February. Also in February appears "To a Lady" (the last of the *Moral Essays*). Volume II of Pope's collected *Works* is published in April. In May appears Curll's unauthorized edition of Pope's *Letters*.

1737   "Epistle II.ii," another Horatian satire, appears in April, followed in May by "Epistle II.i: To Augustus," which is aimed at George II. Also in May, Pope publishes his own edition of his *Letters* to replace the earlier, spurious collection. The identity of the author of *An Essay on Man* is now known; opponents of the poem's religious views launch an attack.

1738   Four satires are published: "Epistle I.vi: To Murray"; "Epistle I.i: To Bolingbroke"; "1738 (Epilogue to the Satires)," Dialogues I (May) and II (July). Warburton, a clergyman, defends *An Essay on Man*.

1740   Pope meets Warburton. He also refurbishes his famous grotto at
         Twickenham.

1741   Pope publishes *Memoirs of Martinus Scriblerus* and his correspon-
         dence with Swift. With Warburton's help, Pope revises *The
         Dunciad*.

1742   *The New Dunciad* (i.e., Book IV) appears in March.

1743   The final four-book version of *The Dunciad* appears in October,
         with Cibber replacing Theobald as "hero." Pope's health declines.

1744   Pope spends the last five months of his life revising his works for
         publication; Warburton compiles accompanying notes. The *Essay
         On Criticism*, *An Essay on Man*, and the four *Moral Essays* are
         completed and published before the poet, suffering from asthma
         and dropsy, dies at Twickenham on May 30.

Contributors

HAROLD BLOOM, Sterling Professor of the Humanities at Yale University, is author of *The Anxiety of Influence, Poetry and Repression*, and many other volumes of literary criticism. His forthcoming study, *Freud: Transference and Authority*, attempts a full-scale reading of all of Freud's major writings. A MacArthur Prize Fellow, he is the general editor of *The Chelsea House Library of Literary Criticism*.

MAYNARD MACK, Sterling Professor of English Emeritus at Yale University, is a critic well known for his work on Pope and his contemporaries. Among his books and articles on the eighteenth century is *The Garden and the City*, which establishes the relationship between "retirement," politics, and Pope's poetry.

W. K. WIMSATT, JR., was Professor of English at Yale University. His books include *Hateful Contraries: Studies in Literature and Criticism* and *The Verbal Icon: Studies in the Meaning of Poetry*.

EARL R. WASSERMAN was Professor of English at Johns Hopkins University. His books include *Shelley: A Critical Reading, The Subtler Language*, and *The Finer Tone*, a study of Keats.

THOMAS R. EDWARDS is Professor of English at Rutgers University. In addition to his book on Pope, *This Dark Estate*, he has written extensively on poetry and politics.

MARTIN PRICE is Sterling Professor of English at Yale University. His books include *Swift's Rhetorical Art, To the Palace of Wisdom*, and *Forms of Life: Character and Moral Imagination in the Novel*.

DAVID B. MORRIS teaches at American University. He is the author of *The Genius of Sense*, a study of Pope.

C. E. NICHOLSON is a lecturer at the University of Edinburgh.

MELINDA ALLIKER RABB is Assistant Professor of English at Brown University.

ROBERT GRIFFIN teaches at Bowdoin College and is completing a study of Dr. Johnson's criticism.

Bibliography

Aden, John M. *Pope's Once and Future Kings: Satire and Politics in the Early Career*. Knoxville: University of Tennessee Press, 1978.

Auden, W. H. "A civilised voice." In *Forewords and Afterwords*, selected by E. Mendelson. London: Faber, 1973.

Ault, Norman. *New Light on Pope*. London: Methuen, 1949.

Battestin, Martin C. "The Transforming Power: Nature and Art in Pope's Pastorals." *Eighteenth-Century Studies* 2 (1969): 183–204.

Bogel, Frederick V. *Acts of Knowledge: Pope's Later Poems*. Louisberg, Penn.: Bucknell University Press, 1981.

Bogel, Frederick V. "Dulness Unbound: Rhetoric and Pope's *Dunciad*." *PMLA* 97, no. 5 (October 1982): 844–55.

Bogue, Ronald L. "The Meaning of 'Grace' in Pope's Aesthetic." *PMLA* 94 (1979): 434–48.

Brett, R. L. "Pope's 'Essay on Man.' " In *Reason and Imagination: A Study of Form and Meaning in Four Poems*. London: Oxford University Press, 1960.

Brower, Reuben A. *Alexander Pope: The Poetry of Allusion*. Oxford: Clarendon Press, 1959.

Brown, Laura. *Alexander Pope*. Oxford: Basil Blackwell Publisher, 1985.

Byron, George Gordon, Lord. "Reply to Blackwood's *Edinburgh Magazine*" (1819). Printed as appendix 9 in *The Works of Lord Byron: Letters and Journals*, edited by R. E. Prothero. 6 vols. London: John Murray, 1902–4.

Dixon, Peter. *Alexander Pope*. London: G. Bell & Sons, 1972.

Empson, William. "Wit in the *Essay on Criticism*." In *The Structure of Complex Words*. London: Chatto & Windus, 1977.

Erskine-Hill, Howard. *The Social Milieu of Alexander Pope*. New Haven: Yale University Press, 1979.

————. "Alexander Pope: The Political Poet in His Time." *Eighteenth-Century Studies* 15, no. 2 (Winter 1981–2): 123–47.

Erskine-Hill, Howard, and Anne Smith, eds. *The Art of Alexander Pope*. New York: Barnes & Noble Books, 1979.

Fairer, David. "Imagination in 'The Rape of the Lock.' " *Essays in Criticism* 29, no. 1 (1979): 53–74.

Goldberg, S. L. "Integrity and Life in Pope's Poetry." In *Studies in the Eighteenth Century*, edited by R. F. Brissenden and J. C. Eade. Canberra: Australian National University Press, 1976.

Griffin, Dustin H. *Alexander Pope: The Poet in the Poems*. Princeton: Princeton University Press, 1978.

Hotch, Ripley. "Pope Surveys His Kingdom: An Essay on Criticism." *Studies in English Literature* 13, no. 3 (Summer 1973): 474–87.

Johnson, Samuel. *Lives of the English Poets*. Edited by G. Birkbeck Hill. 3 vols. Oxford: Clarendon Press, 1905.

Jones, Emrys. "Pope and Dulness." In *Pope: A Collection of Critical Essays*, edited by J. V. Guerinot. Englewood Cliffs, N.J.: Prentice-Hall, 1972.

Kallich, Martin. *Heaven's First Law: Rhetoric and Order in Pope's Essay on Man*. Dekalb, Ill.: Northern Illinois Press, 1967.

Kenner, Hugh. "Pope's Reasonable Rhymes." *English Literary History* 41 (1974): 74–88.

Knight, G. Wilson. *Laureate of Peace: On the Genius of Alexander Pope*. London: Routledge & Kegan Paul, 1954.

Krieger, M. " 'Eloisa to Abelard': The Escape from Body or the Embrace of Body." *Eighteenth-Century Studies* 3 (1969): 28–47.

Leranbaum, Miriam. *Alexander Pope's Opus Magnum, 1729–1744*. Oxford: Clarendon Press, 1977.

Lovejoy, A. O. *The Great Chain of Being: A Study of the History of an Idea*. New York: Harper, 1960.

Mack, Maynard, ed. *Essential Articles for the Study of Alexander Pope*. Hamden, Conn.: Archon Books, 1968.

————. *The Garden and the City: Retirement and Politics in the Later Poetry of Pope, 1731–1743*. London: Oxford University Press, 1969.

————. "On Reading Pope." *College English* 22 (1960): 99–107.

Mack, Maynard, and James A. Winn, eds. *Pope: Recent Essays by Several Hands*. Hamden, Conn.: Archon Books, 1980.

Marshall, W. Gerald. "Pope's 'Windsor Forest' as Providential History." *Tennessee Studies in Literature* 24 (1979): 82–93.

Martindale, Charles A. "Sense and Sensibility: The Child and the Man in 'The Rape of the Lock.' " *Modern Language Review* 78, no. 2 (April 1983): 273–84.

Nicolson, Marjorie Hope, and G. S. Rousseau. *'This Long Disease, My Life': Alexander Pope and the Sciences*. Princeton: Princeton University Press, 1968.

Nuttall, A. D. *Pope's 'Essay on Man.'* London: George Allen & Unwin, 1984.

Park, Douglas B. "'At Once the *Source*, and *End*': Nature's Defining Pattern in *An Essay on Criticism.*" *PMLA* 90 (1975): 861–73.

Price, Martin. *To the Palace of Wisdom: Studies in Order and Energy From Dryden to Blake*. Carbondale and Edwardsville, Ill.: Southern Illinois University Press, 1964.

Rawson, C. J. "Pope's Waste Land: Reflections on Mock-Heroic," *Essays and Studies* 35 (1982): 45–65.

Reid, B. L. "Ordering Chaos: *The Dunciad.*" In *Quick Springs of Sense: Studies in the Eighteenth Century*, edited by Larry S. Champion. Athens, Ga.: University of Georgia Press, 1974.

Rogers, Pat. *An Introduction to Pope*. London: Methuen, 1975.

————. *The Augustan Vision*. London: Weidenfeld & Nicolson, 1974.

Rousseau, George S., ed. *Twentieth-Century Interpretations of The Rape of the Lock*. Englewood Cliffs, N.J.: Prentice-Hall, 1969.

Sherburn, George. *The Early Career of Alexander Pope*. New York: Russell & Russell, 1963.

Siebert, Donald, Jr. "Cibber & Satan: *The Dunciad* and Civilization." *Eighteenth-Century Studies* 10, no. 2 (1976–77): 203–21.

Sitter, John. *The Poetry of Pope's 'Dunciad.'* Minneapolis: University of Minnesota Press, 1971.

Sitwell, Edith. *Alexander Pope*. Harmondsworth: Penguin, 1948.

Spence, Joseph. *Observation, Anecdotes, and Characters of Books and Men*. Edited by James M. Osborn. 2 vols. Oxford: Clarendon Press, 1966.

Tillotson, Geoffrey. *Pope and Human Nature*. Oxford: Clarendon Press, 1958.

Varey, Simon. "Rhetoric and *An Essay on Man.*" In *The Art of Alexander Pope*, edited by Howard Erskine-Hill and Anne Smith. New York: Barnes & Noble Books, 1979.

Wasserman, Earl. "The Limits of Allusion in 'Rape of the Lock.' " *Journal of English and Germanic Philology* 65 (1966): 425–44.

————. *Pope's 'Epistle to Bathurst': A Critical Reading of the Manuscripts*. Baltimore: Johns Hopkins Press, 1960.

Weber, Harold. "The Comic and Tragic Satirist in Pope's *Imitations of Horace.*" *Papers on Language and Literature* 16, no. 1 (Winter 1980): 65–80.

Weinbrot, Howard D. *Alexander Pope and the Traditions of Formal Verse Satire.* Princeton: Princeton University Press, 1982.

White, Douglas Howarth. *Pope and the Context of Controversy: The Manipulation of Ideas in 'An Essay on Man.'* Chicago: University of Chicago Press, 1970.

Williams, Aubrey. *Pope's 'Dunciad': A Study of Its Meaning.* London: Methuen, 1955.

Wimsatt, W. K., Jr. *The Portrait of Alexander Pope.* New Haven: Yale University Press, 1965.

————. "Belinda Ludens." In *Day of the Leopards.* New Haven: Yale University Press, 1976.

————. "One Relation of Rhyme to Reason: Alexander Pope." *Modern Language Quarterly* 5 (1944): 323–38.

Acknowledgments

"Wit and Poetry and Pope" (original title " 'Wit and Poetry and Pope':
  Some Observations on His Imagery") by Maynard Mack, from *Pope and
  His Contemporaries: Essays Presented to George Sherburn*, edited by James
  L. Clifford and Louis L. Landa, copyright © 1949 by The Clarendon
  Press, Oxford. Reprinted by permission.

"Rhetoric and Poems" (original title "Rhetoric and Poems: Alexander Pope")
  by W. K. Wimsatt, Jr., from *The Verbal Icon: Studies in the Meaning of
  Poetry* by W. K. Wimsatt, Jr., copyright © 1954 by The University
  Press of Kentucky. Reprinted by permission of the publisher.

"Windsor Forest" (original title "Pope: Windsor Forest") by Earl R. Wasserman, from *The Subtler Language* by Earl R. Wasserman, pp. 101–
  113, copyright © 1959 by The Johns Hopkins University Press, Baltimore and London. Reprinted by permission.

"The Mighty Maze: *An Essay on Man*" (original title "The Mighty Maze")
  by Thomas R. Edwards from *This Dark Estate: A Reading of Pope*
  by Thomas R. Edwards, copyright © 1963 by The Regents of the
  University of California. Reprinted by permission of the University of
  California Press.

"Character and False Art" (original title "Pope: Art and Morality") by Martin
  Price, from *To the Palace of Wisdom: Studies in Order and Energy from
  Dryden to Blake* by Martin Price, copyright © 1964 by Martin Price.
  Reprinted by permission of Southern Illinois University Press.

Index